Actors and Onlookers

Actors and Onlookers

Theater and Twentieth-Century Scientific Views of Nature

Natalie Crohn Schmitt

Northwestern University Press
Evanston, Illinois

Northwestern University Press
Evanston, Illinois 60201

© 1990 by Natalie Crohn Schmitt
All rights reserved.

Printed in the United States of America

Library of Congress Cataloging-in-Publication Data

Schmitt, Natalie Crohn.
    Actors and onlookers: theater and twentieth-century scientific views of
nature/Natalie Crohn Schmitt.
        p.   cm.
    Includes bibliographical references.
    ISBN 0-8101-0836-4. — ISBN 0-8101-0837-2 (pbk.)
    1. Experimental theater—United States. 2. Wooster Group.
3. Acting. 4. Spolin, Viola. 5. Cage, John. 6. Aristotle. Poetics.
I. Title.
PN2266.5.S36   1989
792'.015'0973—dc20   89-38955
                                                            CIP

Contents

Acknowledgments

I would like to thank Jonathan Arac, Joel Berman, Judith Kegan Gardiner, Anthony Graham-White, and editors Jonathan Brent and Anne Geissman Canright for critical readings of this manuscript; John Cage, R. Victor Harnack, Marjorie Perloff, and Robert Winter for their encouragement; Charles R. Lyons, the Institute of the Humanities at the University of Illinois at Chicago, and the National Endowment for the Humanities for release time in which to work; and the Theater on Film and Tape Collection at the New York Public Library of the Performing Arts, particularly Betty Corwin and Richard Ryan.

A portion of Chapter 1 originally appeared in "John Cage, Nature and Theater," *Triquarterly* 54 (1982): 89–109. A portion of Chapter 3 originally appeared as "Push-down Stacks in Contemporary Theater," *Centennial Review* 31, no. 4 (1987): 338–54.

Introduction

> We must become conscious of the
> fact that we are not truly
> observers but also actors on the
> stage of life.
>
> Werner Heisenberg, paraphrasing
> Niels Bohr, *The Physicist's
> Conception of Nature*

Underlying an important segment of contemporary theater (variously referred to as antitheater, postmodern theater, or simply, new theater) are aesthetic principles consistent with contemporary scientific views of nature and our place within it. To suggest such a relationship, the title and epigraph of this book are taken from a theatrical allusion used by a physicist. Bohr's own phrasing of the theatrical image—"we are both onlookers and actors in the great drama of existence"[1]—coupled with the excitement he displays in his writing, suggests that for him "the great drama of existence" obtained in no small part in the newly conceived relationship between subject and object, between that which the mind produces and that which lies outside the mind. Like Bohr, the creators of the new theater do not mourn the loss of old ideas about the place of human beings in the universe: they do not share Camus's idea that man is in "irremediable exile, because he is deprived of memories of a lost homeland as much as he lacks the hope of a promised land to come," or believe that "this divorce between man and his life, the actor and his setting, truly constitutes the feeling of Absurdity."[2] They neither bemoan the disappearance of a metaphysical setting nor pine for teleology. The image of the actor on the stage of life is both more solid and more immediate. And it embraces a world subject to our participation and invention. Like Bohr, the creators of the new theater redefine and relocate the drama of existence.[3]

The vast number of Western dramas that can be rewardingly analyzed in terms of Aristotle's *Poetics* makes clear the extent to which one can speak of a coherent Western theatrical tradition. The *Poetics* is the first significant work of Western theater theory. Not only have the central concepts and lines of argument of this treatise exerted an enormous influence on theater theory over the centuries,[4] but to a considerable extent Aristotelian theory has shaped Western drama as well. Indeed, even audiences, wholly innocent of theoretical consciousness, continue to demonstrate Aristotelian expectations.

While Aristotle insisted that art should imitate nature by adhering to its principles of operation, the view of nature everywhere implicit in the *Poetics* is one that, even today, is taken for granted rather than examined.[5] New theater perfor-mances violate not only Aristotelian aesthetic principles but also the view of re-ality that they imply, thus profoundly disturbing many audience members. Ronald Hayman, for instance, presumes that whereas traditional Aristotelian theater shows us reality, contemporary theater, "anti-theatre," is "hostile to real-ity, though the anti-world it creates can never provide a viable alternative to real-ity." In Hayman's view, contemporary theater is "negative, destructive,... reductionist and abstractionist."[6] And Robert Brustein, who regards himself as a champion of the new theater, nevertheless asks: "Should the theater artist, whether for purposes of celebrating or criticizing reality, present life as it really is? Or should he show us life as it should be, an alternative world as imagined by a unique, sometimes visionary mind? This argument reflects the irreconcilable conflict between realism and anti-realism, between mainstream culture and avant-garde experimentation." Thus Brustein assumes that whereas the "cher-ished dramas of the past" present reality, the avant-garde imagination presents merely "fantasies and magical transformations."[7] In short, Hayman and Brustein share not only Aristotle's commonsense idea that reality is a given—that is, that we possess means that are not problematic both for knowing as fact what exists or happens and for representing it in art—but also the view of reality implicit in Aristotle's aesthetic.

The description of contemporary theater as "anti-reality" presumes the exis-tence of an earlier theater that was "for" reality and also represented it. In this book I retain the radical antithesis implied in such description because I share the belief that there is something fundamentally different about the new theater but which the term *antireality* belies. To characterize this difference as I see it, I begin in Chapter 1 by contrasting the Aristotelian theater aesthetic with the con-temporary theater aesthetic provided by John Cage.

Although a musician whose writing on aesthetics relies largely on a vocabu-lary and analysis applicable most obviously to music, Cage considers his theoriz-ing to be more inclusive. In fact, he thinks of his musical performances as theater, which for him is the "obligatory" art form, "because it resembles life more closely than the other arts do, requiring for its appreciation the use of both eyes and ears, and space and time."[8] Cage's naturalistic aesthetic opposes that of Aristotle virtually point for point, not because Cage set out to be defiant, as it may seem, but because his aesthetic is—as he claims, like Aristotle's—based on the idea that art should imitate nature in its manner of operation. Our under-standing of this manner of operation, Cage observes, "changes according to ad-vances in the sciences."[9] And on this account, he would argue, the guidelines of the *Poetics* are not so much violated by contemporary theater practice as they are simply superseded; they have ceased to show us the world and to help us live in it. Cage has continually sought to understand what the implications of scientific discovery are for our ordinary modes of thought and, of all theorizers, has most boldly and fully envisioned an art that reflects this thought.

Accordingly, as Charles Hamm notes, Cage "has been at the centre of the avant garde in the USA for several decades," and "the influence of his compositions and his aesthetic thought has been felt all over the world, particularly since World War II."[10] Richard Kostelanetz likewise asserts that "no American has done more to forge an esthetics of post-World War II advanced art than John Cage."[11] Yet Cage's ideas are evident in contemporary theater not because all theater practitioners have been directly influenced by him, although many have, nor even because these practitioners have been influenced by contemporary science, although some have; rather, new theater simply manifests what the eminent biologist C. H. Waddington describes as "changes of the world view that have been occurring in the last fifty years [and that] are amongst the most far-reaching in the whole history of human thought"—changes that are similarly encapsulated in Cage's aesthetic theory.[12]

Chapter 2 explores how this conceptual revolution has received theatrical expression, by setting a contemporary American theater piece, the Wooster Group's *Rumstick Road*, as a Cagean analytical exemplar against Eugene O'Neill's *Long Day's Journey into Night*, which yields readily to an Aristotelian analysis. Contemporary perceptions of reality and of our relationship to it provide explanation for the heightened interest among avant-garde theatergoers in performance theater (that is, in works like *Rumstick Road*, which exist primarily as event rather than as object)[13] as well as a basis for understanding its structure, its treatment of point of view, its use of objects and space, the interpenetration of this theater and life, the acting style it employs, and even certain of its rehearsal techniques.

Even though the aesthetic principles I describe have their most radical application in theaters like the Performing Garage where the Wooster Group works, theaters attracting a coterie audience, they are not limited to such theaters. Performances based on this aesthetic also attract sizable audiences in regional theaters and at international festivals, and many college productions use some of these aesthetic principles as a matter of course. The students, raised on the postmodern elements of "Sesame Street" and rock video, are undaunted. In Chapter 3 I show how the same contemporary aesthetic has shaped even some of the most popular commercial theater, through examination of *A Chorus Line*.

Although my examples here are drawn primarily from U.S. theater, the theater with which I am most familiar, they need not be so limited. Pinter and even Beckett, for instance, inhabit the same aesthetic territory, and Pinter's astute comments appear throughout this book. My focus on performance theater rather than dramatic texts, however, is pointed, for performance theater provides a more marked elaboration of the perception of reality in terms of events rather than objects.[14]

Chapters 4 and 5 shift attention from theatrical works to acting techniques, which have likewise been permeated by major changes in world view. This examination of acting techniques complements both the contemporary interest in theater as event and the new theater's own self-reflexivity: the examination of the relationship between subject and object as an integral part of the works themselves. Not surprisingly, ideas about acting and the particular aesthetic theory they serve or of which they are a part—whether traditional or postmodern—are correlated. To demonstrate this, I contrast the acting theories of Constantin Stanislavski with those of contemporary theorists. Stanislavski sought to base his system of acting in nature, and much of its force derives from the coherent Aristotelian cast of his ideas about nature. Whereas no contemporary acting theory, by contrast, is as well developed as Stanislavski's, the most influential theories all derive from the same assumptions about nature that underlie Cage's aesthetics. Nonetheless, at present much teaching of acting is based unwittingly on conflicting aesthetic principles, a combination of old and new.[15] We do not abandon one world view to take up another.

Many modern scientists, undeterred by the notion of two unbridgeable cultures, have been interested in exploring the philosophical implications of their ideas, believing along with Bohr that this new knowledge has profoundly shaken the very conceptual foundations of our ordinary modes of thought. Bohr's theatrical image, for instance, follows from his conviction, generalized from atomic physics, that the relation between subject and object forms the core of the problem of knowledge.[16] This view, which denies for science a mere objectivity, has lent new force to the idea that the spirit of the times brings out certain features of the world in both the sciences and the arts. It is this idea of a correspondence between science and art, as opposed to a unidirectional influence of scientific ideas *on* art, that forms the critical basis of this study.

1 .... *John Cage, Nature, and Theater*

Both Aristotle and Cage assume that art should imitate nature's processes. There that similarity ends, however, for the two men see nature so differently that their views of art are antithetical. Yet because Aristotelian concepts are so entrenched in our culture, Cage is often depicted as having set out not to imitate nature, but to defy Aristotle.[1]

Despite Cage's statement that his interest lies in theater, and despite the frequent acknowledgment by others of his influence on theater,[2] only Michael Kirby has systematically analyzed the relationship between Cage's views and the new theater, and his analysis is limited to the relationship between Cage's views and Happenings.[3] The outright resistance to serious analysis of Cage's ideas and accordingly of their relationship to theater follows from the belief many hold that Cage's work is simply anti-art. Virgil Thomson, for instance, has asserted that Cage's aim has long been clearly destructive, and Donal Henahan has likened appreciation of Cage to "a worshipping of wildness, a romanticizing of the savage."[4] The view of Cage as merely anti-art seems to be borne out by his unserious demeanor, which appears to mock traditional aesthetics—not withstanding his statements that he has never been interested in anything simply for its shock value and that he is a naturalist following the findings of science.[5] One often encounters judgments on Cage rendered as general philosophical opposition: "Nature as anything but the bringing of order out of chaos is inconceivable," writes one critic.[6] So much for Cage—and for the second law of thermodynamics as well.

A more considerable objection has been put forth, however: that while the *Poetics* may be understood as consistent with the view of reality expressed in Aristotle's scientific writings, Cage's ideas cannot in the same sense correspond to the view of reality described by the physics of Einstein or Heisenberg, because in all likelihood Cage cannot understand the mathematics in which these theories are expressed, and if he can, he cannot literally translate them into aesthetic terms, since they are inherently mathematical concepts.[7] Although this objection does have some force, it must be noted that any number of distinguished scien-

5

tists, including Einstein and Heisenberg, have attempted to explain their discoveries, together with their import, in ordinary English. In part, this effort has been made in the belief expressed by the Nobel Prize–winning physicist Percy Bridgman that "the conceptual revolution forced by recent physical discoveries in the realm of relativity and quantum effects is not really a revolution in the new realms of high velocities or the very small, but is properly a conceptual revolution on the macroscopic level of everyday life. . . . We have to find how to deal with the new things on this level . . . the common sense level of everyday life."[8]

The vocabulary of this revolution has certainly affected contemporary theater. Richard Schechner, for example, begins his book *Environmental Theatre* with a chapter entitled "Space," in which he makes frequent use of the term *space-time field*, and he follows that chapter with one called "Participation." Richard Foreman employs the words *field* and *quanta* and tells us that he wishes us to "see small," because to see small means to enter the realm where contradictions are seen to be at the root of reality; likewise, he wishes his audiences to become aware of perceptual acts instead of focusing on objects.[9] Foreman claims that his reading in the philosophy of contemporary physics has influenced his theater work.[10] More significantly, a view of reality consistent with that provided by contemporary physics is evident in contemporary theater works themselves.

Cage's aesthetic theory serves to make clear the relationship between these works and contemporary science. Although Cage refers to no one scientist or science, it would seem that he, in agreement with Bridgman's suggestion, has tried to understand the macroscopic implications of physical discoveries in the realms of high velocities and the very small. Of all aesthetic theorists, he has most cogently envisioned an art that is a part of the resulting conceptual revolution.

Figure 1 contrasts Cage's views with those of Aristotle, the arrows indicating the transformations of Aristotelian concepts. Because Cage believes that all things flow and interpenetrate and cannot finally be set into categories, any schematic arrangement of his ideas misrepresents them. Certainly his own writing is not schematic; moreover, it is ostensibly about music and makes no mention of Aristotle. Yet it is in many ways a deliberate response to traditional Aristotelian ideas, and my organization aims to make this clear.

All of Aristotle's thought is primarily functional and biological, aimed above all at understanding life, particularly human life. According to John Herman Randall, Aristotle approaches every subject matter from the standpoint of living, knowing, and talking—knowing and talking being in his view the distinctive attributes of human life. "His whole philosophy is built around the categories of life."[11] Life can be understood in terms of motion, the subject matter, then, of Aristotle's natural science. By motion Aristotle meant any transition from potential to actual being, a change from one state of affairs to another. Indeed, for Aristotle, nature itself is a principle of movement.[12] The wide scope of the

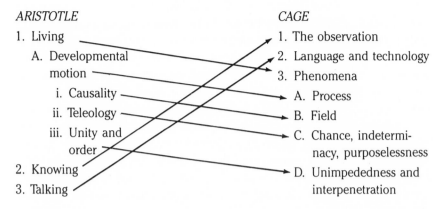

Fig. 1. Contrast Between Aristotle and Cage

ARISTOTLE

1. Living
   A. Developmental
      motion
      i. Causality
      ii. Teleology
      iii. Unity and
          order
2. Knowing
3. Talking

CAGE

1. The observation
2. Language and technology
3. Phenomena
   A. Process
   B. Field
   C. Chance, indetermi-
      nacy, purposelessness
   D. Unimpededness and
      interpenetration

Aristotelian concept of motion is perpetuated in the later scholastic adage "who knows not motion knows not nature." But since Aristotle wanted most of all to understand life, his account of motion had to explain what he considered to be the characteristic change of earthly living things, namely, developmental change. He wanted to understand the "motion" of eggs, not just of billiard balls.

In Aristotle's view, the most complex and developed forms of change and motion are living and knowing. It is these above all other motions that he believed science must explain. Not accidentally, it is also these that he saw drama as imitating. All art, according to Aristotle, imitates human life—not its outward acts, but these acts as they represent spiritual movements, the activity of the soul. The art of poetry in particular, including drama, "imitates men who *live at the level of action*, for whom action is the goal and the principle of life: 'men in action' but also 'men of action.' "[13] Dramatic action, however, should not be understood in any shallow sense: what human beings delight in is imitation of human powers of operation. Of these, knowing is one of the most important, for, according to Aristotle, it is the nature of human beings to seek knowledge. Thus it is that recognition, or coming to know, plays such an important part in the best dramas and that it is closely allied with an important part of their structure, the reversal. The best drama necessarily entails growth and development of character.

Aristotle's concept of action in drama shares its primary characteristics with the primary characteristics of his concept of motion in nature. Each is central to the analysis of the matter at hand, each is understood as an innate principle, a way of acting, a finite process defined by its end, determinate, continuous in time, and unified. Given Aristotle's idea of nature as change or process and his idea that drama is an imitation of nature—that is, of an action, a complex human motion—we should not be surprised that among the arts his first interest was in the drama, or that in the drama the first principle is plot. According to him, all the poetic arts imitate action, but drama evidently reproduces it most completely.

Although Cage agrees that art should imitate nature in its manner of operation, it is noteworthy that he, along with the theater he represents, takes as his scientific model not biology, as Aristotle did, but physics, the science that has most captured our imaginations in this century. This shift in scientific basis has considerable significance for theater. Physics, in its study of nonprogressive events, turns the emphasis away from living things to the larger universe, a universe conceived of as infinite and therefore without a center. In this perspective, both man, the highest living form in Aristotle's view of nature, and the idea of developmental change diminish in significance. These and other important shifts as they relate to theater are the subject of this chapter.

The Observation

Following what has seemed common sense for thousands of years, Aristotle gave primacy not to the act of knowing, but to what he wanted to know. By contrast, Jacob Bronowski has explained why observation, the very act of perceiving, should be the first category: "All the currents of science flow together in this: that the analytical and impersonal view of this world is failing.... The basis of the world is the observation."[14] Relativity derives essentially from the philosophic view that events do not possess discrete facts and discrete perceivers; rather, the two are joined in an observation. And just this is what the principle of uncertainty explains in atomic physics, that the event and the observer are not separable. Or, as Cage puts it aphoristically, "people and sounds interpenetrate."[15] Science no longer studies nature in itself but the interplay between nature and ourselves. At the atomic level the observer interacts with the system to such an extent that the system cannot be understood as having an independent existence. Whereas for Aristotle knowing entails a comprehension of nature apart from the questions we put to nature, an absolute description of what is out there, an exact correlation between our understanding and the physical world, physicists have come to regard theories about natural phenomena, including the so-called laws, as creations of the human mind: properties of our conceptual map of reality rather than reality itself. In the quantum domain, as physicist Henry Stapp explains, "the observed system is required to be isolated in order to be defined, yet interacting in order to be observed."[16] Thus, at the most elemental level, the description of nature necessarily becomes the description of experienced phenomena, not a representation of something more fundamental, an independent physical reality. Bohr said, "There is no quantum world. There is only an abstract quantum physical description. It is wrong to think that the task of physics is to find out how nature *is*. Physics concerns only what we can *say* about nature."[17] All that can be determined is whether or not the logically derivable consequences of the statements correspond with the empirically observed consequences of the phenomena for which the statements have been designed. Reality itself is unknowable; there is no exact correspondence between the world outside and that in our minds. Thus we must turn from the idea of knowing reality in itself to an account of the observation of it.

If the basis of the world is the observation, the imitation of nature must include that observation. So, for Cage, art is not an object distinct from ourselves, but an experience, an event that includes the observer. Percy Bridgman explains his proposed inclusion of himself as observer along similar lines: "It was my original intention to present my analysis of doings or happenings exclusively in the first person singular, the doings or happenings being doings by me or happenings to me. My reason for this was, among others, my desire to secure the greatest possible immediacy in description."[18] What the interaction of observer and observed means to Cage, and to contemporary theater in general, is that the performers overtly participate in what they are performing. They do not perform roles that are separate from themselves; they interact with the roles and are present along with them. Live performance, which includes both performers and observers, becomes far more important than script or score (or film or phonograph record). The script is but a report on a performance, not itself the art object to be presented. To ensure that the audience members, like the performers, consciously interact with what they observe, they are not set apart from the performance. Arrange the presentation, says Cage, "so that the physical circumstances . . .do not oppose audience to performers but dispose the latter around—among the former."[19]

If the idea of reality depends on the observer, the best we can do is report as fully as possible on our actual experience of it. "Our description," says Bridgman, "is not complete unless we can specify what we see or feel or hear or smell or taste."[20] With respect to theater, then, we should not pretend that we are elsewhere than in a theater watching a play. All that is actually occurring and present should be acknowledged. To emphasize this idea, the lighting, the backstage area, actors not performing, other audience members, and the house are all exposed to view. Cage is particularly interested in revealing those parts of reality that have heretofore been hidden, ignored, or degraded.

If no occurrence or object can be defined apart from an observer, the idea of a single true account of reality is challenged. Bridgman explains: "The meaning to be attached to reality is to a large extent a personal matter and changes with time, but I believe it fair to say that the sense in which every one used reality a few years ago and the sense in which the majority use it to-day has 'uniqueness' as a minimum connotation. It would not have been admitted that two entirely different explanations of the universe could each be equally real."[21] The major challenge to the idea that there is one true account of reality inheres in the concept of complementarity. The different intuitive pictures used to describe atomic systems—wave and quantum theory—although each fully adequate for different explanatory situations, are nevertheless mutually exclusive. Each picture is legitimate when used in the right place, and so the theories are said to be mutually complementary. A further challenge to the idea of a single true account of reality is posed by the difficulty, particularly acute in the realm of small-scale phenomena, of verification by repetition or by co-observation; in other words, because an elementary event in the microscopic world may be witnessed by only one observer, confirmation by public report becomes impossible.[22] Support for the idea that the world is at its foundation pluralistic also comes from the realm of the very large, for which Einstein showed that there is no universal "now," only "here and now" for each observer.

Conventional theater, with its frontality and single focus, implies that what is to be understood about reality is its uniqueness—one thing at a time, to which everyone is to attend from the same "right" perspective (although some seats are better than others). "The assumption," says Cage, "is that people will see *it* if they all look in one direction"; but in fact, he goes on to say, each "consciousness is structuring the experience differently from anybody else's in the audience."[23] If reality is perspectival, the value of art cannot derive from its universality. As Cage observes, the very "possibility of conversation resides in the impossibility of two people having the same experience whether or not their attention is directed one-pointedly."[24] Similarly, the composer does not experience his music as does an audience member, "for the composer was not in the same position as [the listener] was with respect to it—on the most mundane level, not in the same part of the room."[25]

Composing, performing, and hearing are separate experiences. Accordingly, Cage believes that instead of presenting reality as yielding to a single account or perspective, theater ought to attempt to provide experiences that reveal reality as it is known—that is, as pluralistic. Seats, sights, and sounds should not be so arranged as to provide everyone with the same experience; neither should there be "right" or "best" seats at a performance, just as there are none for experiencing reality. Rather, the performance should impress on the listener that "the hearing of the piece is his own action—that the music, so to speak, is his, rather than the composer's."[26]

In Cage's music, one of the purposes of nonintentionality is to emphasize that the experience of it is our own and not determined by the external occurrences—sounds. To conform with the idea of a perspectival reality, the performance ought to have more than one thing happening at a time, so that, as in life, our respective attentions are divided. The effort in conventional theater to maintain consistent performances throughout the run of a show is aimed at providing every audience member with an ideal and identical experience, but in fact this is impossible; not only do not all audience members have the same experience at any one performance or at different performances, but an individual who returns will not have the same experience a second time. For Cage, the effort to present a single ideal view represents a falsification of reality. Audience members should be made aware that the performance is different for each observer and from performance to performance. This variance, together with theater's inherent three-dimensionality, makes performance a particularly suitable means for representing reality, because it underscores the fact that there is no one right perspective from which to view reality. Theater performance, then, Cage remarks, is more indicative of our relationship to the world than a painting, which can only be viewed from the front.

Not only is the idea of a constant, discrete, and single identity for any portion of the external world challenged by the role of the observer in the observation, but that of the observer is as well. The observer is not a recording consciousness, a fixed entity; observation, requiring interaction, necessarily affects the observer. Cage elaborates on this idea: "If you do not change your mind about something when you confront a picture you have not seen before, you are either a stubborn fool or the painting is not very good." Self-preservation is "only a preservation from life."[27] "An individual, having no separate soul, is a time-span, a collection of changes. Our nature's that of Nature. Nothing's fixed."[28] Art should heighten our awareness that our identity is not separate from that of nature and not fixed. It should change us, extending our perceptions of reality. We are as we experience. Just as observers are part of what they observe and are changed by their experience, so actors must regard the characters they play not as "other," but as manifestations of themselves in relation to their roles. Actors grow and change as they simultaneously reveal themselves and take on this "other" in their roles; the actors and the roles are not distinct. This, in part, is what Cage has in mind when he says that "the distinctions between self and other are being forgotten."[29]

The corollary of the observer's need to report fully on all that he or she actually experiences is the need to restrict the report to *only* that experienced. Bronowski tells us that Einstein was in fact the first to take very seriously the view that science must get rid of abstractions and make its system only out of what is in fact observed.[30] Similarly persuaded, Cage seeks to free himself of abstract ideas about sounds and instead listen to sounds themselves in all their acoustical detail.[31] He finds art that is "anthropocentric (involved in self-expression)" trivial and lacking in urgency.[32] It asks us to appreciate not sounds but the way in which the composer used the sounds to express himself—his musical ideas, meanings, and feelings; and worse, it conceals this request, requiring us to confuse ourselves "to the same final extent that the composer did and imagine that sounds are not sounds at all but are Beethoven and that men are not men but are sounds."[33] Cage wishes to move away from subjective concerns toward the world of nature and society of which we all are a part and in which there are things as well as people. He has, he says, come to be interested in anything but himself as art material.[34] The world does not express meaning, and it has no essence. On this account, Cage believes that art which imitates nature cannot reveal essence or express meaning either. As the painter Frank Stella succinctly comments, "What you see is what you see."[35] Concepts of meaning and essence are inseparable from, and rely on, a subjective selection and ordering of the possible material. To be sure, says Cage, movements, sounds, and lights are expressive, but what they express "is determined by each one of you—who is right, as Pirandello's title has it, if he thinks he is."[36] "The meaning of something," Cage says, echoing Wittgenstein, "is in its use, not in itself."[37]

To Cage, anthropocentrism is expressed by far more than the desire to find the meaning or essence of experience. The old mainstays of art and of an "objective" view of reality—the ideas of order, of causality, of force, of the possibility of isolating objects, of continuity, of purpose, and of absolute space and time—must be surrendered, understood as intrusions of the self rather than as manifestations of the external world. One must give up on the "desire to improve on creation and function as a faithful receiver of experience."[38]

Accordingly, Cage attempts to compose music that does not express himself, music originating in no psychology, motive, dramatic intention, or literary or pictorial purpose. "I had," he writes, "taken steps to make a music that was just sounds, sounds free of judgments about whether they were 'musical' or not, sounds free of memory and taste (likes and dislikes), sounds free of fixed relations between two or more of them (musical syntax, or glue, as Henry Cowell called it)."[39] To compose such music, Cage has had to find ways to remove himself from the sounds that are his working material, and to that end he uses "non-art" resources, which allow one to perceive art with a certain freshness. For Cage, one such resource is noise: sounds that are not officially designated as musical and that therefore can be heard directly without automatic conceptualization. Another is silence, by which he means any sounds not intended, inasmuch as actual silence does not exist.

To further free sounds from himself, Cage employs means to make composition chancy and indeterminate and, thus, freer of his intention. He explains the distinction between chance and indeterminacy thus: "In the case of chance operations, one knows more or less the elements of the universe with which one is dealing, whereas in indeterminacy, I like to think...that I'm outside the circle of a known universe and dealing with things I literally don't know anything about."[40] Naturally, Cage is more interested in methods of indeterminacy than of chance because they are freer from intrusions of himself. For example, by providing various sounds at one time and placing the sound sources in various parts of the room, Cage ensures that what each audience member hears is a function of his or her location and attention—the final effect, in short, is beyond Cage's control and hence his intention.

Like the composer, the performer must work to relinquish control of the material. Discipline for the performer, then, does not mean incorporation of a technique but, rather, self-renunciation, the ability to give oneself up to the material. Cage elaborates: "It is precisely what the Lord meant when he said, give up your father and mother and follow me. It means give up the things closest to you. It means give yourself up, everything, and do what it is you are going to do."[41] The performer is likened to a religious figure.

The widely used physical exercises of Jerzy Grotowski and the vocal exercises of Kristin Linklater are designed to bring actors to precisely this state of self-renunciation.[42] By freeing the self from physical and psychosocial barriers and developing a far wider range of movement and sound than was previously thought humanly fitting or possible, the actor, it is thought, can respond more directly, without restraint, to the material at hand. This relinquishing of control is what is meant when acting is referred to as risk-taking. Moreover, if self-renunciation provides a more direct, "honest," response to the material, a response that neither participant nor audience expects, the ultimate effect may not be "believable" (thus flouting the sine qua non of the Stanislavski method)— because believability is, after all, a function of our expectations.

The audience, too, must learn to experience art, and consequently nature, disinterestedly. To become fluent, confluent, with nature, one must give up one's desires, expectations, and valuations with respect to it, give up one's presuppositions regarding its orderly, continuous, purposeful character (presuppositions that Cage calls "clap-trap") and assume what, borrowing from Zen Buddhism, he calls the condition of "no-mindedness."[43] "A sober and quiet mind is one in which the ego does not obstruct the fluency of the things that come in through our senses and up through our dreams."[44] "With a mind that has nothing to do, that mind is free to enter into the act of listening, hearing each sound just as it is, not as a phenomenon more or less approximating a preconception."[45]

It is no easier for an audience member to achieve the condition of no-mindedness than it is for a composer or performer. As Cage observes, "Not all of our past, but the parts of it we are taught, lead us to believe that we are in the driver's seat. With respect to nature. And that if we are not, life is meaningless."[46] Although the cessation of the application of mind seems at first to be a giving up of everything that belongs to humanity, Cage believes that actually it leads to the world of nature, where, gradually or suddenly, it becomes clear that nothing is lost when everything is given away; in fact, everything is gained, because life is more interesting than humanmade structures.[47]

It is Cage's hope that art can teach us to check our habits of seeing, to encounter them for the sake of freshness, to be unfamiliar with what we see. And indeed, we *are* learning not to ask what a Pinter or a Foreman play means, and we are learning not to analyze all plays as if they could be understood as logical sequences located specifically in time and place. Eventually, Cage believes, by ceasing to ask that art be meaningful, logical, and so forth, we will cease to ask those things of nature. The grand thing about the human mind, Cage says, "is that it can turn its own tables and see meaninglessness as ultimate meaning."[48] While no-mindedness, poverty of spirit, or silence of the ego (the condition necessary for the art experience) may be understood as a kind of passivity, it is also a condition of extreme alertness and activity. When the material is not controlled by the composer, when observers are not provided with ready-made meaning or logic, far more active observation is required.

A no-minded observer has a lesser role in the universe than does Aristotle's knower. In a universe that has no center, human beings lose their own centrality: they have no special vantage point; they are part of nature, neither set off from it nor its focal point. Nor can human beings be the measure of that universe, which is both infinitely large and infinitely small. If reality is perspectival and continually changing, no human can know it once and for all. Because there is no correspondence between the mind and nature, human beings cannot find their unique, essential purpose and pleasure in knowing; like the rest of nature, they have no ulterior purpose. They have no more importance in nature than any other part. "Life goes on very well without me," Cage observes.[49] In Cage's view, human beings cannot comprehend or grasp nature; to see it they must "keep humble":[50] give up such desires and become no-minded participants, accepting their situation within nature without desire to elevate themselves above it. Pascual Jordan remarks that the scientist's change in attitude "may be characterized in a single phrase that also suggests its human content; it is a turn from arrogance to humility."[51] It is precisely this necessary humility that keeps Cage's writing unpretentious, even seemingly lacking in seriousness, and revelatory of a comic sense of life.

Critic Jill Johnston claims that the most advanced thought and art of our time serve to bring people back to their proper situation within nature.[52] If art by example is to serve this function, then artists must be de-deified: they cannot be those who show us what life means or how it is ordered, nor can they be regarded as distinct from the rest of nature and with views superior to our own. "Someone," observes Cage, "said, 'Art should come from within; then it is profound.' But it seems to me Art goes within, and I don't see the need for 'should' or 'then' or 'it' or 'profound.' When Art comes from within, which it was for so long doing, it became a thing which seemed to elevate the man who made it above those who observed it or heard it."[53] If art, like nature, is a process, a continuing, changing event, and the artist a participant in nature, the artist is not one who makes special products but one who participates in the process. There is no distinction between living and making; art is a way of life and can be anyone's. "But seriously," remarked one reviewer, understanding that Cage meant music to be just sounds, "if this is what music is, I could write it as well as you." And Cage agrees.[54] The act of creation is not special; we are to think of all others, everyone, as artists. "Imitation of nature in her manner of operation, traditionally the artist's function, is now what everyone has to do."[55]

Following this argument, we find that the division between composer, performer, and audience disappears.[56] Viola Spolin, the Judson Dancers, Anna Halprin, and others have devised means for amateurs to create and perform in theater events and dances. And technically trained performers have given up their stylized movements and stage voices to appear as amateurs. Robert Wilson used texts written by a brain-damaged boy; the Wooster Group has sought inspiration from children. Cage would approve: "We begin," he says, "to be keenly aware of the richness and uniqueness of each individual and the natural capacity in each person to open up new possibilities for another."[57] Art as participation requiring no special people can be communal. Art as a way of perceiving, of framing, moreover, need not be restricted to objects made by humans, and can be found anywhere. The role of humans (if they can be said to have one) is simply to become more aware, more curious, and more in accord with nature; and the role of artists (if they can be said to have one) is to help us to be so.

Just as Cage wants us to model our art on nature, including the fact of our participation in nature, so does he want us to model our society on art. Aristotle thought of the Greek city-state as a natural creation: not only the highest form of political life to date, but the highest form of political life possible.[58] Cage believes that although some art is now in accord with nature, our society is not in accord with art. "Our poetry now is the realization that we possess nothing," he writes; "the very practice of music...is a celebration that we own nothing." The world must be seen as a process in which we participate and we are accordingly to give up our possessive, grasping, self-important habits of mind: "To imagine that you own any piece of music is to miss the whole point." We must likewise give up the idea of ownership with respect to nature, for without ownership there is greater abundance: "If one maintains secure possession of nothing...then there is no limit to what one may freely enjoy."[59] In place of ownership, Cage says, we must substitute the idea of use.[60] If there is abundance and we understand that life is purposeless, then art, like all of living, is just something to do. The artist is de-deified indeed.

Although Cage does not assume the same correlation between man's mind and nature that Aristotle thought enabled us to know the world as in itself it really is, Cage does believe that there is one convenient correspondence between world and mind which Aristotle did not acknowledge. The world, Cage asserts, is a complex interrelationship of discontinuous events in time and space, with analyses in terms of discrete linear actions being particularly unsuited to the modern electronic age, where "everything happens at once."[61] As luck would have it, moreover, we are omniattentive; we do not perceive only one thing at a time, but many things at once and discontinuously. Perception is not sequential like language (or like an Aristotelian action); rather, the electronic analogy—that everything happens at once—is more apt. And unlike print, the electronic media condition us to the multiplicity of simultaneous perceptions of which we are capable. Thus, for any theatrical activity, Cage believes, the minimum number of necessary actions going on at once is about five, since "bright people can clear up rather quickly perplexity arising from lower numbers."[62]

Language and Technology

Aristotle assumed that language, like mind, corresponds to and reflects the world exactly, and that the world, with its logical, discursive character and systematic structure, lends itself to the grasp of language. A thing is known when one can state in precise and singular terms what that thing is and why it is as it is. In the final analysis, the structure of the Greek language and the structure of the world are identical.

Linguists and scientists have made us aware of many ways in which language shapes our view of reality. Because language has meaning and intention, we have assumed that reality does also. Yet insofar as language is objective— "There is a horse," as opposed to "I see a horse"—it is misleading. Syntax is a system of subordination that because we describe things in sentences, suggests an equivalent system of subordination in nature. Language presents things one at a time and sequentially and so has suggested the linearity of experience. Language analyzes events into static, clear, and discrete elements, and so we have seen reality in these terms rather than as continually flowing, dissolving, and reforming: the word *horse* is misleading in its creation of a category. Our language is committed to three-dimensional space and the forward flow of time, but present scientific research suggests that the images and concepts of ordinary language following from this commitment must be abandoned in order to understand nature.

Theater has traditionally reflected the belief that language accurately captures reality; the principal medium of drama, as Aristotle believed it should be, has been language. We have been able to regard the text as the play itself, to analyze a play in terms of its meaning, and a speech or a character in terms of its single unified action or intention. Finding that language does not faithfully represent experience—that, as Cage puts it, "if before you live you go through a word then there is an indirection"— the arts in general have moved away from language and have tended toward the condition of music: they have become more self-referential and untranslatable.[63] The influence of the visual arts, moreover, has caused theater to become more spatial, and the influence of dance has caused it to rely more on kinesthetic expression. Because Cage emphasizes music as a performance art and has conceived of it in visual and spatial terms, he, of all musicians, has most directly influenced contemporary theater.

At the same time that nonverbal modes of expression have gained importance in theater performance, the use of nondescriptive or nonanalytic language has also increased. Cage has been influential on, and representative of, these efforts as well. Aristotle regarded poetic language highly because it was refined; Cage, in contrast, insists on language more reflective of experience, objecting for example to language organized rhythmically because it suggests a reality of great regularity.[64] His recent experiments using language thus reveal simultaneity, odd juxtaposition, repetition, and lack of progression or subordination of parts. In *M* (1974), Cage relies almost entirely on musical or visual effects of language: graphics that leave sentences unreadable, experiments with nonsense words and sentences. In *Empty Words* (1979) and *X* (1982), his goal was to construct a language "saying nothing at all," a language "without sentences and not confined to any subject."[65] These books constitute a transition from language to music, with much of the writing intended for performance. For not only do voice and gesture provide a more personal and fuller response to experience than words alone, but spoken language, unlike written, is continually flowing, dissolving, and re-forming, in this respect more closely reflecting our actual experience of reality.

Between the observer and the world observed, Cage introduces a new consideration: technology. Like language, technology can be an instrument of perception. It also has the same limitations: measurements "measure measuring means."[66] Aristotle believed that nature is as we can know it experientially; Cage, conversely, holds that all we can know of nature is our experience of it. Aristotle believed humans to be so suited as knowers that their naked eyes and ears would suffice; Cage sees technology as a means for extending our nervous systems into the environment, allowing us to experience events more directly. Electronic music, for instance, is sound without middlemen, without interpreters—people subservient to the sounds they produce.

The real significance of technology, however, lies in its power not just to change our perception of nature but to change nature itself. The "only chance to make the world a success for humanity," says Cage, "lies in technology, [in the] grand possibility technology provides to do more with less, and indiscriminately for everyone. Return to nature as nature pre-technologically was, attractive and possible as it still in some places is, can only work for some of us." Even though much technological development is very recent, some very serious errors have already resulted as a consequence of it. "We are in our technological infancy," says Cage. "Telsa, who discovered alternating current, did so in this century. . . . Technological errors made by government, industry (DDT, ABM, SST, CIA, etc.) are those of children, who even though they don't know what the score is, go on playing pre-technological games of power and profit."[67] Nevertheless, technology affords us a significant opportunity: "The question really now—the most urgent thing—is getting us to shift from an economy of scarcity to an economy of abundance; and this is going to mean an utter change of our minds with regard to morals and everything."[68]

The abundance afforded by technology has great potential impact on art, for in the midst of this plenty the masses can cease to strive. Perhaps, as Richard Foreman suggests, the drama of conflict will then become less interesting.[69] If leisure increases, people will have more time simply to experience the world and need no longer perceive it strictly in terms of its usefulness for their livelihood. Like Aristotle, Cage believes that the highest experience lies not in striving to change the world but in knowing or experiencing it as it is. His argument that we must improve technology so that we can change the world in order better to appreciate it, therefore, is paradoxical, as, for that matter, is the idea that the highest experience for human beings—in a valueless world—is to appreciate the world as it is. Cage acknowledges the existence of such contradictions in his writing and, indeed, makes no claim to logical consistency—although he is for the most part extremely logical. Rather, he thinks of these paradoxes as correlates or complements, and has in mind the complementarity in descriptions of the quantum world.[70]

Phenomena
....

When physics is taken as the model science, life loses its central importance. This loss of centrality is evident in the arts, although least in theater, perhaps because the general reliance on human bodies and speech as the primary media of theater suggests that human life should be its primary subject matter as well. Nonetheless, the dispassionate and distant view of humanity conveyed by some contemporary dramas and performances, in which human and nonhuman are viewed equally as objects or humans serve to represent the nonhuman, become more comprehensible when not life but phenomena constitute the central reality. Playwright Heiner Müller, believing that "the history of mankind can no longer be separated from the history of animals (and plants, stones, and machines) except at the price of its fall," celebrates Robert Wilson's art as "the only truly Communist theater," a theater that represents not only all people, but also all species and even all elements equally.[71] The focus on phenomena also acknowledges the essential role of human participation in what we perceive and emphasizes the analysis of reality in terms of occurrences.

Process   Aristotle's analysis of nature concerns motion, the motion of matter: to him, the world is essentially substantial. According to contemporary science, however, the unit of things real is the *event*—energy, not matter, constitutes the basic datum. Particles are not material stuff, but dynamic patterns or processes. In contrast to Aristotle's assumption that motions are discrete and finite, occurring in an essentially unchanging universe, contemporary physics holds that all particles can be transmuted into other particles: they can be created from and vanish into energy. Classical concepts like "elementary particle," "material substance," and "isolated object" have lost their meaning; the whole universe appears as a dynamic, endlessly changing web of inseparable energy patterns. "No greater revolution has occurred in the history of human thought than the radical shift from a fixed, stable cosmology to a dynamic, evolving ever-changing cosmogenesis," the eminent biologist Ernst Mayr observes.[72] As Bridgman puts it, the present situation is characterized by an intensified conviction that in reality new orders of experience do exist, which we may expect to meet continually.[73]

The belief that reality is an endless process in which the observer plays a part has deeply affected Cage's view of art, leading to his emphasis on performance rather than art object. There is, he says, an unfortunate "tendency in painting (permanent pigments) as in poetry (printing, binding) to be secure in the thingness of a work."[74] The value of art cannot be its timelessness, for that which is fixed misrepresents reality. For this reason, Cage thinks of literature already written as material rather than as art and tells us that the phonograph record is not the music. "A finished work," he says, "is exactly that, requires resurrection."[75] "We are having art in order to use it. . . . Art for the now-moment rather than for posterity's museum civilization."[76] This immediacy, he says, is the very nature of dance, of music-making, or of any other art requiring performance.[77] Art as process is the idea behind Happenings and also partly explains theater in which the director assumes as important a role as the playwright—or even more important. It is the idea behind works specific to particular places and particular performers, works that are deliberately specific and temporary. It is the idea behind theater works that are called "works in progress," in which theoretically no effort is made to stabilize performances; on the contrary, productions are actively allowed to change over time, as does everything else in nature. Art in process, because it is like nature, can, Cage hopes, help us to adapt to a continually changing world. With respect to change, Cage, as usual, has no regrets that nature is as it is: "What permits us to love one another and the earth we inhabit is that we and it are impermanent."[78] "Life without death is no longer life but only self-preservation. . . .The acceptance of death is the source of all life."[79]

Because language works on the principle of repetition, it misleads us about nature. In reality there is no repetition; everything, including ourselves, is always changing. Reality is dynamic, not static. The tree makes no two leaves exactly alike. Cage is especially interested in art that highlights those aspects of reality that we tend to overlook, in this case the particularity of things. Generalizing about all the leaves on a tree, we distance ourselves from each individual leaf, forfeiting its immediacy. Cage is fond of using apparent repetition because it makes clear that actual repetition does not occur; rather, as things change in time and in relation to other things, we perceive varying aspects of all those things and, over time, we also change. Thus Cage, borrowing from Zen, requests, "If something is boring after two minutes, try it for four. If still boring, try it for eight, sixteen, thirty-two, and so on. Eventually one discovers that it's not boring at all but very interesting."[80] Bridgman observes that what we perceive changes with time, not just if we stay still but especially if we move about ourselves or manipulate things.[81] As if to heighten audience awareness of this particularity of events, Richard Schechner and Andrei Serban, among others, have contrived environments that encourage audience members to move about to see the theater performance from various perspectives.

If the world is an endless dynamic process, with all particles transmutable into other particles, then only transformation or creation by transformation exists; there can be no creations or annihilations.[82] When applied to performance, this means that a work can have no clear beginning or ending. Whereas Cage's early works had beginnings, middles, and endings, the later ones do not: they begin anywhere and last any length of time. A critic of Cage's work explains, "The whole performance is an excerpt; indeed the piece is an excerpt. . .from everything. It begins nowhere and ends nowhere. It has always been in progress; it is only that it became audible just recently. It is, in fact, still in progress."[83] Cage describes a 1965 performance, which was to begin without the audience knowing it had begun and was to conclude when the last audience member had left. "When only twelve people were left, we arranged to serve refreshments: all those people had a party."[84]

Such overt transformation became de rigueur in American theater of the late sixties and early seventies. As the audience arrived, the actors were seen to be warming up; gradually, in plain view, each assumed a character; at the end the character was transformed into the actor, and the audience members were invited on stage to dance or have a party with the actors, presumably until everyone got tired and went home. Without a curtain and with no dimming of houselights or perceptible brightening of stage lights, it became difficult to establish just when the theater event began or ended. Robert Wilson and the Wooster

Group, respectively, have characterized their body of works as all one work.[85] Likewise, actors may not describe themselves as creating a role, which they then drop out of at the end of the evening and at the end of the run; instead they may say they are transformed through transaction with a role.[86] The Living Theater's *Mysteries and Smaller Pieces* (1968) contained a section variously entitled "Lee's Piece" or "Sound and Movement," in which one actor improvised a gesture or sound and "gave" it to an approaching performer; that person "picked up" the gesture, transformed it into a new expression, and passed it on to another actor; and so on. Alternatively, a player may in the course of a single performance undergo a number of transformations, changing roles with each change of costume—as the particles of an atom might change. The player does not need an hour before the curtain goes up to get into the role. Such transformations prevent us from seeing the play as an object and urge us to see it as unbounded process in which actor, character, and audience all play a part.

Field   In relativity theory, time as a one-dimensional continuum is considered an artificial construct; rather, space and time are both part of the same continuum. At the atomic level, nature is perceivable only as discontinuous; there, apparently, no law of causality obtains. Force and matter are but different aspects of the same phenomenon, and matter and space are inseparable and interdependent parts of a single whole—the field. The concept of the field, then, replaces the idea of continuous motion in linear time, in which the single chain of events is causally linked.

The notion of linear time is inconsistent with time as we experience it. Bridgman tells us that

> the time of the mathematician is a one-dimensional continuum, reaching forward and backward to plus and minus infinity, everywhere homogeneous, and with an origin which may be situated arbitrarily. The time of the mathematician seems to have got itself ineradicably embedded in the thinking of modern civilization, for apparently we all nearly always think of time as a homogeneous and unlimited one-dimensional sequence, all past time on one side, all future time on the other, separated by the present which is in continuous motion from past to future. What could be more unlike the time of experience, apprehended with true freshness, which consists of a blurred sequence of memories, culminating in the budding and unfolding present?[87]

Furthermore, contrary to experience, events cannot be ordered in time independent of their location in space. Space-time is a four-dimensional continuum of events. The distinction we make between space and time thus ultimately reflects a peculiarity of our mental functioning. As physicist H. Minkowski tells us, "Henceforth space by itself, and time by itself, are doomed to fade away into mere shadows, and only a kind of union of the two will preserve an independent reality."[88]

If each moment includes our memories and anticipations and we do not actually experience time as a continuum, then in drama that imitates nature the emphasis must shift from recounting chronology to presenting that which is immediate. "When life is lived," Cage remarks, "there is nothing in it but the present, the 'now-moment.' "[89] Director Richard Foreman has tried to make his drama immediate—an account of all that is experienced at any one moment, including the remembered past and that anticipated. The account takes time but is essentially spatial. Furthermore, Foreman is interested in creating not memorable work, but work that involves us rigorously in all its moments.[90] Similarly, in a Pinter play such as *Old Times,* the characters' stories of past events should be understood as serving the characters' present interaction and self-definition; the play as a whole may be usefully understood as an account of all that takes place in but a moment—the moment frozen in a pose at the end of the play. Gertrude Stein would have referred to *Old Times* and to Foreman's performances as she referred to her own plays—as "landscapes": "A landscape does not move, nothing really moves in a landscape, but things are there, and I put into the play the things that were there."[91]

Cage believes that the distinctions we make between the spatial arts (visual) and the temporal arts (aural) at present are oversimplified. He therefore works to intermix spatial and temporal arts "in order to show a musical recognition of the necessity of space, which has already been recognized on the part of the other arts, not to mention scientific awareness." Accordingly, he composes guided by the imperfections in the paper because, he says, he is "thus able to designate certain aspects of sound as though they were in a field, which of course they are."[92] His music, he says, is performance for both the eyes and the ears.

From quantum mechanics we learn that change is discontinuous; a system passes from one state to another, not smoothly, but by a series of jerks or jumps. When we wish to determine the order in which the jumps will occur, no exact laws apply, and we are compelled to appeal to statistics and probabilities. In the realm of the subatomic, in short, we appear to be confronted with total chaos and anarchy. Even Erwin Schrödinger, who sought to eliminate from physics the random, unvisualizable, and unanalyzable quantum leaps, called on science to eliminate such connecting terms as *how, because, so, in order to, suppose, as a result of, although,* and *when* from the description of nature because, he says, these logical connectives are in people's minds, not in nature.[93] Likewise, Cage wishes to devise an art that is free of such connectives: "Where people had felt the necessity to stick sounds together to make a continuity, we...felt the opposite necessity, to rid them of the glue so that sounds would be themselves." The "privilege of connecting two things," he says, "remains [the] privilege of each individual (e.g.: I: thirsty: *drink a glass of water*); but this privilege isn't to be exercised publicly except in emergencies (there are no aesthetic emergencies)."[94] Cage does not feel the necessity to present sounds (or, for that matter, ideas) so as to ensure continuity. In fact, he believes that it is more important to present sounds in no particular order, just as they appear in nature. If sounds and musical events are simply placed one after another they will be seen as related through their coexistence in space. "The problem of modulating from one key to another 'very distant' one was discussed. After an hour, the instructor asked Ruggles how he, Ruggles, would solve the problem. Ruggles said: I wouldn't make a problem out of it; I'd just go from one to the other without any transition."[95] Discontinuity in art makes the work unpredictable and therefore conveys no sense of movement toward an endpoint, leaving us to attend to the moment, to individual elements without regard for what they portend. It also divorces the elements from the burden of psychological intention, making clear that the act of connection is our own.[96] As we become aware that nature is essentially discontinuous, we notice that our attention and even personality are too. "We jump," says Cage[97]—or, as popular psychology puts it, "today is the first day of the rest of our lives": we can be different from what we were yesterday. Hence character in drama need not be "consistent" to be realistic; we become as interested in the transformations actors can make as in the single coherent characters they can develop.

The idea of causality has changed beyond recognition. Erwin Schrödinger observes that the widespread belief in causality at the molecular level arises simply from the custom, inherited over thousands of years, of thinking causally; that this custom makes the idea of undetermined events, of absolute, primary casualness, seem complete nonsense, a logical absurdity; but that the habit of causal thinking was derived from observing over millennia precisely those regularities in natural events which, in the light of our present knowledge, most certainly are not governed by causality—or at least not essentially, since we know them only as statistically regulated phenomena.[98] Bridgman, taking a radical view of the matter, tells us that whenever the physicist "penetrates to the atomic or electronic level in his analysis, he finds things acting in a way for which he can assign no cause, and for which he never can assign a cause, for which the concept of cause has no meaning, if Heisenberg's principle is right. This means nothing more nor less than that the law of cause and effect must be given up."[99]

The traditional understanding of causality has lost its foundation. Accordingly, Cage desires an art in which cause and effect are not emphasized, in which, instead, one relates to what is here now. We are getting rid of the habit we had of explaining everything, he says. The custom of asking why disconnects us from and prevents us from identifying with experience.[100] Previously, when the important question was why, the what was taken for granted; contemporary theater does not let us assume the what.

Whereas before when physicists spoke of force the concept was inherently related to causality, we learn now that in the subatomic world the concept of force is better understood as describing mutual interactions between particles. Hence physicists today prefer to speak about interactions rather than forces, and the laws of force in turn become but formulas for denoting the ways in which things are interdependent as they exist together in areas of spacetime that they create about themselves. When time as a continuum separate from space, the continuity of motion, causality, and force lose their potency as scientific ideas, so does the centrality of action. In place of these is substituted the concept of the field.

The field theories of modern physics "force" us to forsake the classical distinction between material particles and the void. Einstein's field theory of gravity and quantum field theory both show that particles cannot be separated from the space around them. On the one hand, those particles determine the structure of that space, but on the other, they must be conceived of, not as isolated entities, but as condensations of a continuous field present throughout space.[101] This field is seen as the basis of all particles and their mutual interactions. Matter and space thus become inseparable and interdependent parts of a single whole. Fields and bodies co-determine one another. And the concept of empty space, which once appeared unavoidable, now appears to be no more than an artifact of thought.

Cage has often expressed his ideas about the "void": "The sand in which the stones in a Japanese Garden lie is also something."[102] "No silence exists that is not pregnant with sound."[103] There is, Cage believes, no such thing as non-activity: in art as in nature, no space, no sound, no activity can be discounted as background, as inconsequential, irrelevant, or nonexistent. Indeed, Heisenberg tells us that "the primary reality is the field and not the body."[104] And Cage would have us see that the stones in the Japanese garden are there to delineate the sand. His own work places considerable emphasis on "empty" space, "silence," and "non-activity." Contemporary theater generally has turned its attention to the examination of the relationships between space and mass, sound and silence, and motion and non-activity. The scenery is no longer the background for the action; the total space, including the audience space, may be used as the environment in which actors, audience, light, and sound all interact. There may be no backstage or hidden space. Frequently, actors remain visible throughout a performance and make their costume changes, such as they are, in full view. No curtain keeps set changes unseen; the changes become part of the performance. Sound sources are often visible, and sound produced by the actors themselves may be preferred to recorded sound.

The field is unbounded, "so that when one says that there is no cause and effect," explains Cage, "what is meant is that there are an incalculable infinity of causes and effects, that in fact each and every thing in all of time and space is related to each and every other thing in all of time and space."[105] Because everything causes everything else, however, we do not speak of one thing causing another.[106] The physicist David Bohm reiterates this idea: "Thus far, no evidence has been discovered that the possibility of tracing causal relationship...will ever end. In other words, every causal relationship, which necessarily operates in a finite context, has been found to be subject to contingencies arising outside the context in question."[107] Aristotle was a contextualist, but there is no end to the context envisioned by Cage or the physicist. The idea of discrete actions therefore comes to seem an artifice. In space, as in time, action has no end. "Whoever makes the stretcher isn't separate from the painting. (It doesn't stop there either.)"[108] Cage finds the series (i.e., chromatic music) objectionable because it suggests that it is the principle from which all happenings flow; he would accept the series were it to appear as part of a field situation. "Everything happens at once," he says. "Image is no longer stream falling over rocks, getting from original to final place; it's...a vibrating complex, any addition or subtraction of component(s), regardless of apparent position(s) in the total system, producing alteration, a different music."[109] "There is no need to minimize the complexity of the situation, but rather a great need to make this complexity something we can all enjoy. If our arts introduce us to it, then I think they are performing a useful function. But if they continue...to provide an escape from the actual complexity in which we live, then I think they are to be avoided."[110]

If the field is unbounded spatially, then everything truly belongs together at once and no element of the field can be considered an interruption or irrelevancy. Says Cage:

> The moment it becomes a special continuity of I am composing and nothing else should happen, then the rest of life is nothing but a series of interruptions, pleasant or catastrophic as the case may be. The truth, however, is that it is more like Feldman's music—anything may happen and it all does go together. There is no rest of life. Life is one. Without beginning, without middle, without ending. The concept: beginning middle and meaning comes from a sense of self which separates itself from what it considers to be the rest of life.[111]

Cage's music is not interrupted by the sounds of the environment, which are discounted as noise or silence in the concept "beginning middle and meaning." Because natural boundaries do not exist, there are none between art and life, foreground and background, self and other, space and time, performer and audience, or different art forms. When Cage talks about music, then, he is quite naturally talking about theater as well.

Aristotle thought of drama as a temporal art because the presentation of a single action's development takes time. Of course, the single unified action occupies finite space too, but space is merely the background, the context; the action is not as closely related to space as it is to its own past and future. The field concept, by contrast, makes all that occurs at any one time as worthy of examination as that which takes time. The performance thus becomes spatially more complex in order to articulate "the vibrating complex of events happening at one time."[112]

As always, Cage wishes to extend the principles of art—that is to say, of nature—into society as a whole. "If, for instance, you made a structure of society which would be interrupted by the actions of people who were not in it, then it would not be the proper structure."[113] And there is no natural boundary between nations; people ought to be able to come and go quite freely. "In removing the boundaries is the preservation of the World."[114] "Freedom of movement, you see, is basic to both this art and this society."[115] Our sense of the necessity of action, in life as in art, confines us to the road and thus limits our sense of the abundance of the world, most of which, of course, lies off the path.[116]

Chance, Indeterminacy, Purposelessness Heisenberg explains that in the domain of quantum mechanics the present state of a system does not determine its future state: "In the strict form of the principle of causality, 'If we know the present exactly we can calculate what will happen in the future,' it is not the conclusion but the premise which is false. We cannot, even in principle, know every detail of the present."[117] Predictability, and therefore determinism, occur only on a limited scale, when precise describability and isolatability or control of external factors can be obtained. More and more it is coming to be understood that it is the nature of knowledge to be subject to uncertainty.[118]

Art, in Cage's view, must similarly demonstrate nature's chanciness and indeterminacy. Such art is not easy to create, however, because artists, like all persons, have intentions. Cage uses methods of chance to make his music, but these are useful only when the overall number of possibilities is limited. To render art even less subject to human control, Cage utilizes the performers' intentions, at variance from one another, to make the performance, like much of daily life, nonintentional and unstructured. "A performance of a composition which is indeterminate of its performance is necessarily unique. It cannot be repeated. When performed for a second time, the outcome is other than it was. Nothing therefore is accomplished by such a performance, since that performance cannot be grasped as an object in time. A recording of such a work has no more value than a postcard; it provides a knowledge of something that happened, whereas the action was a non-knowledge of something that had not yet happened."[119] An indeterminate work, Cage writes, is truly experimental because it does not develop in terms of approximations and errors, as an "informed" action by its very nature must. No mental images of what will happen are set beforehand; the outcome is not foreseen.[120] Techniques of indeterminacy allow sounds to exist autonomously without subordinating them to sentiments and ideas of order. Cage, accordingly, likes his music to be called experimental.

Apart from dance pieces, only a few theatrical works have employed chance and indeterminacy to the extent that Cage's compositions have. The most successful theater using chance in actual performance that I know of is that of At the Foot of the Mountain, a women's collective. In one production, for example, the group requested audience members to stop the performance whenever it elicited a recollection of having been raped and to narrate that experience; in another production the group asked the audience to volunteer the names of persons they wished to have commemorated by the performance; and in another they invited audience members to complete sentences beginning "Mother always said...," "Mother never said...," "I never said to my mother...," and "Mother, I want you to know that...." In each case, audience participation constituted a moving, though circumscribed, part of the performance.

Other groups have focused on creating innovative audience spaces, moving the audience about within the theater, and structuring works in unfamiliar ways, thus allowing the audience no predetermined responses and putting them necessarily in a condition of non-expectation. Performances that are in any sense truly dependent on audience participation are, in these respects, chancy or indeterminate. There has been considerable interest as well in improvisational rehearsal techniques, which result in interactions that cannot be anticipated by the actors, the director, or an author. Whole works have been created by improvising with collected material objects or texts. As in biology, chance has come to be understood as a truly important creative element.

In dramatic texts indeterminacy has replaced teleology in various ways. Pinter's later plays, for instance, like cubist paintings, are composed from a variety of perspectives outside of which no superordinate authorial point of view exists. As in life, it is impossible to specify precisely what happens in these plays, let alone why, for without determinism no action can in retrospect be said to have been necessary. Even probability may be so weakened that suspense no longer functions as an organizational principle of the dramatic work. The end of a play, then, may seem unclear or unresolved. Likewise, characters become truly free and can in no sense be said to "miss the mark" of their destiny. As Lincoln Barnett writes, "One by-product of this surrender [of cause, effect, and prediction] is a new argument for the existence of free will. For if physical events are indeterminate and the future unpredictable, then perhaps the unknown quality called 'mind' may yet guide man's destiny among the infinite uncertainties of a capricious universe."[121] To the extent that "mind" does guide human life, it is not determined and, accordingly, is often not represented as such in art.

Here again, Cage would have us incorporate the principles of nature into our lives, agreeing with Bridgman, who writes:

> An integral component of this budding and unfolding present is an attitude of expectancy toward the future, which we shall accept without cavil or argument, no matter what it brings. The instinctive urge of our minds to believe in a future causally determined by the past is obviously opposed to our simultaneous recognition that the future can only be accepted no matter how it breaks with the past, and is just another example of the incompatibility of some of our strongest mental impulses....The recognition that the only possible attitude toward the future is one of unreserved acceptance, no matter how distasteful or contrary to expectations, is fundamental to all sane thinking.[122]

As usual, Cage is aphoristic: "If I can't take what happens, I'm not ready for anything."[123] Unlike the existentialists, who express a tragic sense of loss at the absence of ultimate certainties, Cage would welcome Alvin Toffler's future of endless change and not find it shocking.[124] Cage wants art to teach us to accept—or rather, to love—nature precisely for all its endless change and unpredictability.

If there is endless change, things do not move toward a finite end. And nature at large, being indeterminate, cannot be purposeful. There is no day of reckoning. Nature cannot mete out retributive justice to those who fail to meet the mark. Indeed, what mark? Human life, being part of nature, is purposeless, a fact that does not grieve Cage. "The highest purpose is to have no purpose at all," he says paradoxically.[125] Purposeless, one is in accord with nature's manner of operation. Only when we give up the idea that we are moving toward some end are we truly able to live.

Art, Cage says, must teach us to cease defining our lives in terms of ends and to appreciate our purposelessness. What we are doing is living; rather than moving toward a goal, we are, so to speak, at the goal constantly and changing with it—and art, if it is going to do anything useful, should open our eyes to this fact.[126] Cage's own work, therefore, moves toward no end; in contrast to traditional European music, it is static. Whereas in conventional music works are "whole," having a beginning, middle, and end, and progressive, with a climax or climaxes (that is, point or points of special interest), Cage's music is monotonous, or else so continually changing as to seem always the same and to be going nowhere. Cage approvingly quotes Christian Wolff's description of his music: "There is no necessary concern with time as a measure of distance from a point in the past to a point in the future....It is not a question of getting anywhere, of making progress, or having come from anywhere in particular, of tradition or futurism. There is neither nostalgia nor anticipation."[127]

Many consider this static quality irritating. Cage, however, believes that it is not irritating to be where one is, that it is only irritating to think that one would like to be somewhere else. In other words, the static quality of his music is annoying only if one steadfastly refuses to accept the present. Gertrude Stein was troubled by traditional plays because, watching them, she felt at every moment called on to be affected by her memory of the preceding action and her anticipation of future action, so that she could never be fully in the present time of the play. She was always in syncopated time with respect to the play and that irritated her. "The business of Art," she wrote, "is to live in the actual present, that is the complete actual present, and to completely express that complete and actual present."[128] Stein and Cage (who was strongly influenced by her) want art to allow us to be just in time with it, in the present. Cage, admiring a performance of his own and telling us how we are to listen to it, notes, "Slowly, as the talk goes on, we are getting nowhere and that is a pleasure."[129] Performance is pleasing because it, particularly, is an art of presentness. Of contemporary theater, the work of Robert Wilson most especially gets nowhere, slowly.

If nature is purposeless, what can be the function of art that is like nature? This art, too, is purposeless. Continuous with life and like the rest of life, it is just something to do. Still, art has what Cage paradoxically calls a purposeful purposelessness. It is useful in connection with our daily lives; it teaches us to live in accord with life. Art can "quiet the mind thus making it susceptible to divine influences," to "the environment in which we are."[130] Thus the purpose of theater, as one form of art, is to increase our perceptual awareness of the world. The various kinds of theater, moreover, are ideally not to be distinguished with respect to purpose, one from another. "The obligation—the morality, if you wish—of all the arts today is to intensify, to alter, perceptual awareness and, hence, consciousness...of the real material world....Our minds are going to be stretched. We are going to stretch ourselves to the breaking point."[131]

Aristotle too, in his respect for nature, envisioned an art that would enable us to appreciate it. His aim was to understand, not to subdue or alter nature. Yet by Cage's standards, Aristotle, in his efforts to represent nature in its essence (i.e., idealized), by no means portrayed it as it was. Art that is separate from and better than nature, Cage objects, does not enable us to become fluent with life but is, rather, an escape, setting us in a dream world. "And what, precisely, does this, this beautiful profound object, this masterpiece, have to do with Life? It has this to do with Life: that it is separate from it....When we see it we feel better, and when we are away from it, we don't feel so good. Life seems shabby and chaotic, disordered, ugly in contrast."[132] One comes to see such art, he says, as if it were a salvation. There is an "extraordinary contradiction between this work and the world around us—to which Duchamp's willingness to sign anything was the best of all possible introductions."[133]

According to Cage, by contrast, art has no special materials, topics, or form; it does not idealize nature but instead introduces us to it. "Art and our involvement in it will somehow introduce us to the very life that we are living...[so] that we will be able without scores, without performers and so forth simply to sit still to listen to the sounds which surround us and hear them as music."[134] If observers assume that the beach is theater and experience it in those terms, Cage remarks, then he doesn't see much difference between the beach and theater.[135]

Sights and sounds immediately set the theorizing mind to theorizing, and the emotions of the human being are continually aroused by encounters with nature. Sounds, when allowed to be themselves, "do not require that those who hear them do so unfeelingly. The opposite is what is meant by response ability. ...Where the bird, flies, fly"—if it makes you feel like doing so.[136] Emotion takes place in the person who has it. New art and music, following Cage, do not communicate an individual's conceptions in ordered structures; rather, they implement processes that, like our daily lives, are opportunities for perception and emotion. Cage admires Marshall McLuhan, for one reason among many, because he emphasizes this shift from life that is shaped and made meaningful for us to life that we must shape and make meaningful for ourselves.

Aristotle believed that society was part of nature; Cage does not. Whereas Aristotle's art reconciles human beings to nature and society, Cage's art, modeled on nature, suggests, by means of analogy, drastic changes in society. Cage's art is first of all a means to self-alteration: it alters mind, which is in the world and is a social fact.[137] Moreover, we are to apply the facts of nature/art to society at large:

> Try them in economics/politics, giving up, that is, notions about balance (of power, of wealth), foreground, background.... In music [for example] it was hopeless to think in terms of the old structure (tonality), to do things following old methods (counter-point, harmony), to use the old materials (orchestral instruments). We started from scratch: sound, silence, time, activity. In society, no amount of doctoring up economics/politics will help. Begin again, assuming abundance, unemployment, a field situation, multiplicity, unpredictability, immediacy, the possibility of participation.[138]

Interpenetration and Unimpededness Interrelations in a space-time field are so complex that contemporary physics has replaced the idea of unity, which depends on discrete wholes, the integrity of entities, with that of interpenetration, and the idea of order with that of unimpededness. "Unimpededness," Cage explains, "is seeing that in all of space each thing and each human being is at the center and furthermore that each one being at the center is the most honored one of all. Interpenetration means that each one of these most honored ones of all is moving out in all directions penetrating and being penetrated by every other one no matter what the time or what the space."[139] Nothing in nature is inherently peripheral. "Activities which are different happen in a time which is a space: are each central"; hence "each person is in the best seat."[140] This centrality of each thing, moreover, is related to the idea that nature is purposeless: no part exists simply to serve some whole; there is no natural hierarchy or subordination. Why is it so necessary, Cage asks, "that sounds should be just sounds? There are many ways of saying why. One is this: In order that each sound may become the Buddha. If that is too Oriental an expression, take the Christian Gnostic statement: 'Split the stick and there is Jesus.' "[141]

In Cage's art no part is subordinate to any other. Thus harmony, which is a system of subordination, is eliminated, as are the development to an overwhelming climax and the *Hauptstimme*. Where structure is employed, it entails no subordination; rather, structure must be symmetrical in character, or canonic, with all parts, whether at any one instant or successively over time, assuming equal importance. Similarly, Cage rejects the subservience of one element in a work to any other—of dance to music, for instance. Jazz, he remarks, exhibits such subordination: one part is free while the others are not. "Observe," says Cage, "that the enjoyment of a modern painting carries one's attention not to a center of interest but all over the canvas and not following any particular path. Each point on the canvas may be used as a beginning, continuing, or ending of one's observation of it."[142]

Central focus in space, like central focus in time (climax), is a system of subordination of all the rest of the space or time, controlling the audience's attention. But if the audience itself is not to be subservient to the work, the idea of getting and holding their attention must be relinquished. Cage also insists that the performer not be subordinated to the work. Nevertheless, in at least one instance his efforts to eliminate central focus and climax by means of chance unexpectedly brought about the performer's *increased* subordination: "The *Music of Changes* is an object more inhuman than human, since chance operations brought it into being. The fact that these things that constitute it, though only sounds, have come together to control a human being, the performer, gives the work the alarming aspect of a Frankenstein monster."[143] Likewise, the subservience of performer to the conductor (who is himself subordinate, not to the composer—another human being, at least—but to the composer's work) Cage considers quite undesirable.

In performance, the spatial separation of ensemble players encourages each performer to initiate actions independently without waiting to be told what to do. Silence, too, like space, can make for unimpededness, by emphasizing the equality of separate sounds. Employing the idea of unimpededness in theater performance, Richard Schechner, for example, instructed the performers in *Dionysus in 69* to say only those lines from *The Bacchae* that they found meaningful. Thus the actors were subordinated neither to the script nor to their characters. In performance they referred to themselves as "I, William Finley/Dionysus," and so on; and because they rotated roles, no actor regularly had a secondary part. Ostensibly, in fact, the players were coequal with Schechner in the creation of both the work itself and the book that describes the work.[144]

Extending to society the lesson that in nature each thing is central, Cage finds social systems of subordination outdated. The structure of the contemporary performance, then, should illustrate an improvement in society in this regard, and ideally the ensemble should function as a miniature society of equality.

To Cage it is not only hierarchical structures that are unnatural, but structure altogether, which is the imposition of man's self on nature. Bridgman tells us that nature is intrinsically and in its elements neither understandable nor subject to law; chance, indeterminacy, and chaos are as real as order.[145] Accordingly, Cage seeks to provide sounds without the imposition of human-made structures, "improvements," on them. "The requiring that many parts be played in a particular togetherness, is not an accurate representation of how things are."[146] Cage wants to free sounds of fixed relations between two or more of them, to free sounds of conventional harmonies and progressions, to let them occur in any combination or continuity. "The structure we should think about is that of each person in the audience. In other words, his consciousness is structuring the experience differently from anybody else's in the audience. So the less we structure the theatrical occasion and the more it is like unstructured daily life, the greater will be the stimulus to the structuring faculty of each person in the audience."[147] We must, he says, give up our presuppositions about what things go together. Dissimilarities can coexist, and the central points where they fuse are many: the ears of the listeners, wherever they are. The disharmony of unstructured sounds, he comments, paraphrasing Bergson's statement about disorder, is simply a harmony to which we are unaccustomed. When our attention is inclusive rather than exclusive, when we attend to all the things going on at one time, including those that are environmental, no question of making understandable structures can arise; one is, as it were, a tourist or experimentalist, ready to accept the unexpected. The relationship of things in time and space, we see now, is far more complex and interesting than humanmade structures have allowed. Art should represent the complex interrelationships present in reality: "total field, nonfocused multiplicity."[148] As Cage puts it, "Complicate your garden so it's surprising like uncultivated land."[149]

If no hierarchy exists in nature, then there are no higher forms, no things more worthy of attention than others, no things that are inherently beautiful or good. Nature has no value system, and if we apply one we only disconnect ourselves from experience. In Cage's view then, the task of art is to reflect nature without distancing us from our experience of it. For this reason he admits all kinds of sounds into his compositions, in the belief that the materials and subjects of art should be no more limited than those in life. Nature does not exclude things as banal, beside the point, or ugly. Indeed, to challenge the presumption of such values and to bring us to a condition of no-mindedness, art may deliberately focus on the conventionally unpleasant or commonplace. Cage observes, for example, that

•••••••••••• with the help. . . of some American paintings, Bob Rauschenberg's particularly, I can pass through Times Square without disgust. And, similarly, having written radio music [a composition using radios as instruments] has enabled me to accept, not only the sounds I there encounter, but the television, radio, and Muzak ones, which nearly constantly and everywhere offer themselves. Formerly, for me, they were a source of irritation. Now, they are just as lively as ever, but I have changed. . . . My work. . . [is] an affirmation of life.[150]

Because he is not concerned with valuation, criticism that consists of such valuation—this work is good, this portion of it excellent—does not interest him either. "The big thing to do actually is to get yourself into a situation in which you use your experience no matter where you are, even if you are at a performance of a work of art which, if you were asked to criticize it, you would criticize out of existence. Nevertheless, you should get yourself into such a position that, were you present at it, you would somehow be able to use it."[151] The best criticism, he believes, is a reply in the form of a work of one's own.

If value does not exist in nature, neither do proper proportion and magnitude, for these are aspects of valuation. "How in heaven's name," asks Cage, "did anyone get the idea that proportion took place in an object outside of him?"[152] And likewise, "significant" size or scope of any artwork is not a property innate to the work but a function of one's response to it. Challenging our Aristotelian idea about proper magnitude, theater artists have turned from "full-length" works to short ones or, in Robert Wilson's case, to ones as long as 168 hours. Bridgman believes that "there are still many new and revolutionary things to be said which have escaped us because they are so close, ubiquitous, and constant that we have not been able to see them."[153] Cage would agree. Modern and pop art in this country hold interest for him, for example, because they have trained our eyes to see not the most noticeable things, but the things *generally overlooked.* Cage also wishes for artists to attend to those things that are either too big or too interior (too small) for us to have noticed and related to our daily experience. The complete and actual present includes those small things that the sweep of an Aristotelian action necessarily discounts. Once we give up our ideas about what is important, Cage says, everything becomes more interesting: "Boredom dropped when we dropped our interest in climaxes."[154]

Finally, if we abandon the idea of discrete unified wholes for the ideas of unimpededness and interpenetration, it becomes impossible any longer to conceive of the parts of those wholes. An elementary particle is not an independent analyzable entity, a basic building block of matter, but rather a set of relationships extending outward to other things. As David Bohm observes,

●●●●●●●●●●●● one is led to a new notion of unbroken wholeness which denies the classical
idea of analyzability of the world into separately and independently existing
parts. . . . We have reversed the usual classical notion that the independent
"elementary parts" of the world are the fundamental reality, and that the
various systems are merely particular contingent forms and arrangements of
these parts. Rather, we say that inseparable quantum interconnectedness of
the whole universe is the fundamental reality, and that relatively independently behaving parts are merely particular and contingent forms within
this whole.[155]

Reflecting this idea, Cage tells us that with respect to music we need not be in a twelve-tone or any other discrete situation.

●●●●●●●●●●●● Musical habits include scales, modes, theories of counterpoint and harmony, and the study of timbres, singly and in combination of a limited number of sound-producing mechanisms. In mathematical terms these all
concern discrete steps. They resemble walking—in the case of pitches, on
steppingstones twelve in number. This cautious stepping is not characteristic of the possibilities of magnetic tape, which is revealing to us that musical
action or existence can occur at any point or along any line or curve or what
have you in total sound-space; that we are, in fact, technically equipped to
transform our contemporary awareness of nature's manner of operation into
art.[156]

Nature does not consist of discrete entities but of interpenetrating processes. Accordingly, it is misleading to create art works with discrete parts; art that reflects nature must consist of interpenetrating processes. It is, in essence, performance.

Cage's aesthetic program opposes that of Aristotle virtually point for point, although both are correlated with an understanding of nature. Cage's aesthetic may be explained as a response to previous art; more significantly, however, it is—as he would have us understand it—a response to life. Cage would agree with Jacob Bronowski that "present and future, cause and effect, order and disorder, time and space, the uncertain, the average and the unexpected, are notions which any philosophy must consider; and if contemporary science has given them new forms, they must influence all philosophy."[157] Cage is generally of the opinion that "art changes because science changes—that is, changes in science give artists different understandings of how nature works."[158] Nevertheless, it would not be accurate to explain all theater that is consistent with Cage's ideas as deriving from contemporary science. I am more comfortable with the idea of interpenetration: the idea that changes in both the sciences and the arts are dependent on the technical and ideological possibilities of their time and place, that the questions which scientists and artists pose are a part of the history they all share.

"Present and future, cause and effect, order and disorder, time and space, the uncertain, the average, and the unexpected" are notions that influence philosophy and also the way in which philosophy is written. Aristotle not only believed that art should imitate nature, but he also seems to have followed his stated intention of arranging the *Poetics* itself in accordance with the order of nature as he saw it.[159] As Gerald Else convincingly argues, the text remaining to us constitutes "a single, coherent piece of argument."[160] Indeed, it is chiefly on the basis of the logical structure of this argument that some portions of the text have been argued to be later interpolations by Aristotle or another and that latter-day extrapolations on the nature of comedy have been made. The argument that constitutes the structure of the essay is the equivalent of the action of a drama. It is written in such a way that we attend to its structure and to the meaning of the words, with a linear progression focusing on ever smaller parts of the whole: first poetry, and drama in particular; then tragedy, the highest form of drama; and then each part of tragedy in order of importance, plot first. Each part is clearly delineated and follows from the preceding part either necessarily or probably. The argument is presented primarily in terms of universals, and it is meant to be timeless. Early in the argument (chapter 4) Aristotle provides a history of poetry, and of drama in particular, it being important in understanding anything to know its cause. The tone of the whole is authoritative and serious; Aristotle is confident in his powers of knowing and his role in nature to define, explain, and show significance.

Unlike Aristotle, Cage understands that language is inherently related to our perception of reality and accordingly, deliberately and increasingly, has imitated what he understands to be nature's manner of operation in his writing as well as in his music. He states that he often says what he has to say in a way that will exemplify it, hoping to enable the audience to comprehend his ideas through experiencing them.[161]

In accord with his belief that reality does not consist of discrete and unified wholes, Cage's books *Silence, A Year from Monday,* and *M* do not consist of unified linear arguments; rather, they are compilations of essays, lectures, anecdotes, day-to-day observations, and poems. The books are not distinguished by subject matter, except insofar as Cage's thought has changed with time (it has, he observes, become more political). They are, as it were, one work continually in process. Ideas and even exact sentences are repeated. The work is in effect spatial, not progressive; it seems to extend by accretion and permutation. While each collection offers variety and a careful elaboration of ideas, no bases for judgment about the completeness or orderliness of presentation are provided. Believing that the complexity of the interrelationship of ideas should not be oversimplified by a particular idea of "relationship" in any one person's mind, Cage invites the reader of one essay to read it "in whole or in part; any sections of it may be skipped, what remains may be read in any order."[162] Indeed, that invitation might well apply to the whole of the book, for without an overall argument to which each essay or anecdote is subordinate, each is the center of interest in its own right. In the "Diary," begun in *A Year from Monday* and continued in *M*, the style grows more aphoristic: each sentence becomes the center.[163]

The writings include anecdotes about Cage's mushroom collecting, Zen, music classes, his friends. His writings on aesthetics, that is to say, are not distinct from the rest of life; there are no boundaries. "My intention," says Cage, "in putting the stories together in an unplanned way was to suggest that all things—stories, incidental sounds from the environment, and, by extension, beings—*are* related."[164] In the "Diary," observations about life are intermixed with those about art. Nothing is too small or lacking in drama to be worthy of Cage's attention.

References to contemporary technology and to particular people establish the anecdotes clearly in time and place. The longer pieces are dated and the occasion for which each was written explained. The process of composition, including rejected possibilities, is noted. The writing is not presented as universal and timeless; instead it is specific to a time, a place, his person and methods. Cage calls our attention to writing as an act. Because print, despite its fixity, does not give the final word, or even Cage's final word, on any subject, his tone is not authoritative. Cage does not think that his role in the universe is central. Human beings, he says, have no special role as knowers; writing is merely something to do, and given humans' place in the universe, he thinks it had best be done with modesty and humor.

Until recently, in *Empty Words* and *X*, Cage's writing style did not approach the radicalism of his music. It conveyed meaning. "If you're going to have a discussion, have it and use words," he said earlier, respecting the distinctive capabilities of language.[165] Jill Johnston describes his work as "some of the most crystal-cut prose of contemporary writing" and believes that this keenness accounts in part for his influence on so much of contemporary art.[166] Clarity and logic do not, however, illustrate Cage's meaning; such illustration is provided in a number of other ways. For example, one piece, which he considers particularly pontifical, he had set in very small type, thus mocking his own pontification and making the piece virtually impossible to read without accidental rereading of some lines; hence our reading does not have the orderliness of the composition and we can hardly attend only to the sense.[167] In another piece four speeches are interlaced, each set in a different type to give the effect of voices in a choral work—that is, of field multiplicity, juxtaposition, and simultaneity. "The texts were written to be heard as four simultaneous lectures. . . . The presentation here used has the effect of making the words legible—a dubious advantage, for I had wanted to say that our experiences, gotten as they are all at once, pass beyond our understanding."[168] Elsewhere Cage provides a sense of performance by including directions for sound effects and gestures. And in another case normal English word order—left to right and top to bottom—is adhered to, but the specific placement of the few phrases on the page is determined by chance, making the arrangement spatial in effect, though still linear in fact. The arrangement of words, phrases, or sentences so as to make space and silence as noticeable as words is common.

The title of Cage's first book, *Silence*, is of course central to his thought; the title of the second, *A Year from Monday*, is indeterminate; and that of the third, *M*, was obtained by subjecting the twenty-six letters of the alphabet to I Ching chance operations (it is coincidentally related, too, to Cage's interests in music and mushrooms). The book titles are indicative as well of Cage's stylistic development. In *M*, for example, there are parts where the manner of operation finally rules out the possibility of inherent meaning: "Mureau" is "a mix of letters, syllables, words, phrases, and sentences. I wrote it by subjecting all the remarks of Henry David Thoreau about music, silence, and sounds he heard that are indexed in the Dover publication of the *Journal* to a series of I Ching chance operations."[169] The words, then, are found words, not words of Cage's choosing—except that he chose their source. Their I Ching–determined arrangement is not syntactical; although the words provide certain recognizable sounds and associations, they do not make sense. *M* also contains "mesostics" (acrostics, but with the "row not down the edge but down the middle"; each line across, then, necessarily has a random determinant). For one mesostic, Cage tells us, he uses over seven hundred different type faces and sizes in an effort to give "each letter undivided attention" rather than leave it subordinate to a word.[170] Together the words serve as graphic art. Of the three books discussed here, *M* intends the least meaning. It is more art than theory, in sections most closely approximating his ideas of poetry: "I have nothing to say and I am saying it and that is poetry."[171]

2 .... *Family Plays:* **Long Day's Journey into Night** *and* **Rumstick Road**

Rumstick Road (1977) is a work that exemplifies many of the characteristics of new theater and clearly illustrates Cage's aesthetic principles in theatrical practice. Furthermore, it readily lends itself to comparison with Eugene O'Neill's *Long Day's Journey into Night* (1941), a work of traditional theater regarded by many as the greatest American play. Such an exercise in comparison and contrast will allow us more easily to identify the departures from traditional work entailed in *Rumstick Road*.

Rumstick Road was developed by the Wooster Group, a highly acclaimed American avant-garde theater group. It was part of a series of four related pieces making up *Three Places in Rhode Island*, the work that first established the group's reputation. Separately or in series, the pieces—which included, in addition to *Rumstick Road*, *Sakonnet Point* (1975), *Nayatt School* (1978), and an epilogue, *Point Judith* (1979)—were performed at intervals between 1975 and 1982. *Rumstick Road* was performed in New York both downtown at the Performing Garage, the group's home theater, and, in 1980, uptown at the American Place Theatre. I have chosen *Rumstick Road* for analysis not only because of its comparability with *Long Day's Journey*, but also because the production has been well documented and the work of the Wooster Group has been highly influential. Avant-garde director Peter Sellars, for instance, whose individual work has had considerable impact, regards the group as "the most important theater company" in the United States today.[1]

There are many similarities between *Long Day's Journey into Night* and *Rumstick Road*. For one thing, both are closely tied to autobiographical material, the explicit use of which has, until quite recently, been uncommon in the theater. The reasons for this are fairly obvious. The mode of drama is objective: the play provides the illusion that the action is happening directly before us; the dramatist speaks only indirectly, through character, action, and theme. The story of a life, particularly an author's often sedentary and solitary life, may not take the form of dramatic action and may lack magnitude. Performance, unlike diaries or letters, is an inherently public art, providing no privacy either for the author or for others included in the autobiographical work and presenting the prospect of having oneself or those close to oneself impersonated by others. Thus Eugene O'Neill's understandable—though not honored—request that *Long Day's Journey* not be published or performed until twenty-five years after his death.

Contemporary theater practices, however, facilitate the use of autobiographical material. Here, performances may rely on narrative, may have no conventional dramatic action, and may be small in scope. One may be asked to take a special interest in the storyteller's own limitations in perception and understanding and in the personal nature of the work. The hand of the creator may be clearly visible. Indeed, playwright-director Richard Foreman believes that all creative work should be about "the author trying to *CREATE* his subject and structure."[2] In his view all art, whatever its ostensible subject matter, is necessarily also about the person who represents that subject matter. It is thus in the strongest sense autobiographical, and should be so forthrightly. If the artist is involved in the artwork not only as its maker but also as its subject, it becomes, in the words of Spalding Gray, co-author of *Rumstick Road*, the study of the "one who sees himself seeing himself."[3]

Reacting against the idea of anthropocentric art, Cage says that he has become interested in anything but himself as art material. Many artists wishing similarly to eliminate the presupposition of human centrality embedded in earlier art take the opposite tack, examining not only themselves as art material like any other and but also their own inevitable participation as creators. Indeed, by choosing obviously personal subject matter, they have foregrounded the interaction between creator and creation, observer and observed, thereby forcing our and their own examination of it.

Scientists have likewise responded in contrasting ways to their awareness of the extent to which, in Arthur Eddington's words, "the mind has but regained from nature that which the mind has put into nature."[4] Schrödinger, for instance, calls for renewed efforts to leave subjectivity out of scientific accounts,[5] while Heisenberg insists that we must attend more fully to the way in which humans are inevitably part of the account. Heisenberg's most solipsistic-sounding statement on the matter of participation—"*the object of research is no longer nature itself, but man's investigation of nature*"[6]—which is echoed in Foreman's statement that all art should be about the author's attempts to create it, serves to correct the presumption of objectivity in earlier views.

Although *Rumstick Road* is, like *Long Day's Journey into Night*, autobiographical, it is so in a far more radical sense. Both plays are family studies. Yet *Rumstick Road* has a dual character: while it is based on actual records of Spalding Gray's family—audio tapes, slides, and letters —as well as on Gray's own memories, it is also about the aesthetic responses to these records of the Wooster

Group, a group whom Gray regarded as his second—his theater—family. O'Neill makes an artwork out of his family history, which provides us with the perspective on his family he intends for us to share with him. The Wooster Group, however, leaves the audience to interpret and integrate the documents and the group's responses to the documents.

Spalding Gray is aware that the autobiographical material in *Three Places in Rhode Island* can be compared with that in O'Neill's play: "There's so much for me to identify with in *Long Day's Journey*: the tormented mother going mad, the cold father, the actor whose career has gone off course."[7] In addition, Gray performed the role of Edmund, O'Neill's persona, in 1966. And *Point Judith*, the epilogue to *Three Places in Rhode Island*, contains a sixteen-minute parody of *Long Day's Journey*.

As in *Long Day's Journey*, the autobiographical material in *Rumstick Road* centers on the mother's final descent into madness. In both plays the examination of the autobiographical material is conducted by a son who perceives physical and psychic resemblances between himself and his mother—an identification that, to a certain extent, seems to have motivated the examination. In both plays the mother's illness is regarded as a family event, with religion and doctors, unequal to their tasks, figuring as outside forces. The mother attempts to represent herself as normal; one of the family members tries to perceive her in that way as well. In each case, moreover, the mother experiences some conflict between her religion and her relationship with the father. It is the father, unwilling or unable to provide for the mother's emotional needs, whom the son blames, at least in part, though in the end he comes to see the older man in a more complex and sympathetic way. In both plays, too, the health of the son who conducts the examination is left in the balance. That son, further, regards himself as an innocent in whatever family dynamics may have caused the mother's destruction, yet his examination is partly an attempt at self-purgation before others.[8]

Although many contemporary works have experimented with unfamiliar spatial relationships between the audience and performance—providing, as Cage would have it, no single right perspective from which to view the performance and thus facilitating the interpenetration of perceiver and work—the spatial relationship between *Rumstick Road* and its audience is for the most part conventional, like that envisioned by O'Neill for *Long Day's Journey*. Both works are played in front of the audience, separate from it in space. For both, a box set represents the New England house that spatially delimits the action and acts on the mother as a confining space.[9] Although the house in *Rumstick Road* is indicated merely by raw plywood walls and doors, Gray does project a slide of the actual house onto the back wall, and his accompanying description of its interior might be a stage direction written by O'Neill. The house figures significantly as an image, as well it might where analysis of reality in terms of the family is central.

In both plays the mother's descent constitutes a single action. As the very title of *Long Day's Journey into Night* emphasizes, that action moves forward in time. Broadly speaking, the temporal movement in *Rumstick Road* is also forward, extending as a whole from dream images of the past, to more recent, realistically presented, interviews with family members, and to present time in the theater. The work also moves from the storyteller's youth to his manhood, and from playfulness to seriousness. The mother's end is associated with darkness and cold, just as in *Long Day's Journey* it is associated with night and the end of summer.

The autobiographical origins, the similarities in the autobiographical material, and its structuring provide a strong basis for comparison of *Rumstick Road* and *Long Day's Journey*. Certainly the obvious story and the conventional features in the structuring of *Rumstick Road* make the work accessible to a larger public than that typically attracted to the Performing Garage and other contemporary theater, and probably accounts for the fact that the Wooster Group was invited to stage the work at the American Place Theatre, which, although it does put on works by new playwrights, does not ordinarily present contemporary performance pieces.

Relationship of Work to Text

Rumstick Road and *Long Day's Journey* share many aspects of plot and theme, but their relationship to their texts is so different that they need to be understood as existing in different media. *Long Day's Journey* was written to be performed, but it exists as a literary work composed by Eugene O'Neill. *Rumstick Road*, in contrast, created through improvisation by a group—three performers, a director, and a technical director—can only be understood to exist in performance by that group. The published text of *Rumstick Road* (credited to Spalding Gray, who collected the documents, and Elizabeth LeCompte, the director) consists of the tape segments chosen for presentation arranged in the order of their presentation; Gray's brief introduction to each of the segments; the biographical information that appeared in the program; an outline of the "organization of the text and movement," with segments entitled "House Slide," "House Dance," "Flying the Tent," and the like; and a chart of that organization. This twenty-page "script" is accompanied by five photographs taken during the performance under conditions of extreme light contrast and is followed by a request that permission to perform the work be directed to its "authors." But the script, which, like a conventional one, contains all the words spoken in performance, does not serve as a guideline for performance, even to the limited extent that, say, that of a classical Greek play or even a Jonsonian masque does. On the basis of it, one can assume that in performance Gray's narration and the tape segments were heard by the audience in the sequence provided and that there were slides and "dances." But since nothing except the narrated portion was spoken live, there is no indication of what the other actors spent their time doing. The text, which followed from rather than preceded the work of actors and director, is a meager document of work done rather than either a guideline for performance or a coherent art object in its own right.

Moreover, performance by others, even an attempt at exact imitation, would result in a wholly different work, regardless of the fact that the words spoken were the same, because the tapes would not be the actual tapes, the slides the actual slides, and Gray would not play himself. The knowledge (or at least the belief) that the documents actually are from Gray's collection and that the performer truly is Spalding Gray is essential to our experience of the work.

So slight, or unfamiliar, is the relationship between contemporary performance and text that Michael Kirby, as editor of the *Drama Review* from 1971 to 1985, came to see the journal's function as providing running accounts of performances, not analyses. A new text may convey no indication of the nature of its performance (*Film Is Evil: Radio Is Good*), a text may be unreadable (*Einstein on the Beach*), there may be almost no text (*Sakonnet Point*), or an old text may be radically reinterpreted in performance (*The Gospel at Colonus*). Indeed, the contemporary emphasis on performance encourages the reading of all plays as limited documents of work done, providing no guidelines for contemporary performance. All old texts become, as Cage would have it, material for new art works.

The focus on performance is consistent with the scientific perception of the world in terms of events: the object has disappeared from modern physics, replaced by a whole range of energies, an interplay of continuous happenings, as the motivating force of a complex and many-faceted reality. Richard Foreman explains why it is important to make performances rather than dramatic texts, by reference to contemporary perceptions of reality:

•••••••••••• Art shouldn't add new objects to the world to enslave men. It should begin the process of freeing men by calling into doubt the solidity of objects—and laying bare the fact that it is a web of relations that exists only; that web held taut in each instance by the focal point of consciousness that is each separate individual consciousness. . . . The relationship between consciousness and "world" is the relation between two intersecting force fields, neither of which is a thing, both of which are systems of relations.[10]

Separability of the Artwork

Long Day's Journey into Night is an isolated system, a work separable from its creator and from life, despite the fact that the material on which it is based is autobiographical and the author by then famous and his autobiography known. With the deaths of himself and his family, performance or publication of *Long Day's Journey* could affect none of them. In his dedication of the play O'Neill describes it as having been written "in tears and blood": we are to understand that the work is personal and painful. Yet we are also to understand that it is written with the appropriate objectivity even about himself: he was finally able, he says, to "face [his] dead at last and write this play—write it with deep pity and understanding and forgiveness for all the four haunted Tyrones." The work, O'Neill suggests, serves as a turning point in his relationship with his family; it provides closure: he understands and forgives. And when we read or see *Long Day's Journey*, we too have the sense of a finished work, one that successfully encapsulates O'Neill's past. No parts seem to have been left out, to not belong, or to go unexplained. The work does not extend beyond the space of the text or stage. It has a clear beginning and end; it is framed, contained.

In the play, the character who represents O'Neill is named Edmund, after O'Neill's real-life brother who died in childhood—an expedient that presumably allows O'Neill to establish a proper perspective on himself and his family situation. To write the play, O'Neill delves into his past; yet the character Edmund moves forward in time and, by means of the understanding he acquires in the course of the play, overcomes his fate: he gains release from his family, even if then only to go to a tuberculosis sanatorium. The author is separate from the time and place of the play's action, and detached by the synthesis and interpretation that the act of writing represents. Indeed, achievement of this distance is an important object of O'Neill's writing of the play.

The work is also separable from the time, place, and persons of the performance, for it exists in words alone. Everything in the performance is inherent in the words, which delimit the action, character, style, tone, and thought of the play.

In this traditional play, the audience is separated spatially and temporally from the performance as well. The play is in four acts, with each opening and closing of the curtain between acts distinguishing audience-time from play-time. Act breaks used as intermissions call attention to this distinction even more strongly. In the performance style envisioned by the author, the actors tacitly acknowledge and so reinforce the separation between performance and audience: actors speak loudly and distinctly, directing most of their action so that it can be seen clearly by the audience. The subject matter, too, is presented, or arranged, for our benefit. The actors interpret the material for us; they show us the motivation for what they do. When the play is over, the audience has a sense of completeness, a clear understanding of what has happened and why. It feels right for the curtain to close. Although the family ends in darkness and fog, we see its members clearly and completely. The play exists in our minds as a discrete entity.

The work is distinct, then, from those about whom the story is told (including the author), from its performance, and from the audience. It is distinguished from life by being raised to a higher form that presents life as art, life in its essence. The title makes clear that a single action or event—the thirty-five-year marriage of O'Neill's parents—is unified and so compressed that it takes place in but a single day. (Presumably O'Neill's own first marriage is not mentioned because it is not relevant to the single action he wishes to describe.)[11] O'Neill changes the family name from O'Neill to Tyrone, thus to make clear that his account is raised to the level of fiction: it isn't only about his family; it is about the complex psychological interactions in all families. The singleness, unification, and compression result in great intensity in the action portrayed. As the title further suggests, the tone of the work is unified: the action is a descent into darkness, a tragedy. It is teleological: the journey can be understood in terms of its end. In the play we learn the causes of the action, including the end. The dialogue is less repetitive and more rhetorical than real speech. People articulate arguments and explain their motivations. The play demonstrates the mother's observation that "the past is the present, isn't it. It's the future too."

Not only the playwriting but also the performance tradition in which O'Neill worked serves to raise art above life. In it actors are valued for their pleasing voices, good looks, and charisma. Setting, costumes, and lighting are designed to present a balanced, unified, and varied effect with clear symbolic meaning.

Those elements that raise *Long Day's Journey* above life and separate it from performance, author, and audience are Aristotelian. O'Neill's play is realistic, and while realism is not in all respects Aristotelian, from the perspective of contemporary theater performance the requisites are closely related. I agree with C. D. Innes that while "it is normal to date modern drama from Ibsen. . .naturalism was actually the final phase of traditional theater" and that "it is more accurate to take the Dada movement as the starting-point of these attempts to find theatrical correlatives for the new consciousness."[12]

The differences between the requisites of Aristotelian and realistic drama bear elaboration, because they suggest some ways in which the new theater can be understood as an outgrowth of realism. In realism, for one thing, there is a deliberate emphasis on unconscious motivation. For this reason the language cannot adhere so closely to the rhetorical tradition of earlier theater, and the actor must interpret what is said and show what is not said. Thus this emphasis gives a new importance to the actor as creator and to performance as a creative act.

Furthermore, realism imitates not just nature's manner of operation, but also its appearance. Although the realistic work is separate from life by being better than life, it is nevertheless intended to provide the illusion of reality; it must not appear to be contrived. We must be less conscious than in other theatrical conventions of the means by which life is epitomized and presented to us. Hence, speech should be realistically motivated. In *Long Day's Journey*, for instance, the revelations at the end which serve to explain the action must seem to be motivated by the fact that the characters are given naturally to talk: they are actors and a poet, self-pitying and self-dramatizing; it is late, and they are desperate and drunk; Edmund is leaving and may die. The set, while it must serve as an image of their world and must be aesthetically pleasing, must also seem to be a real and particular place.[13] We must be able to understand the night and the fog as actualities as well as images. And at the end, the lighting must allow us to see, but it must also suggest that the father is miserly even with the electricity. All the characters and design elements, while subordinate to the play, must seem to exist in their own right. The performers must be seen and understood to be characters moving and speaking with only one another in mind. No attention can be called to the means of the performance: actors' efforts, actors not in character, crew, backstage, all are to be hidden so as not to suggest that the artwork is anything but a real entity existing on its own. The play is an illusion of reality, and any reality breaks the spell of the illusion.

Imitation of the appearance of nature means that greater emphasis is necessarily placed on the visual and aural aspects of performance. But the most serious effect of this tenet of realism is the diminishment of the magnitude of drama. Realistic works become more specific and less universalized. There are no larger-than-life declamations, gestures, and masks. The characters are not ruling class but middle class; their problems are miserliness, alcoholism, drug addiction, and tuberculosis, not the destruction of a reign or the disruption of nature. The realm is a house, not a kingdom. And compared to the catastrophe of a lost reign or ravaged nature, the import of the action is diminished.[14] Fog and darkness symbolize internal states, but the causal relationship between these states and nature is weakened or nonexistent. It is not the universe that is troubled by a fall, only the individuals involved. The idea of fate is thus weakened. And actions are more easily understood as sick or healthy than as immoral or moral. In sum, the emphasis on the unconscious, on realistic appearances, and on middle-class subjects results in a greater emphasis on performance as creation, a diminishment of dramatic magnitude, and a weakening and reinterpretation of the ideas of fate and causality.

Contemporary performance theater places even greater emphasis than realism on performance as creation, further decreases the magnitude, and weakens the concept of causality still more, but for different reasons: its creators are interested in pressing on behind appearances.

Because of its emphasis on performance, *Rumstick Road* is not an autonomous art object, a closed system, to the extent that *Long Day's Journey* is, but a process, inseparable from its performers and this period of their lives. It is not a representation of a text, of something beyond the performance; instead it is an exploration of the relationship between the presentation and the very means of its presentation, including the particular persons, space, objects, and technology through which the material is perceived and presented. The word *performers* rather than *actors* is sometimes used in contemporary theater to make clear that the persons in question are not pretending to disappear into or become their roles; on the contrary, they know and show *through themselves*. Such contemporary theater performance takes to heart Percy Bridgman's observation that "the participation of the individual is necessary in every process of intelligence, not merely in the processes of science," and makes that participation overt.[15]

The presence of the performers is intimately related to the perception of reality as process. Percy Bridgman explains that his own "resolution to use the first person was one of the outcomes of the attempt to see things in terms of activities. A spoken or a written word was spoken or written by someone, and part of the recognition of the word as activity is a recognition of who it was that said or wrote it."[16] Performance is an essential means for the exploration of the process of knowing or making. In that sense, as Gray tells us, "the 'finished' piece is never completed. Opening and closing dates are its arbitrary frame."[17]

Although it is not as autonomous an artwork as *Long Day's Journey*, *Rumstick Road* is unmistakably a theatrical performance and does not deceive us into thinking otherwise. The work is shown in a theater, at specified times and before an audience. Two events in the performance are dramatized to give the appearance of actual occurrences, but these are framed in such a way that we are made conscious of their being part of a theatrical presentation. Nine years after his mother's death, Gray sought out a psychiatrist who had treated his mother shortly before her suicide, and he taped the resulting telephone conversation with that psychiatrist. That tape is played in performance; Gray's portion of the tape is edited out and he speaks it live, reconstructing as accurately as possible his gestures and movements during the actual conversation. LeCompte, the director, was present at the time of the telephone call and helped Gray with the reconstruction, which Gray refers to as "direct representation of life...true naturalism."[18] In performance, however, Gray begins his conversation by supposedly telling the psychiatrist that he, Gray, is in the theater with members of his company, performing before an audience; yet it is clear from what the psychiatrist says that Gray told him no such thing and that the psychiatrist had no idea that the conversation was being taped or would be made public. In the other instance Gray, as himself, and Ron Vawter, as his father, lip-synch to a tape of a conversation Gray had with his father. The passing of the microphone between Gray and Vawter apparently reconstructs the passing of the microphone between Gray and his father, for the volume changes are synchronized exactly. Vawter wears the same attire that he wears for his other roles; we do not assume that he is really the father. And the lip-synching constitutes a precise and obvious artifice. In both instances the technician playing the tapes sits front stage center and we are aware that the voices of the psychiatrist, the father, and, in the second instance, Gray are taped, not live. We are never encouraged to believe that we are seeing the actual encounters between Gray and the father or the psychiatrist, no matter how meticulous the reconstruction. Elsewhere in the performance we have no sense that a past reality is represented; instead the performance becomes an elaboration of, a personal response to, that reality.

Nonetheless, the use of actual documents of Gray's family rather than fabricated art materials supports the notion that *Rumstick Road* is not an autonomous art object but an event continuous with life. The documents consist of home-quality slides from Gray's childhood in Rhode Island, a letter to him from his mother following one of her (probably early) hospitalizations for manic depression, a letter Gray received from his father during the last stages of her illness, a more recent letter from a former neighbor listing possible origins for the street name Rumstick Road, taped conversations Gray had individually with his father and his paternal grandmother (including the grandmother's commentary on the old family slides when Gray showed them to her), a tape of his maternal grandmother reciting from memory from Mary Baker Eddy's *Science and Health with Keys to the Scriptures*, the taped telephone conversation Gray had with a psychiatrist who attended his mother, Gray's memories, and music from the period. The documents provide almost all of the text of the eighty-minute-long play. The program notes include dates of family births and marriages as well as dates and places of residence and the dates of the paternal grandmother's divorce and of Gray's mother's death.

These documents are raised to the level of art only through selection, editing, and arrangement, and by our consideration of them as such. Gray accidentally showed his grandmother a slide upside down, and it is left that way for us. There are accidental noises on the tape, some of them fortuitous: as the grandmother identifies the slide of Christmas 1951, a clock chimes. The documents reveal the wonder of reality, not as raised to the level of art, but in and of itself, recalling Cage's idea that the beach is theater if we only regard it as such. It would be hard to create a more arrogant, uncomprehending, thoughtless psychiatrist, who is nevertheless trying to help, than the one Gray actually called; nor a more striking letter from a manic woman—too enthusiastically reassuring her son that she is well—than the one Gray actually received from his mother on her release from the hospital (it begins, "Hi Darling! I'm home and all well and deliriously happy to be here!").

Insofar as an artwork calls attention to the means of its creation, it is not autonomous. As a multimedia production employing tapes, slides, and phonograph records as well as actors, props, a set, and lighting, *Rumstick Road* calls more attention to the means of production and communication than does realistic theater, which hides the source of the light and uses no music in the course of the work unless the characters have reason to hear it. In *Rumstick Road*, in contrast, the sound equipment and technician are placed front stage center. When the mother puts a record on the phonograph, she does so just after the tape of the record is started by the technician, thus specifically calling attention to the fact that the sound comes from the tape. Set changes are carried out in full view by the performers and constitute a part of the action. Similarly, some lighting effects are implemented by the actors and constitute a part of the action. The performers focus the slide projector themselves. Light and sound changes are often

Fig. 2. Set for Rumstick Road: *Bruce Porter/Sound Operator above, center; Ron Vawter/ Quack Doctor and Libby Howes/Patient below; Spalding Gray beneath table. Photograph courtesy Ken Kobland from the collection of The Wooster Group.*

abrupt, the abruptness calling attention to them as effects. No attempt is made to harmonize the hodgepodge of records and media effects to make them less obtrusive. We are deliberately made conscious of them as effects.

Because the performers just happened to be part of the Wooster Group at the time, they, like the documents, are in a sense found objects, as are the props with which they work. Some props are left over from the previous work, *Sakonnet Point*: a red dome tent, white sheets, a miniature house, a phonograph, a flashlight.[19] There are also a telephone, a wheelchair, a stool, and some chairs. No prop is specially made for this production, nor is any recognizably a theater prop; except for the miniature house, the objects are all everyday objects. Although used in various ways and suggesting various images, the objects are always resolutely themselves. The red dome tent, for instance, evokes the mother, moving day, and the garage in which the mother committed suicide. But a red dome tent is not an obvious symbol for these things: it cannot disappear into that which it represents; it is always there as itself.

While the imagery evoked by the narrative in *Rumstick Road* is of a suburban boyhood—summer at the beach, tying a neighbor girl up in an old chicken coop—the objects on stage are urban and technological. Theater itself is by and large urban and increasingly technological, and no effort is made here to pretend otherwise. Indeed, the often innovative technology or use of it is shown to be interesting in itself. In *Rumstick Road*, for instance, a slide of the mother's face is projected onto the face of the performer who plays the mother: the slide come to life. Another slide is projected simultaneously onto a wall and onto a door in front of and parallel to the wall, thus onto two parallel planes.

Similarly, objects are shown to be interesting as such, and not only insofar as they represent other things. For instance, the various potentials of the red tent are explored: when two performers are inside the tent with a light, we can see their shadows; when the tent is slowly lifted, it appears to be flying. Just as the performer can play many roles, so each object can suggest many things, however unlike its immediate referent it may look and however different its intended use. Robbe-Grillet expresses this interest in things apart from what they "mean" thus: "Let it be first of all by their *presence* that objects and gestures establish themselves, and let this presence continue to prevail over whatever explanatory theory that may try to enclose them in a system of references.... Gestures and objects will be *there* before being *something*; and they will still be there afterwards...mocking their own 'meaning.'"[20] Like performers, objects, because they are not submerged in what they represent, are not subordinate to what they represent. They are not transformed into that which they portray; consequently, their usefulness in eliciting subjective responses, rather than in presenting the illusion of objective reality, is emphasized. And because they, like the performers, are presented as objects in their own right rather than as mere representatives of another set of things, and because the technical means of presentation are not concealed, the idea that the work does not exist as an independent art object is reinforced.[21]

The set in which the action takes place is the only thing specifically built for the play. Elizabeth LeCompte refers to this set as "the House":

••••••••••••   The House is divided into two rooms on either side of a platform from which the operator runs the lights, the tape recordings, the records, and the slides. Behind this platform is a third room which can only be seen via mirrors on the insides of the doors which open into the rooms on either side. Scenes are played in all three of these rooms, on an examination table in the center in front of the operator's panel, and in a long tunnel which stretches behind the picture window in the back wall of one of the rooms.[22]

The walls of the house are shown in forced perspective, and, to increase this sensation, the lights above the set diminish in size the farther they are from the audience. The set is unpainted plywood. No one would mistake this set for a house; it is patently a set. Three years after *Rumstick Road* was first performed, an audience member next to me, seeing the set at the American Place Theatre, asked me whether the play was still in previews. In fact the play had not changed perceptibly since the year before. But this idea that the play is still in rehearsal, in process, is reinforced by the casual beginning of the performance, by our sense that the performers are not fully transformed into their roles, that the props are rehearsal props—things that just happened to be lying around, not really the things they are supposed to represent—and by the exposure of the "backstage" technology. The unfinished quality is consistent with the fact that Gray's investigation into his family and its effect on him is unresolved: everything can change, it is suggested, including Gray's life. The unfinished look is also consistent with the fact that the work does not (yet) exist in its own right apart from its makers and their means. It appears to be unremoved in time or space from its creation. We see, as it were, not only the brush strokes, but the canvas and painters as well; they are as much a part of the work as is that which they portray. Insofar as the work seems to be in progress, incomplete, it invites our participation in the act of completing it. We become part of the process.

No superior clarity serves to distinguish *Rumstick Road* from life outside the theater. The taped language is not clear in its intention. We can infer a great deal from how some things are said and from what is not said, just as in real life. But the speaker's intention is not always as clear as it is made to be in traditional playwriting. We do not know why the grandmother says she cannot make out a slide that seems plain enough to us or why she mistakes a slide of a bear head for one of Gray—perhaps she simply does not see well. Nor do we know why Gray several times says "Forty-six" when he means Sixty-six Rumstick Road. Did he once live at some number Forty-six? As the import of such remarks is not always clear, we have no way of judging their relevance or irrelevance.

From *Rumstick Road* we can construct something of a history, though not a complete one, and we cannot know its causes. Gray recalls his mother telling him that when he was a young child and the family dog died he stopped talking for so long that the family considered sending him to a psychiatrist. Gray seeks confirmation of that event from both his grandmother and father, apparently believing that such a depression, if it occurred, might be causally related to his mother's illness. But the grandmother cannot remember such an incident, and his father characteristically avoids or forgets unpleasant truths. Nor can Gray learn precisely what happened the night his mother died. The data are not clear; the fragments of information do not fit together into a logical whole. The incomplete facts are simply presented to us as such. On the basis of this material, Gray's interpretation cannot be sure. Pinter, remarking on the theatrical convention in which characters can explain or come to learn everything about themselves, the tradition in which O'Neill worked, writes: "A character on the stage who can present no convincing argument or information as to his past experience, his present behaviour or his aspirations, nor give a comprehensive analysis of his motives is as legitimate and as worthy of attention as one who, alarmingly, can do all these things."[23]

The performance of *Rumstick Road* does not clarify or explain the documents. The relationship between the tapes we hear and the actions we see is not explicit; rather, it is allusive and elliptical. Far less than in conventional theater do movements here reiterate, or otherwise reinforce or clarify, the verbal. Indeed, the staging heightens our sense that more is going on than we can see or hear plainly. Because music is sometimes played over the taped voices, we feel we cannot hear all that is being said. Part of the action takes place inside the back-center room, and all but what is partially reflected in the Mylar mirrors on the room's doors is lost to us. Gray and Vawter have a scene inside the tent during which we see only their shadows.

In the New York Public Library of the Performing Arts taped discussion following one performance, an audience member said apologetically, "I'm sure I didn't get everything." Whereupon Gray responded, "No one ever does. It's a metaphor for the quality of memory"—thereby denying the clarity of events represented in tranquility. The performance also accurately represents the multiplicity and lack of clarity in real-life events as they occur. Pinter reminds us that the assumption behind traditional playwriting, "that to verify what has happened and what is happening presents few problems[, is] inaccurate."[24]

Rumstick Road is not larger than life; the subject matter is restricted and close to home. As the painter Dubuffet remarks, "I cannot help feeling that the things closest to us, the most constantly before our eyes, are also the ones that have at all times been the least perceived, that they remain the least known."[25] The theater space and the playing area are small, audience seating limited. The cast consists of only three performers and a technician. Everything looks home-made and easily come by; there are no special art materials. The seating in the Performing Garage is on risers; the whole space is unpretentious, not to say poor. The performers are close to the audience; they wear ordinary-looking clothing and they move the set pieces themselves. Nothing about their acting suggests anything larger than life. Certainly, one cannot speak of the greatness or inten-sity of the acting. Nor is there a sense of the performers as personalities. Gray's face and manner are not striking, and his delivery is rather flat. His family is un-remarkable. Gray himself has no heroic action or recognition. His investigation is inconclusive. Nothing in his comprehension changes in the course of the play except perhaps his opinion of his father. The work lasts somewhat over an hour; it is not "full length."[26]

Rumstick Road is not distinguished from life by its universality and timeless-ness. Instead it is tied to its particular performers and director, who present their personal responses to various segments; they do not try to provide a coherent in-terpretation. Just as the responses of the Wooster Group members are presum-ably impermanent, moreover, so is the group itself impermanent. We are made aware that perception is personal, emotional, fragmentary, and transitory. Gray's interpretation is not final. He lacks the perspective of the deified playwright. He does not know, for instance, why his mother committed suicide or why his father is so reluctant to talk about it. On the basis of the evidence provided we are no more able than Gray to form any conclusive interpretation, much less to general-ize from his family to all families. Absent the causal explanations, or the evi-dence that would allow us to provide such explanations, *Rumstick Road* cannot serve as a case study for a class on family psychology, as *Long Day's Journey into Night* can and does.[27]

The personal and intimate nature of *Rumstick Road* justifies aesthetically (if not morally) the invasions of privacy involved. The effect is that of a private ex-amination of personal matters, with our help. These necessary qualities of inti-macy and privacy, together with the sense of impermanence and lack of performance conveyed, are destroyed when works of this kind, on becoming successful, move to large, permanent, and elegant theaters. Since they have so little magnitude, such works cannot fill spaces where the architecture leads us to expect something larger than life.

Although *Rumstick Road* cannot be mistaken for life outside the theater, nei-ther is it distinguished from actual experience by being raised to a higher form. The materials it uses are by and large not distinctly the materials of art; nor is the work separated from the means of its making. The work is not made to tran-scend life through imposition of a greater clarity or magnitude. In what follows I will show that neither those about whom the story is told, including Spalding Gray as one of the playwrights, nor the performers, again including Gray, nor the spectators are distinct from the work. In the final section of this chapter, "Point of View," moreover, I will show that the work is not clearly distinguished from life itself by time, place, or action, nor raised above it by their unity or by a unity of tone.

The work plays a part in the lives of those whose story is told. Gray's father was extremely reluctant to talk about his wife's suicide at all, much less on tape; Gray's maternal grandmother did not want her recitation on tape of a portion of *Science and Health* by Mary Baker Eddy to be made public; the psychiatrist did not even know that he was being recorded. We must wonder what effect the public performance of the tapes had on these people. The violation of privacy involved—that is to say, the particular nature of the intimate relationship between art and life—was such that it struck members of the Obie awards committee as "unethical as well as illegal."[28] Gray's relationship with the father, grandmother, and psychiatrist must have been affected by his intentional violation of their privacy and trust. His work is a part of his relationship with them. By playing the tape of the conversation with the psychiatrist, Gray attacks the psychiatrist—or, rather, permits the psychiatrist to incriminate himself. In its way, conversely, Gray's reading of a letter from his father, in which the older man is revealed as more comprehending, sympathetic to the mother, and pained by her illness than Gray had previously allowed or understood, is a public expression of respect and love for the father while they are both still living. Emotionally Gray protects neither himself nor others, not even those close to him.[29] Rumstick Road is an act in Gray's life very different from what Walter Kerr saw as O'Neill's in *Long Day's Journey*: "to be reassuring their ghosts, wherever they may be, that he knows everything awful they have done, and loves them."[30] With *Rumstick Road* Gray destroys the possibility of any further contact with the psychiatrist and alters his relationship with living family members.

Rumstick Road intimately involves Gray's relationship not just with others but with himself as well. When Gray first brought the taped material into the theater, he says, he was passionately concerned with it. The work suggests that he is no less involved at the conclusion of each performance. His search for the cause of his mother's illness, manic depression, remains unresolved. Moreover, the sickness is inherited, as the psychiatrist explains; if Gray's fate is determined by his genes, no understanding he might have concerning his past will free him of it. The relationship between his past and his future is uncertain, as it is for us all. In this respect the work must remain unresolved. Gray cannot move out of his past as do Edmund the character and O'Neill the playwright. If one function of performance is, as Gray says, confessional, one cannot know how many performances will suffice, whereas presumably one finished *Long Day's Journey* sufficed for O'Neill. In this respect, too, *Rumstick Road* is unresolved.

Gray is present both as persona from the past, with no attempt made to "be" his younger self, and as narrator now. No distinction between the two is made: performer and role are both present; subject and object are merged. Gray's examination of himself both as perceiver and as object of study entails his having several overlapping roles. Indeed, in contemporary theater performance the roles of playwright, character, and performer often converge. The playwright may appear in person, and in his own person may speak directly to the audience—about himself. Acting then becomes, in the words of the influential actor and director Joseph Chaikin, "a demonstration of the self with or without a disguise."[31] It entails taking risks, including that of being made vulnerable directly before the public. One's self is not a discrete and inviolable entity. The performance is not separate from the rest of life; it is part of the ongoing process of life and may interact with and have repercussions on the rest of one's life.

Although Gray is the only performer who plays himself, the two other performers are not separable from the work either. They were not selected for any role-specific appropriateness. In fact, the play was not cast; Gray and his colleagues simply began by free-associatively improvising to Gray's tapes. No attempt is made to make up or costume Libby Howes (the mother) and Ron Vawter (the quack doctor, the father, and the paternal grandmother) to look like their personae. They are not transformed into and submerged in their roles. Whereas presumably O'Neill's elaborate descriptions of the looks of the characters and their clothing is important to a production of *Long Day's Journey*, in *Rumstick Road* it is enough for us to make the identification of performer and character: that Libby Howes is female and, as Gray seems to remember his mother, attractive and sensual, and that Ron Vawter is male and apparently as restrained as Gray's father. We do not get a sense of "acting," of virtuoso performance, in any familiar sense at all. Indeed, Howes and Vawter were not trained actors.

Director-choreographer Meredith Monk explains the value of working with untrained performers: "Maybe, ten years ago, I was starting to understand how skills could get in people's way, and how my own skills were even getting in my own way to finding new ways of doing things. . . . I felt that seeing people that had a more natural presence, where you were able to see the human being in them more than people that had certain persona's like 'I am a dancer . . .' was a necessary step in artistic development."[32] That this persona, which separates the performer from the performance, is present even in the most realistic theater is made clear only when one sees a contemporary theater performance, in which it is not.

Before *Rumstick Road* begins, the performers lay out a few items of clothing in the house; Gray turns on a light on the set; and then the performers sit or stand to the side of the audience. No distinct space or time demarcates their role playing, nor does anything about their manner indicate whether they are performing in a character role or as themselves. The performers are so close to the small audience that they need not raise their voices or gesture largely. They wear what might be street clothes. Ron Vawter plays the father and other roles in the same glasses, perhaps his own. We cannot say whether he, Vawter, is playing quack doctor or whether he has assumed the role of a particular quack doctor. He plays the grandmother in mask, wig, and wheelchair, with restrained movement. He is not, however, further disguised, nor do we assume that the grandmother's face looks like the mask, or her hair like the wig. We know that in seeing the performers we are not seeing the people. In addition, none of Vawter's roles is sustained. Suddenly, in the midst of playing the grandmother, Vawter hops onto a table and displays his flexed arm as if it were that of one of Gray's heftier brothers. At one point he goes in and out of the center playing area performing various tasks, without making clear whether he is "in character" or not.

Libby Howes, rather than literally representing the mother, seems more to evoke her image. Whereas we might praise an actress for personifying Laura in *The Glass Menagerie*, it is to the point that Gray's mother is not so incarnated. Gray seeks to know her and why she committed suicide, and cannot. Her elusive presence and unexplained suicide suggest that the definition of character which drama provides is a fiction. Libby Howes's performance is a personal response to the tapes. For instance, Howes provides an image of the mother's madness by standing and repeatedly throwing the upper half of her body forward toward her knees until we think she and we cannot tolerate the action any more. There is no intimation that this repetitive masochistic behavior literally represents the form that the mother's mania took; instead the actress provides a correlative action, which, we are aware, inflicts discomfort, if not violence, on the actress's own body. Similarly, when the quack doctor osculates or sucks on the mother's body, Libby Howes is left with red marks on her flesh. Vawter's sucking causes Howes to laugh hysterically. Perhaps the hysteria suggests something of the mother's response to one or more of the various treatments she received, but her actual responses are unknown and no attempt is made to represent them literally.

Howes and Vawter, representing the mother and the father, appear nude at separate times, but as always when we see nude performers we are aware that both the character and the player are nude. A nude performer has no disguise, and we are interested in the person's body in and of itself, and not just as an emblem. In this case, in fact, it seems unlikely that Gray's puritanical father ever walked around in the nude. Hence we get a performer's correlative expression of the father's sexuality, here represented as rather needy and comic: Vawter carries a large phallic-shaped flashlight at genital height and never removes his socks or glasses. Elsewhere, when Vawter puts his fingers in Gray's mouth to display Gray's fine teeth, he dramatizes the grandmother's remark to Gray that he has fine teeth which he inherited from his mother (like manic depression?); but we are also aware that he puts his by now probably not very clean hands into the mouth of an actor.

Not only are the boundaries between performers and performance elided, but those between audience and performance are as well. Although the audience occupies a separate physical space, there is no barrier between it and the performing space. The steeply raked bank of seats begins at playing-space level, with the first row only a few feet away; there is no raised stage or curtain. No audience member is farther than thirty or so feet away. The actors stand to the side of the audience before the play begins, and Vawter, holding a slide projector, walks back into that space during the performance. A curtain or an intermission would mark play time and place as distinct, turn the performance on and off, and make it into an object rather than a process. *Rumstick Road* does none of these. The play takes place in real time, and the action is set in the theater at the time of the performance. Gray narrates directly to us; we are not voyeurs seeing as if through a fourth wall. The actors do not so much represent as illustrate, suggest, present. No artificial or trained manner distinguishes them from ourselves. Vawter, the quack doctor, speaks to us as if we were part of the action, attendants at a medical lecture perhaps. Insofar as the performers do not assume a role, their relationship to us is more direct.

But the most important sense in which the boundaries between work and audience are indistinct is that the work is to a considerable extent of our own making. We do not get a poet's transformation and interpretation; we get the same tapes, slides, and letters (at least a portion of them) for interpretation as the improvising performers had originally. Gray's narration invites us directly to examine the material with him, and his closing "Thank you for coming" acknowledges and so calls attention to our participation in his unfinished investigation. Further, the audience members must make their own connections and associations among the tapes, slides, and letters and between these documents and the performers' activities. No logical connections are provided; the work of interpretation and association is left to the audience, requiring more active participation than is called for traditionally and thus shifting the audience's attention away from anticipation to what Cage calls the "now-moment."

Point of View

Like most traditional plays, *Long Day's Journey into Night* has a single clear point of view. O'Neill's role, Edmund, is largely that of sensitive observer who comes to understand everything. He has a kind of moral or psychological superiority that seems to promise him escape from his family situation. As the author, O'Neill already knows everything. That Edmund comes to know everything serves to substantiate O'Neill's authorial omniscience. There is no apparent inconsistency between the views of the young Edmund and those of O'Neill at the time he wrote this work, or between the view provided of Edmund as a sensitive young observer and O'Neill's omniscience as author. Because the playwright can see everything, so can we—and it is his intention that we see it as he saw it. His view is single, unambiguous, and presumably all-encompassing. We are not supposed to question O'Neill's veracity as an observer. "Edmund" was there; he is honest and intelligent. The story concerns the past, which is over and done with. We know what became of "Edmund": he survived his tuberculosis and became a famous playwright. O'Neill's efforts to keep the play from being published or performed until twenty-five years after his death suggest that he sought to protect his family, whereas any urgency to publish the play might have indicated his need to indict them, thus calling into question the judiciousness of his account. At the same time, the rawness and brutality of the play's confrontations and revelations give the work the appearance of being honest, at least in the dramatic tradition in which O'Neill writes. (Confrontations do not seem to have been characteristic of Gray's family; hence the family would not be suitable subject matter for traditional drama, in which conflict is central.)

Although the action of the play is past for the playwright, we see it happening before our eyes, and the enactment serves to convince us that the action is plausible. Thus one important measure of the success of a production of this play is that it be believable, that is, acceptable as truth.

The uniform tone, logical presentation, and ready comprehensibility of *Long Day's Journey* also assure us that O'Neill's account is reliable. The play puts into words O'Neill's strong feeling about the material: the play is a tragedy, as the title suggests. The sureness of tone expresses the playwright's ability to see the material in perspective, to interpret it with certainty. His account is systematic and causal. We are given the information we need to make sense of the action only when, in the course of the action, we need to know it.

The very familiarity of the dramatic form that O'Neill employs enhances his account's credibility, since we are more likely to believe something that is presented in a recognized form. The psychology inherent in O'Neill's analysis of the characters is familiar to us as well: his view of fate—the past is the present—is both traditional in drama and a part of Freudian psychology. The detailed descriptions of set, costumes, manner of delivery, if reproduced in comparable detail in performance, make us further trust the account with which we are provided; nothing is left vague or sketchy. The consistency, detail, and clarity of O'Neill's script provide the impression that he has written for all time: this is the mark of the greatness of *Long Day's Journey*. One can speak comfortably of great dead authors in the present tense, because what they say is deathless.

The shortcomings of the play's characters other than Edmund/O'Neill are either that they cannot see reality or that they cannot accept it and so must escape into drink, drugs, or women. The distinction between illusion and reality is clear; the protagonist, the author, and the audience see—or come to see—the truth. Drama's frequent theme of illusion versus reality is natural when dramatic action is structured so that it leads to a recognition, and when drama, by means of illusion, presents reality.

Mel Gussow of the *New York Times* provides the criticism of *Rumstick Road* that results when the point of view inherent in *Long Day's Journey* is universally applied.

•••••••••••• Many of the images seem like random notations from a different interpretive work. Mr. Gray and Miss Howes chase each other around the stage with the athleticism of adolescents. Miss Howes lies on a table and Ron Vawter "plays doctor." The actress sits in a small tent and ritualistically removes her clothing. These may be impressions from Mr. Gray's youth or his reflections on his mother's psyche, but the symbolism, if any, is not apparent to the audience. The scenes divert our attention from the biography. Repeatedly in this short play, Mr. Gray seems to be on the verge of communicating a dramatic truth about his mother and his family—and then pulls back.[33]

The criticism is based on the assumptions that the work is interpretive, that the play is Gray's, that it is about his biography, that there is a dramatic truth about his mother and his family, that Gray can know what it is, and that the symbolism should be made clear. These assumptions, however, are at odds with the aesthetic principles underlying *Rumstick Road*.

The very staging of *Rumstick Road* should alert us to the fact that the play provides no single point of view for interpretation. Libby Howes, illustrating the mother's madness as previously described, stands directly in front of the projected slide of the house. She is three-dimensional, the slide two-dimensional; she places her hand so that she appears to be grasping the top of the roof. At the beginning of the play we can see, through the back window of the stage-left room of the house, a very small house, which we take, in the forced perspective of the whole set, to be a house in the distance. Later the red tent, large enough for Libby Howes to lie in, is put in the same space. Also, because simultaneous actions often take place in the two rooms of the house presented to view, the audience members have a choice of what to watch; it is therefore unlikely that any two viewers will focus on precisely the same things throughout a performance.

For *Rumstick Road*, that which dramatic tradition leads us to analyze in terms of point of view is better analyzed in terms of two distinct categories: (1) the biographical documents on which the performance is based and (2) the theatrical responses of performers, director, and audience. One cannot assume that these people share a single point of view. Indeed, the performers, director, and audience do not even all have the same material to respond to. The performers respond to the set designed by the director and technical director, to the documents, props, and one another. The director responds to the performers' improvisations with these materials. And the audience members respond to everything as it is presented in a structure made by the director.

Roughly speaking, the documents are the objective material, and the performers' and director's perceptions of and responses to that material are the subjective part of the presentation. Objective and subjective are not brought together in performance into a single unified perspective. No longer confident that the shape of the world corresponds to the shape of their reason, contemporary dramatists respond with renewed efforts at objectivity or with examination of the shape of their ideas, or both. Contemporary theater is frequently based on documentary material or uses a dramatic text as document, clearly distinguishing between the text and the theatrical—subjective—response to it. In *Rumstick Road* our sense that the documents are objective is heightened by our awareness that they were not made for performance and, indeed, that a number of them are private. Because performers cannot literally re-create that which is documented or literally represent a text, interpretation is necessarily entailed: they must, as observers, interact with the documents or texts. In *Rumstick Road* the performance is called to our attention as an openly subjective response. The documents are left to speak for themselves.

But of course, the separation of objective from subjective is artificial: the two categories interpenetrate. *Rumstick Road* makes this point even in the presentation of the documents. There, the means of our knowing and the nature of the documentation are essential parts of what we know. As if responding to physicist Jacob Bronowski's observation that "we have all been hagridden with this idea that the world is there and that our modes of perception do not much influence how we interpret it; that we can get at the nature of the world without much bothering about the apparatus that we use,"[34] the technological means—tape recorder, tapes, slides, slide projector, technician—are not hidden from us.

Rumstick Road makes us conscious of the documents as documents. The letter from the female neighbor is read to us by the male technician. The performers pose in front of the screen that they set up, as if they were Gray's family watching a slide show; they thus frame the documents as such. We are made conscious that in seeing them, we do not see reality itself. The documents are not live, not present tense; they are fixed in the past and seem to leave the history largely unrecoverable. The mother, the family member Gray is most interested in, is dead. She speaks through one "ecstatically happy" letter, written when she had just come home from the psychiatric hospital, and through one smiling photo. All the other evidence about her is from secondary sources: her mother-in-law; her husband, who finds it difficult to talk about her; a psychiatrist who treated her but does not remember her; and Spalding Gray, who loved her. Several explanations for the mother's illness are provided: religious fervor, change of life, marital unhappiness, bad genes. Yet there is insufficient evidence to confirm or deny any of these explanations. Neither the father nor the grandmother can or will recall for Gray the early time in his life when, according to his mother, he ceased to speak.

The very opening document in the play, the letter from the former neighbor concerning the street name Rumstick Road, introduces the idea that the documents do not provide ultimate truth but, rather, only limited versions of the truth. The speakers are restricted by available information, belief structures, memory, and the way they wish to be perceived. Families commonly document themselves at particular times, on special occasions—usually happy ones. The family shows itself as a work of art. Thus the slides in *Rumstick Road* record a family gathering, a bear someone shot, a Christmas dinner, the mother smilingly embracing her sons. Gray thought to document on tape the responses of family members to another special occasion: his mother's suicide. He says that he had "no plan or direction in making the tapes"; yet, "using a tape recorder, I had asked them questions about my mother's nervous breakdown and about how her 'madness,' and eventual suicide, had affected them. For whatever reasons, these were questions I might never have asked had there not been a tape recorder present. The tape recorder became a medium, a way of relating and dealing with these very powerful and painful questions."[35]

The documents' particulars constitute an essential part of our understanding. We hear the father refer to the mother, nine years after her suicide, in the present tense. We hear him describe her as having been "a perfectly normal sort of gal." And we hear him say, when Gray asks about his mother's vision of having floated up to the ceiling in the orchestra hall in Providence, that he never "chatted" with her about it. We hear how the father's unwillingness to talk about the suicide constitutes a denial of it: "[You and I] never talked about it and I wish it had never happened." The apparatus of language becomes an essential part of what we know.

The apparatus that we are made most conscious of in viewing and listening to the documents in *Rumstick Road*, however, is our own mind. The documents are presented much as if we were snooping in a drawer (indeed, a couple of them are specifically private, and Gray tells us that he was expressly forbidden to play one of them). Although the documents have been consciously selected, they are delivered neither in a logical order nor through any refining or interpreting sensibility; instead they are presented "as is," for us to make sense of ourselves. It is up to us to structure the material and discard incorrect hypotheses as we go along. Our interpretations are not finally confirmed by an omniscient playwright, and we cannot package them into a single coherent system.

Gray, as investigator, narrator, and son, does not suggest that he is in a better position than we to interpret the documents he provides. In fact, we have one document more than he himself has: himself. Then again, he does not have a clear point of view, even a limited one, that might allow us to see him as a character—whose point of view we might in turn interpret.[36] We see him as a complex of sometimes conflicting sensations. He changes his mind. He does not seem any more articulate or informed than those he interviews. He cannot remember and cannot get information about what may have been an important episode in his own childhood. He was not in the country at the time of his mother's suicide, or living at home during the latter years of her illness. Although Gray seems a reasonable enough investigator, the very question of his sanity is raised by the possibility of his having inherited his mother's illness. His investigation is motivated not by omniscience, but by his lack of knowledge, his inability to interpret, his fear of his own possible insanity, and his passionate involvement. Not even his locus of concerns is specific: "I was not conscious of doing anything in the making of the tapes other than asking questions as they would come up. I asked the first question and out of my father's answer a new question would come. . . . It was a kind of action-reaction process."[37]

Gray does not intellectually dominate the world he reveals; he cannot bring the material under his control. The data do not allow him that privilege any more than us. Far from theater historian Oscar Brockett's view that, especially now when we have ceased to believe that meaning, significance, is inherent in things, the dramatist is "compelled to bring order out of the irrationality and create a framework within which life may be made as meaningful as possible,"[38] *Rumstick Road* does not wrest truth from evidence that cannot provide it. The play does not present the certain point of view of a man who is in no position to have one. Virtually nothing is asserted beyond the raw data. By the same token, the data are presented with a ruthless (and illegal) integrity. Tapes are played without the permission of the speakers and against their will.

Meaning does not exist except in our efforts to make it; dramatic truths are fictions—that is what the documents and Gray's investigations reveal. Jacob Bronowski remarks, "I do not think that there is a God's eye view of nature, that there is a truth, an accessible truth of this kind. . . . While the universe is totally connected, we *cannot* extricate ourselves from our own finiteness."[39] In life there is no single truth about a family, or if there is one, we are in no position to know it. Gray's manner is properly humble, self-disclosing, and self-effacing—not heroic. He cannot explain the evidence and get free of it. He properly thanks us for coming, for participating, in effect, as coinvestigators in an inconclusive investigation.

Traditionally based criticism assumes that *Rumstick Road* is the biographical material and takes Gray to task for failing to interpret that material for us. But the biographical documents are not the play; they are part of the material out of which the play is made. Gray writes: "Finally, if [*Rumstick Road*] is therapeutic, it is not so much so in the fact that it is confessional but in the fact that it is ART. The historic event of my mother's suicide is only a part of the fabric of that ART. Finally, the piece is not about suicide; it is about making ART."[40] In this view, art can be made out of virtually any "fabric." But to make a point, Gray overstates his case: in its similarities to *Long Day's Journey*, the primary fabric of *Rumstick Road* is familiarly dramatic. The work is clearly about something beyond its own making.

Although Spalding Gray brought in the pieces of "fabric," the documents on which *Rumstick Road* is based, the play cannot be understood to be his. Rather, it belonged to Ron Vawter, Libby Howes, and Gray himself, who, as performers, improvised freely in reaction to the material over a period of seven months, and to Elizabeth LeCompte, who, as director, made suggestions and in the end selected the improvisational work she liked and structured it in relation to the documents. The members of the Wooster Group had worked together before and knew one another well. Gray and LeCompte had lived together for about ten years. This commonality surely meant that their improvisations were in some ways limited, but it also made for freer experimentation, as did the long stretch of time devoted to rehearsal. Too, the relative inexperience of Howes and Vawter may have allowed them to work with fewer preconceptions about the nature of performance.

At any rate, it is important to emphasize the freedom with which the performers worked. They were not concerned with Gray's questions about his mother's illness, or with trying to represent the mother's madness or Gray's experience of that madness. They did not begin with any preconceived whole or an agreed-upon overall approach. Nor did they attempt to restrict themselves to interactions that could be verbalized, much less verbalized in psychological terms.

The concept of point of view implies a response that is logical, articulable, and continuing over some time. The performers, as individuals or an ensemble, did not work toward this, however. Their responses could be fleeting, and neither the performers nor the audience needed to be able to translate them into explicit meanings. Because the performers were improvising to spoken words and music, most of their responses were nonverbal. As Spalding Gray explains it, he "had been trained in a kind of psychological encounter with [his] fellow performers":

> We were all encouraged to have a lot of eye contact and to touch each other a lot with great emphasis on psychological honesty and full, emotive expression and feeling. The feeling always had to be recognized and named in a traditional sense. There was a kind of category for feelings. All feelings found their right boxes but at [Robert Wilson's] Byrd Hoffman loft something else began to happen for me. One was that I began to have a flow of feeling that I could not name because the flow, which was directly connected to the physical flow of body movement, happened so quickly and in a continuum that it was more difficult to pin down and name. There was only direct unmediated expression . . . a kind of energy field between us at all times and for the first time I experienced being held together with a group of performers by something other than words.[41]

It was just such "direct unmediated physical expression," rather than an exploration of psychology, that was encouraged in the rehearsal of *Rumstick Road*.

Gray provides an example of the group's exploration of the documents:

> Liz and I began to work with the tapes in two ways. At first we used the unedited tapes as background for theatrical improvisations which we began to do at the Performing Garage with Libby Howes, Ron Vawter, and myself, with Liz acting as director. We would do our regular physical warm-ups while the tapes played and then we would try to explore, through structured improvisations, some of the situations recorded on the tapes. An example of this is the mention of my mother's visitation from Christ and her subsequent healing. We worked on the situation of Vawter being a Christ figure and Howes the mother figure. We read from Acts in the Bible and one image, the image of Christ healing a sick person by spitting in his ear, captured our imaginations. This led to Vawter becoming more directly physical with Howes and expressing a desire to tickle her stomach. Vawter slowly dropped the role of Christ and began to improvise a kind of mad Esalen-type of doctor-healer who both healed and tickled his patient to the point of very real and uncontrolled laughter on the part of Howes, the mother-patient.
>
> In this case, we were discovering images that were immediate to our present work in the space but that had grown out of a personal association with the text. It was a constellation of people again. It was group associations around facts in my life. In a way it was the autobiography of the four of us. It was not just my autobiography.[42]

The situation explored in Gray's example is not that of a speaker speaking (as conventional drama explores) but rather that of something said; moreover, no distinction is made in the choice of material for dramatization between actual occurrence and delusion (or myth). Pinter points out: "There are no hard distinctions between what is real and what is unreal, nor between what is true and what is false: it can be both true and false."[43] Gray's mother, we learn in the course of the work, did visit a number of healers, perhaps all of them charlatans as Vawter's work seems to suggest; but for a time after her visit from Christ, she was evidently "well."

Elsewhere in the production, in a further denial of the absolute distinction between real and unreal, the performers in *Rumstick Road* make the figurative tellingly literal. On the tape the paternal grandmother speaks of the mother "after she left us," euphemistically referring to the time when the mother was no longer in contact with "reality." At this point Howes shows the mother going out the window, literally escaping from the house to a place above the other performers—a dramatization that is consistent with the mother's experience of having floated to the ceiling in the Providence orchestra hall and with her interest in Christian Science, through which, the grandmother says, "she was going to...uh...bring herself to the point where she could just be up above everyone and look down." The dramatization thus points to the way in which literal and metaphorical, objective and subjective, are intertwined.

The performers do not know how Christ healed Gray's mother or how she experienced that healing, much less how Christ may have experienced it, nor do they attempt to represent these things. They selected the image of Christ spitting in the ear because it somehow "captured their imaginations." They focused on material that interested them and responded to it in highly personal ways. But not arbitrarily. Even though chance and free association constitute important creative elements in the work, LeCompte emphasizes, "the tapes indicated the approach. The approach is always indicated by the material."[44]

In *Rumstick Road* the performers do not dominate the material or work without regard for it: they interact with it. C. H. Waddington's comment on the relationship between the methods of modern painters and Alfred North Whitehead's understanding of the act of perception is instructive in this respect. Whitehead, he explains, thought that "in the act of perception, the person involved is neither merely a passive reflector nor a dominating actor who imposes his preconceived scheme of things on his surroundings, but is instead a knot or focus in a network of to-and-fro influences." Waddington observes that this point of view has strong affinities with the attitude of many recent painters toward their work: they start painting without knowing exactly where they want to go, and they allow the painting itself, as it develops, to suggest what the next step should be. He quotes Robert Motherwell: " 'I begin somewhat by chance but then work by logical sequence—by internal relations, in the Hegelian sense—according to strictly held values....A picture is a collaboration between artist and canvas. "Bad" painting is when an artist enforces his will without regard for the sensibilities of the canvas.' "[45] Similarly, Robert Rauschenberg states that he works with materials, not ideas. Whitehead's description of the network of to-and-fro influences, like Motherwell's and Rauschenberg's characterizations of their work, challenges the distinction between creation and perception. They are complementary descriptions of the same phenomenon.

The interaction in Gray's example of the group's work style is very direct—in Gray's word, "autobiographical," a group autobiography—with no single human being at the center of the artwork.[46] The interaction is also highly physical and intimate. The performers do not restrict themselves to realism's usual means of expressiveness: talking, sitting, standing (and smoking and drinking). No kind of response to the material is ruled out, but there is a clear preference for responses that are personal and physical, that provide deeply buried and emotional reverberations with the material rather than literally make sense of the material. A performer does not *assume* the character of the "other," neither adopts it nor presumes to know it. As Joseph Chaikin points out, the playing of the "other" can only result in the playing of a stereotype, because we cannot know the other except through ourselves and to pretend otherwise is to keep reaffirming reality as a given.[47] The relationship between performer and role in *Rumstick Road* is an interaction in which each has some independence. The work provides, on the one hand, the documents themselves and, on the other, the distinctly subjective responses of the performers, responses that, although specific to the material, are primarily direct and intuitive rather than analytical—what Gray calls "mind projections."[48]

The performers' responses deny the absolute separateness, singleness, and inviolacy of persons. While performers and their roles are distinct, they also interpenetrate, as do the various roles and the various performers. Ron Vawter plays the quack doctor, the father, and the paternal grandmother—both sexes, and several ages. The distinction between roles is not absolute, because Vawter is always clearly the same performer. Thus at the same time that he plays the quack doctor treating the mother, he also represents the father having sex with the mother (or at least a child's conception of that act). Of course, the treatment provided by quack doctors (and not only quacks) may entail sexual suggestion or even explicit sex; moreover, at about the same time that the mother stopped "having anything to do with the father," she started seeking various cures. The conflation here makes sense. When Gray runs from wall to wall, as his mother is said to have done during her illness, we do not know whether he is enacting her madness or his own, which may be a response to hers.[49] Gray can be both his mother and himself, his present self and his past self, simultaneously. In each case we understand that the distinction between persons, like the distinction between past and present selves, is not absolute. Joseph Chaikin writes: "When we sat together, we were two. When I am alone, we are both me."[50] The whole question of how the actor becomes the other collapses. Persons are not represented as discrete entities, their bodies as demarcating fixed boundaries.

The performers work with props and the set much as they work with the documents, by letting them suggest actions, allowing them a kind of responsiveness in their own right. Much of the performance results from playing with the props without prior assumptions about their given function. Sheets, a flashlight, and a red tent were present in the space where *Rumstick Road* was developed. In performance these items play a role: Gray plays a ghost under a sheet; sheets cover the chairs when the family moves; the flashlight serves as a phallus, and inside the tent it also serves to make shadows. Gray describes the group's work with props as "free-associating," "playing with images" without prior thought about how to present meaningful constructs for the audience.[51] Objects do not have fixed identities and, like the performers, can undergo rapid transformations, symbolizing first one thing and then another. Because the objects are never disguised or made to represent that which they symbolize, the audience is encouraged to see that they are both object and symbol at once. The flashlight is both light and phallus; the gun is also a phallus: two objects can symbolize one thing. The gun is also a gun, and the fight over it between the father and son suggests the intensity of their sexual competitiveness. An object and a performer can represent the same thing as well: Libby Howes and the red tent are both in some way the mother. Objects coalesce; objects and persons coalesce.

The equipment that projects or plays the documents also allows the performers to respond to the documents: it functions as props. The performers play with the projector: they project the slide of the mother's face onto Libby Howes's face; they project the slide of the house onto two parallel planes. Gray walks away from the projected house, referring to the space into which he walks as the yard. The performers lip-synch to the tape; they intersperse live speech and tape. They pretend to be the family viewing the slides, suddenly cutting the light from the projection screen at the moment of the mother's death. "Teching" is part of the process of creation.

The way the performers work with the materials and actions without regard to an end effect, just letting objects and actions suggest things rather than attempting to substantiate an overriding interpretation, requires extensive rehearsal time. Indeed, much more work with the materials is necessary in such productions than when technical effects are planned in advance and controlled by designers and technical directors. Always, of course, objects have powers and limitations of their own. In conventional theater, efforts are made to anticipate and control these effects; nevertheless, props and costumes may, since they are often specially made and generally brought into the production after it is well under way, possess surprising attributes and prove inappropriate or unusable in the end. In *Rumstick Road*, by contrast, the uses of objects are not determined in advance of rehearsal but are discovered in the process of rehearsal. The potentiality of objects is then explored and exhibited as an integral part of the performance.[52]

The performers also work closely with the set, exploring the qualities of the performance space and letting actions follow accordingly, as well as making the few set changes themselves. No fixed or single time or place is established, and there are abrupt changes in lighting, music, and mood. Like a Shakespearean stage, this one is freely transformed and can be at once itself, a performance space, and some other place. It can also simultaneously be two different places and times in the past; for instance, as we see the mother preparing for her suicide in the background, the grandmother is speaking at a more recent date in the foreground. Sometimes the space is undefined, or, as when Vawter and Howes play doctor-patient or the child's idea of his parents having intercourse, one place on the stage is two places at once—an examining room and a bedroom.

In *Rumstick Road* the communality of the theater enterprise is brought to the forefront. There is little subordination of parts: of performers to ruling ideas, to one another, or to a text, or of technical effects, technician, props, or set to performers. Each thing tends to be the center.

Insofar as any single point of view is expressed, it is that of the director. The text follows from her selection and arrangement of the documents in relation to the performers' improvisations. Hers is not an originating intelligence like that of a playwright; rather, performer improvisation is, along with the documents, the found material with which LeCompte works, with the set being the only thing that she preestablishes. LeCompte's directorial passivity, or Zen no-mindedness, before her material is clarified by remarks Pinter makes about his own authorial no-mindedness: "I am not trying to assert myself when I write, or rarely. [My subjects] present themselves to me in their separate guises. I sharpen my tools for them. I stand them in front of the window with the light behind them, I place them in a corner in the shadows. I am there, of course—I am writing the stuff. . . . [But] I am not a fixed star."[53] Or, as Meredith Monk states it, she puts herself "in a state of receptivity to whatever will happen."[54]

The structure that LeCompte creates is one of montage, of juxtaposition. There are abrupt changes from one speaker to another; tape selections may be cut off in midsentence, a portion of an interview dislocated from its context and replaced somewhere else in the sequence of interviews. The segments of action do not necessarily begin and end with the related segments of tape. We are told about the mother's suicide near the beginning of the work, but we do not see it enacted until near the end. There are discontinuities in lighting, music, use of props, mood, and rhythm. Time and space are variable, discontinuous, and overlapping. There is no hierarchical arrangement of the parts: no focal climaxes, no subordination of the parts to the whole. Multifocus, like the lack of climax, works against centrality, giving a kind of all-overness to the structure. Rather than anticipating the next part, we view each part in itself. Because the montage structure is spatial, the progressive form of the work is deemphasized. (Appropriately, *Rumstick Road* is named after a place.) Further, the montage structure stresses the idea of mere change over that of development. Kaprow observes that frequently in contemporary art "the usually slow mutations wrought by nature are quickened and literally made part of the experience of it.... Reality [is] understood as *constant metamorphosis*."[55]

The montage structure—the artistic arrangement of the material—coexists with the linear structure of the story as we can piece it together and with the circular structure provided by Gray's investigation. At the end, Gray reads the letter from his father written when his mother was hopelessly ill, the letter that shows the father as more comprehending, pained, and sympathetic than Gray had understood him to be. And in view of that letter, Gray suggests that the previous material be reexamined. The conflict between the desire to know and the unyielding data is unresolved.

The investigation moves from the long ago past to the present in the theater; the montage exists in present time; the story of the suicide is set in the past. These three structures—circular, montage, and linear—exist simultaneously. The story of the suicide possesses no primacy. It is distanced from us in time and disjunctured. It holds no suspense. It is not based on conflict. There are, to be sure, conflicts inherent in the story—between sex and religion, Gray and the psychiatrist, the mother's world view and the father's, Gray and his father—but they do not organize or explain the story.

The audience responds to the work as structured by the director, its chief interest being the way it induces not only our active participation but also our awareness of that participation. By means of connections and cross-associations, we hold together—or seek to hold together—document and performance. We receive far less guidance than in conventional theater but must sort through our perceptions and arrange correspondences, continuities, and contraries on our own. In the process, we become conscious of our so doing. Richard Foreman points out that we are generally taught to see objects, not perceptual acts.[56] Seeing *Rumstick Road*, however, we become aware that perception itself is a mechanism by which sensations are instantly interpreted inferentially. Our "mind-projections" connect the freedom of the performers' actions with the text to which they are responding. Gray expresses the faith, too, that the "mind-projections" of the performers in some way connect with our own. He does not assume that playwright, performer, and audience all experience the same thing. Viewers make their own connections. It is difficult, usually impossible, to distinguish what exists by a creator's intent from what we make by our own associations. Our involvement in constructing and reconstructing the work requires concentration. Robert Wilson's extremely long works, in which change seems hardly more rapid than in a blooming flower, provoke reverie and intermittent attention. The active participation required by *Rumstick Road* suggests that the work is appropriately limited in length.

The congruities and incongruities we see in the performance are our own; they differ for everyone. The connectedness of all things includes our connection with the artwork, our participation in it. To this extent, the work becomes everybody's autobiography. Description of the work's resonance, then, is highly personal and subjective. But the associations exist objectively, however particular to each observer, and cannot be omitted from description of the piece. Provocation of those associations is the work's principal purpose.[57]

Some correspondences I make do not relate to the text; their interest is merely formal. Sometimes I perceive discomfiting discontinuities between the formal elements themselves or between the formal elements and the text. Sometimes images inconsistent with the text seem to comment on the text by being so. In some instances I have multiple interpretations of actions seen in relation to the text; these may strike me as mutually incompatible, leaving me unable to decide among them, or they may all seem perfectly appropriate and even inform one another. In short, the relationships between elements approximate in their complexity, lack of clarity, and fixedness the relationships between events as I perceive them in life outside the theater.

Most of all, the connections give the work density. I associate the "house dance," in which Howes holds on to the roof of the projected house and repeatedly throws her body forward from the waist, with the mother's floating to the ceiling in the orchestra hall. The father in his letter to Gray describes his feelings about the mother's last illness but then suddenly switches to a story about a bird he ate, a bird that had crashed through a window to its death in the parents' bedroom. I associate the mother with the bird. I also associate the mother with the tent because the tent "flies" and goes out the window, as does Howes. The mother "left" the family in her madness at about the time of the move— symbolized by the flying tent. Mother and the tent are enclosed red spaces. The nude father goes into the tent, his large flashlight phallus preceding him. Gray goes into the tent also, just after a game of chase with the mother that ends with the two males fighting over the gun. I think the mother dies in the tent/garage. The tent does not stand for anything in the logical way that fog does in *Long Day's Journey*; there are no clear boundaries for the associations. Instead a great many associations are tied together. My responses are multivalent, making the work spatial in form. Foreman remarks that

.... most people like material on stage which is NOT DENSE in the sense we mean, because they haven't used—in their lives—the THINKING that reveals the density of the simplest moment. So to them—the DENSE vision seems confusion, discontinuity, even THINNESS! because it doesn't SEEM (appear) like the life they know. In order to live (in their lives), they depend on various simplification mechanisms that block out everything except the USEFUL signs, pointers, tools they find on the narrow road they have made of their life—all energy directed to being able to continue moving along that NARROW road.[58]

The fact that in the rehearsal so many of the interconnections are found by chance reinforces the idea of the interconnectedness of all things. Naturally, this interconnectedness includes our connection with the artwork, our participation in it.

If it is the case, as Bronowski says, "that the universe is totally connected, that *every* fact has some influence on every other fact, then it follows that any cut you make at all is a convenient simplification. But in essence it is a distortion, and you are now decoding only a part of the total sentences."[59] The associations between objects, performers, actions, and images are not limited by the bounds of the play but also extend to the other works in *Three Places in Rhode Island*. LeCompte states that all the pieces of the trilogy are related to the theme of loss. This relatedness is emphasized by the use of the same performers and objects, repetitions of images and actions and their transformations, in new contexts. The separate pieces are, in a sense, all one work evolving, suggesting that every event is somehow relevant to every other event in the universe, its character determined entirely and completely by the way it relates to everything else. Bronowski again: "The part of the world that we can inspect and analyze is always finite. We always have to say the rest of the world does not influence this part, and it is never true. . . . The world is totally connected."[60] In *Sakonnet Point*, for example, the same red tent is a place from which soft music and peaceful women's voices emanate. I imagine it to be the porch of the summer house outside of which Gray, as a child, plays. Later, in *Nayatt School*, the tent seems to be some cancer or illness multiplying out of control. Yet the tent itself is always resolutely a tent, reminding me that my associations are my own. They are not logical: the mother is the tent; the father and son go into the tent; the tent is a disease; the tent can fly; the tent is a peaceful place; the tent is the place where the mother commits suicide. The density suggests an environment of unseen fields of force. It makes the form of the work spatial.

The activity of making the interconnections is intellectual. This is not to say, however, that the work cannot have powerful emotional effects, if no single unified emotional effect. Materials and actions that perhaps convey no emotion in isolation may when juxtaposed cause unexpected feeling. LeCompte remarks that director Richard Schechner, with whom she, Gray, and Vawter had previously worked, "felt that you had to feel an emotion in order to convey it [the idea, of course, behind Method Acting]. He wanted people to actually experience an emotion before an audience. I believed that an actor didn't have to feel an emotion in order to express it."[61] The smiling face of the mother projected onto the face of Libby Howes is at first amazing, the portrait come to life, and then, in the context of the manic letter, depressing, a mask worn by a suicidal woman. Howes's is merely the face on which the slide is projected. In the "house dance" Howes has a more active role, but she does not have to feel mentally disturbed in order to convey the mother's madness. Rather, the combination of her strong repetitive motion, the projection of the house, and the Bach partita played on the phonograph as if by the mother express this madness quite effectively.

As the images transmute, so does their emotional effect, although there is carryover from one image to another. One's emotional responses, however, are determined by what one thinks happened. In traditional drama what happens is clear; it is the causes that are open to discussion. In contemporary theater, though, the "what" cannot be taken for granted. James Bierman, who describes the woman as bedding down for the night in the tent;[62] I, who perceive her to have bedded down for death; and Mel Gussow, who sees the whole image as irrelevant, clearly had different emotional responses to the image. Conversely, our emotions determine what we see.

By means of the associations we make, the work comes to have density or resonance. This resonance itself provides an emotional effect which Yeats, in a short essay from 1903, called "the emotion of multitude": "I have been thinking a good deal about plays lately, and I have been wondering why I dislike the clear and logical construction which seems necessary if one is to succeed on the modern stage. It came into my head the other day that this construction, which all the world has learned from France, has everything of high literature except the emotion of multitude." For Yeats, this emotion was a kind of ecstasy, a religious experience. He thought that it could be provided by drama in three ways: by the use of a subplot that echoed the main plot, as in Shakespeare's plays; by the use of a chorus that related the enacted characters to other gods and heroes, as in Greek tragedy; and "by the use of vague symbols that set the mind wandering from idea to idea, emotion to emotion, the rich, far-wandering, many-imaged life of the half-seen world beyond the fable," as in Ibsen and Maeterlinck. "Vague, many-imaged things have in them the strength of the moon," Yeats explained, using one of his favorite multitudinous images.[63]

O'Neill, following Ibsen, gave *Long Day's Journey into Night* some density through the use of imagery. *Rumstick Road* gains density or resonance from its multiple structures, confluent roles, and imagery that is less specifically translatable than the imagery in *Long Day's Journey.* The emotion of multitude that this density provides, an important aesthetic value in new theater, thus separates the work from life, or at least from life as we ordinarily experience it.

Because *Rumstick Road* reveals its means and is at the same time about those means, as much as it is about its content, it employs yet another technique to provide the emotion of multitude, one unimagined by Yeats. In *Rumstick Road* we are made aware that the present time in the theater and those past times and places being recalled come together as one, as do performer and role, one person and another, three-dimensional and two-dimensional, object and symbol, subjective and objective, life and art, process and product, live performance and text, our creation and theirs. Other places, times, persons, and objects do not exist as inviolable separate wholes. Whereas dance can present people here now without reference to other circumstances, drama generally provides another context; it refers to something beyond itself, in part because it employs language, which is referential. Part of theater's inherent fascination has always come from the kind of density or interconnectedness that contemporary theater so manifestly provides: however much the actor in traditional theater becomes the role, we still take pleasure in the presence of the actor, in the mystery of actor and role having become one and, at the same time, in their separateness. Contemporary theater performance, however, achieves the emotion of multitude by working against the magic of illusion.

Rumstick Road is, in LeCompte's words, about "Spalding's love for the image of his mother and his attempt to re-possess her through art."[64] Yet it is also about the inevitable failure of such an attempt—that is, about loss. Physicist C. F. von Weizsäcker describes the failure of a comparable attempt in quantum physics: "We wanted to press on behind appearances to the things themselves, in order to know them and to possess them; now it appears that precisely beyond our natural perceptual world the very concept of a thing can be defined only in relation to the man to whom it appears or who himself makes it."[65] This comprehension has profoundly changed our examination of the natural perceptual world, and it lies likewise at the heart of the theatrical means employed in *Rumstick Road*. The union between the material on which *Rumstick Road* is based and its contemporary theatrical means is apt.

I have taken the title of this chapter from an essay by Ted Kalem, formerly drama critic for *Time*, entitled "The Visceral Response." Kalem's essay serves by contrast to summarize the ways in which *Rumstick Road* departs from conventional drama. In it he assumes that the fabric "from which all theatre is woven is the 'fabric of illusion.'"

•••••••••••• What gives drama compelling life?...The sense of imminence....We must feel that we cannot wait to know what is going to happen next....Every play of lasting merit...is a kind of sophisticated detective story, and the dramatist for whom theatre is a true vocation will know how to strew his clues.

In addition to being a master spinner of tales, the great playwright is rather like a god. He creates a unique universe of vision. If, in that universe, the play is the sun, the actor is the magnifying glass. He, or she, transmits the rays of the playwright's vision to the stage in a pinpoint of flame. It seems to me that this is both possible and desirable regardless of the genre of the play....The quality I look for in an actor, above all others, is intensity.

"Give me the family play," Kalem concludes, because drama within the family has the greatest intensity.[66]

Rumstick Road is based on documents of Spalding Gray's family. It was created by the group that Gray regarded as his theater family, who played with the documents over a period of seven months. It is, then, both family play and a family play. For the rest, *Rumstick Road* meets none of Kalem's traditional criteria. It evokes not a primarily visceral response but an intellectual one. It seeks not to move us but to activate us and to make us aware of that activation. It is not illusionistic. Much of the presented material is not live. The work does not gain its interest from suspense. It was not designed to endure; it is personal, restricted to its performer-creators and to a transitory view. Although the work contains a detectivelike investigation, that is not its principal aspect, and the investigation goes unresolved. Indeed, the principal interest of the work is not in the story at all. The perspective that Gray provides is limited, uncertain, and unclear, the material of little magnitude. As co-authors the performers and director present their own perspectives or, hardly that, responses to the various documents and other materials and to the persons with whom they work. They do not strive for intensity.

Kalem's criteria, while appropriate to *Long Day's Journey into Night*, are not "desirable, regardless of the genre of the play." I have therefore tried to show a more appropriate way to value contemporary theater performance.

After completing the trilogy *Three Places in Rhode Island*, the Wooster Group added a fourth piece, "an epilogue" which they entitled *Point Judith*. This epilogue included, as a play-within-a-play, a twenty-minute parody of *Long Day's Journey into Night*. In an epilogue of my own, I shall briefly discuss this parody, for it serves to highlight some additional Cagean characteristics of contemporary theater practice.

Within *Point Judith*, *Long Day's Journey into Night* is introduced as a party skit. As part of the parody, the group heightens the work's theatricality by performing the whole of it to the programmatic Romantic music of Berlioz. For the "skit," Gray selected the lines from *Long Day's Journey* that particularly interested him. The text, then, serves as found material, and no effort is made to effect a coherent condensation of the play; some lines are played on a tape recorder and then repeated by the actors out of synch. Gray takes the role of the father, but for much of the scene he stands aside as an intermediary between the play and the audience, in a way reminiscent of his role in *Rumstick Road*. The mother, who is certainly a sympathetic character in both *Long Day's Journey* and *Rumstick Road*, is here played by Willem Dafoe, who in the part of *Point Judith* that precedes this skit has just played a most unappealing role. He performs in a dress, which he raises to show his man's underpants. The role of Edmund is played by a boy of twelve with braces on his teeth. The house, recognizably the same one as in *Rumstick Road*, is set off to one side; part of it has a floor and part does not. The tempo of the piece is frenzied; in addition, a film that we cannot make out is projected onto the house, providing erratic lighting and, together with the tempo, making the whole seem like an old movie. Objects are out of control: a lawn mower and a garden hose seem to defy their users; the vacuum cleaner used by the maid creates dust or fog and noise. Neither she nor the objects with which she works behave in a subordinate manner. A child, who appears to be a doppelganger of the mother, runs about upstage in shadow, as if the mother (like the tent in the previous play, *Nayatt School*) has in her madness multiplied out of control. Much of the action is set out-of-doors, as if the madness had burst beyond the bounds of the house. Throughout this chaos, the poet son Edmund reads, apparently oblivious to the goings-on.

Nothing is "well" lit or clear. The playing area is very wide, with no central focus, and the audience is close. Multiple focus makes it impossible to take in all the activity in one view. The resolution, however, is very clear: the father, presumably in disgust, shoots all the other characters.

The text is not represented; instead it becomes an object for use in another artwork. The parody of *Long Day's Journey* is quite clearly also a parody of *Rumstick Road*. The sentimentality about the mother and her madness is mocked. The sensitive son is represented as merely oblivious. We see the work from the point of view of the father, who finds the whole family intolerable. Like all parody, this one challenges the magnitude of the original—even the limited magnitude of *Rumstick Road*.

Point Judith demonstrates some characteristics of contemporary theater not present in *Rumstick Road*. The mother's madness, the subject of *Rumstick Road*, here affects the structure and rhythm of the work. So does the energy of the participating child performers, who are co-equal with the adult artists. *Point Judith* takes very seriously Cage's idea that each person can open up new possibilities for others.

Objects, for their part, are no more brought under control than the children, but seem to have an independent life within the work. The traditional text is regarded as an object like any other, something with which to improvise freely. In the process of improvisation, moreover, O'Neill's and Gray's perspectives are mocked, making clear that each contains a point of view which we cannot take for granted. Finally, the size of the playing area and the multiple simultaneous activities within that space allow us no possibility of a single fixed comprehensive perspective. There is no sense that the world represented on the stage is under our control any more than it is under the control of the performers.

Rumstick Road and *Point Judith* are based on a different set of assumptions about the nature of reality and our relationship to it than is traditional theater, and those assumptions are Cagean. In their examination of the role of observation, of language, and of technology; in their structure; in their dedication to process, the field situation, indeterminacy, unimpededness, and interpenetration, they reveal Cage's aesthetic in theater practice. This aesthetic has had a profound influence on contemporary avant-garde theater for a coterie audience, but also, if to a lesser extent, on very popular theater—such as *A Chorus Line*, which I examine next.

3 .... *A Popular Contemporary Work:* **A Chorus Line**

On 29 September 1983, *A Chorus Line* became Broadway's longest-running show. By then, there had been 3389 Broadway performances; it had run for eight years and played in 184 U.S. cities in forty-four states, 24 cities having had three or more engagements. It had been seen by twenty-two million people in the United States alone. The American hostages in Iran, after the New York parade celebrating their release in 1981, chose to see *A Chorus Line* together. Productions of *A Chorus Line* have played in Canada, England, Puerto Rico, Australia, Germany, Sweden, Japan, Brazil, Argentina, Mexico, Spain, France, Norway, and Austria. Now in its fourteenth year of continuous Broadway performance, one cannot doubt that *A Chorus Line* is popular theater. That it has many features of contemporary experimental theater, however—sometimes referred to as anti-theater and anti-reality—may come as a surprise, both to those who have avoided the avant-garde as being too esoteric and to those who have avoided *A Chorus Line* because it is popular theater.

As the aesthetic I explore turns our attention increasingly toward performance, we are not simply free to examine theater works whose reputations depend on something other than literary merit, we are obliged to do so. *A Chorus Line* belongs to a familiar genre: the backstage musical. And like many such musicals, it contains a play-within-a-play. The action consists of an audition for a group of dancers aspiring to work in the chorus line of a new musical. After seven are rejected at the outset, seventeen remain, from whom the director-choreographer will select "four boys and four girls" based on their execution of various dance combinations learned on the spot and the personal impression they make while talking about themselves. At the end, when the eight have been chosen, the whole company immediately appears costumed and kicking in one large chorus line—presumably the one for which the audition was being held.

The Workshop Process

Like *Rumstick Road*, *A Chorus Line* was collaboratively developed over a long period of time, with no set deadline for completion. No script was rehearsed (the word *rehearse*, interestingly, means literally to "reharrow," go over old ground); rather, a show was created during a nine-month period. Choreographers, writers, composer, and dancers were all included at the onset. The result is a show that uses movement and song as much as a script to tell its story.

The way the show evolved has had important ramifications on the overall economics and nature of Broadway theater. The work was initiated in January 1974 when director-choreographer Michael Bennett met with eighteen Broadway chorus dancers. After the dancers took a class together led by one of them, Bennett turned on a tape recorder and asked them to talk about Broadway and their lives. They talked all night. On the basis of the tapes made on that and a subsequent night, Bennett persuaded producer Joseph Papp to fund a workshop in which he could develop a work about dancers auditioning for a musical. Much of the material for *A Chorus Line* was then composed from the tapes.

Bennett worked out a landmark agreement with Actor's Equity Association that officially recognizes the performers' contribution to the creation of *A Chorus Line*. Under the terms of that agreement, the original dancers from the taping sessions and the workshops continue to be paid collectively one-half of the 1 percent of the weekly gross receipts designated as Bennett's author's royalty.[1] In other words, more than twenty people are receiving writers' royalties for their part in the origination of *A Chorus Line*.

Those taking part in the workshop were each paid a modest one hundred dollars a week. Even though the participants had specialized jobs—writer, choreographer, composer—implicit in the equality of pay was an assumption of equality in the work. According to Bennett, a collaborative atmosphere prevailed, probably enhanced by the fact that all the contributors had worked with Bennett before. Defensiveness about the work was little in evidence, Bennett said; no one claimed writing, choreography, or musical composition as his special province—the mere fact that you were in the room meant that you had talent. Anyone could do anything.[2] The development of a work through collaboration, rather than the mounting of a preconceived text in accord with a directorial "concept," of course, takes extensive rehearsal time; the twenty-minute segment "Hello Twelve," for example, took six weeks to develop. The writers, composer, and choreographers thus developed the work slowly through a process of interaction with their materials—in this case, dancers and their stories.

More can be attempted in a workshop situation than when people work under extreme time pressure. Freedom from time constraints expands the range of possibilities: it allows the collaborators to follow their fantasies, to interact with their materials, to make mistakes, and, in general, to try things they could not try were they intent only on immediate success. The work can be more audacious, more experimental, with chance becoming a creative element in the work.[3] In the song entitled "Sing," for instance, the husband of the auditioning character supplies the last notes of each line because the character herself can neither reach them nor carry a tune. The idea for this song came from the actual singing audition held for the first performers in A Chorus Line, one of whom, to the composer's despair, could carry no tune whatever.

Despite the long workshop period, A Chorus Line was mounted relatively inexpensively. Its primary materials were dancers, and everyone participating in the workshop was paid very little. The show opened at a cost of $260,000 at Papp's Off-Broadway Public Theatre—when the cost of opening a standard Broadway musical was about $1 million—and its weekly overhead on Broadway in 1983 was a very modest $150,000.[4] The communal nature of the work and the materials that went into it have strongly affected its financial success.

Since A Chorus Line, Equity workshops have become common. In 1977, when Bennett was working on Ballroom, he refined the agreement by which workshop participants get a cut of the proceeds, and that agreement has become the basis of all Equity workshop agreements.[5] Even where the work has been scripted ahead of time, such Equity contracts have allowed extensive rehearsal time during which directors can indulge in less goal-directed activity and try more innovative approaches; they have shifted the emphasis away from the scripted materials to performance elements; and they have allowed backers to see the shows, and to see that they work. Backers in turn have been willing to finance more original works, including works directed, acted, or choreographed by unknowns. "The workshop process has enabled a lot of Broadway shows [like Nine] to be done that otherwise would be regarded as too risky or too dangerous."[6] The workshop has formalized the idea of rehearsal as a process of creation through interaction with the materials rather than a period during which a preestablished work is mounted. The process is not endless, like Cage's reality, but it is prolonged; and this changed process has had a profound effect on the economics and nature of the Broadway production.

Structure

The script of A Chorus Line itself reflects a contemporary interest in process. Action is minimal. We hear many autobiographical narratives, stories about the past, the arrangement of which provides no strong sense of movement toward a conclusion of the audition. Although the narrated biographies are from progressively later periods in the dancers' own lives, that movement is not reflected in

Fig. 3. From an advertisement for A Chorus Line. *Courtesy of The New York Shakespeare Festival, Joseph Papp, Producer.*

the present action. Nor is it clear either at the time of their delivery or in conclusion how each narrative serves the director's selection process.

The audition is concluded when the director asks some of the dancers to step forward one at a time. We and the dancers assume that these performers are the ones chosen for the chorus line. But the director soon makes clear that it is those left behind that he has cast. By then we hardly have time to see who remains before they all exit. It hardly matters: our interest has been effectively shifted to what happens *as* it happens, and not only insofar as it serves this decisive moment. As with dance, our interest in *A Chorus Line* is in the moments, not in the outcome.

A Chorus Line has so little suspense that any intermission would be inappropriate. Certainly, no break is needed for scene changes: the changes in the extremely minimal scenery are part of the show's visual effect. The various autobiographical narratives overlap and flow into one another. Dance and song occur separately or simultaneously, telling the story apart or together. Dance, song, and narrative coalesce fluidly. An intermission points up the structure of a work, whereas the sense of *A Chorus Line* is that of flow. While many segments of *A Chorus Line* are memorable, it is difficult to identify these as the familiar parts of a dramatic structure.

A Chorus Line is blocked so that it has less central focus than conventional drama. In part, of course, it is a piece about movement, rather than action. The line of auditioning dancers standing equally spaced across the front of the stage has no central focus: as the dancer Cassie would have it, "each one of them is special"—an idea that is reinforced by the fact that the dancers are all listed alphabetically in the program. Bennett regarded all of the dancers in the original cast of A Chorus Line as principals and paid them as such. Their salaries raised the pay scale for all chorus-line dancers thereafter,[7] as if the union could not understand chorus-line dancers as each one special, as principals, so firmly entrenched is the idea of the hierarchy of performers in musicals. In the beginning and later, when the dancers execute various combinations as part of the audition, the foci are multiple as we try to make discriminations among the dancers. We are required to be more active participants than when the focus is single. There are so many dancers doing the dance combinations at once that, like Zach, the director in the play, we must decide which deserve our attention, for how long, and in what sequence. In this way, the form of A Chorus Line, like that of Rumstick Road, corresponds to life outside the theater. Ironically, in the climatic, strictly unison chorus-line finale, which each dancer has striven so hard to become part of, none is central; the dancers perform as a unified mass.

Michael Bennett remarked that the lighting for A Chorus Line provides the equivalent of the film techniques of jump cut, close focus, and dissolve.[8] These effects are not merely imitative of film, however; they are consistent with the very structuring of the material otherwise and are of a piece with the view of reality expressed through that structure. With the aid of lighting, A Chorus Line jumps without transition from theater to dance studio, from internal to external, from the narration of one person to that of another, and, at the end, from the audition to the play-within-a-play. The use of close focus—or rather, its theatrical equivalent, lighting that frames small areas, as opposed to lighting that allows a more general view—is consistent with the shifts in perspective from individual to group and from internal to external. In one striking instance, three performers downstage sing about how "everything was beautiful at the ballet" class, while upstage in a rectangular frame of light we see the feet of a group of dancers at a ballet barre, presumably representing the singer's recollections. Lighting fades in and out, the equivalent of film dissolves, causing the various narratives—and internal and external, and past and present—to interpenetrate.

The filmlike techniques evident in the lighting are employed in other aspects of the work as well. Some of the songs jump from one speaker to another and from external dialogue to internal monologue; in one instance an internal monologue is even cut off in midsentence. The structuring of the work around various autobiographical narratives means that juxtaposition, or jump-cutting, is inherent in the work's basic form. This juxtapositional effect is heightened because instead of narrating each of the seventeen biographies one after another, the co-authors intercut from one to another. Further, there are jumps from the present to the past, which the characters both tell about and represent. And there are abrupt changes in tone—as in life. *A Chorus Line* has no single overall tone; it is a musical, but not a musical comedy; moods, along with characters, are abutted abruptly against one another. Critic Julius Novick observes that *A Chorus Line*'s "wisecracks and heart-tugs and razzmatazz are juxtaposed with the utmost shrewdness."[9]

A high degree of technical sophistication is much in evidence in *A Chorus Line*. The computerized lighting was as elaborately choreographed as the dancers and, like them, calls attention to itself. The set consists of eight tall three-sided structures (*periaktoi*) on one side of which were lightweight mylar mirrors the likes of which the set designer originally saw used by NASA. The space-age mirrors, which can be rotated so as not to be seen, together with the lighting, make the show essentially minimalist high tech. It is not unusual for contemporary theater to rely heavily on the latest sound, video, lighting, and film technology, and to make the use of that technology evident. Both *A Chorus Line* and *Dreamgirls*, another of Bennett's musicals—which has as its set tall moving light towers—have a subject matter that is specifically urban; moreover, the means of production are obviously so as well. There is a kind of integrity in this: the highly sophisticated technology that theater now uses is made part of the show. *A Chorus Line* does not reveal all, however. The musicians in the orchestra pit, who would of course not be present at an audition, are covered by a cloth that lets through sound but not light, so that the theater can be entirely blacked out and the fiction of the audition maintained.

The structure of *A Chorus Line* is more like that of *Rumstick Road* than of traditional drama, in that our interest is not in anticipation but in the moments themselves. The focus is less central, in space as well as in time. The work is juxtapositional with interpenetrating parts. It calls attention to the means of its making.

The Hot Musical

With the success of *A Chorus Line* and *Dreamgirls*, director-choreographer Michael Bennett rightly and proudly proclaimed himself the king of the backstage musical.[10] Bennett liked backstage musicals, he said, because their form is "hot." "In the old-fashioned musical," he explained, "they finish a number with their arms raised in the air, and they stare at the audience, the audience applauds. The audience is acknowledged as being at a musical, whereas one of the dangers of the modern musical is that the audience is somewhat distanced, not acknowledged, more like a voyeur." A hot musical, in contrast, is one, first of all, "with an intense stage-audience relationship, one with a flimsy fourth wall."[11]

Second, the hot musical provides a milieu in which dancers and singers can dance and sing as such: "where," as Bennett explained, "it's not just a bunch of doctors and dentists dancing at an office party. . . . In 'Chorus' the performers are actually dancing for you, the audience, just as Mozart in 'Amadeus' actually plays a piece."[12] In a hot musical, then, the performer and role are made obviously close. As a result, the relationship between performer and audience is also more immediate. The play does not require the willing suspension of disbelief that we (the audience), the actors, and the theater are not there; instead these elements are called to our attention and come to seem related to the text.

The backstage musical acknowledges the audience insofar as the play that the characters put on is for an audience. But the costumed dance number in *A Chorus Line*, the play-within-a-play, comes only at the very end, and it is brief. The presentational effect of the work, moreover, is heightened by our identification with Zach. Shortly after *A Chorus Line* begins he moves out into the audience space, where he remains as an unseen speaker until near the end. The dancers line up across the front of the stage and speak out to him, as to us, in response to his questions about their lives.

When one of the characters, in response to Zach's questioning, narrates or dramatizes something from his past, the other aspirants act as an onstage audience. So close are performers and roles here that we cannot tell whether those standing around listening to the speaker are in character or not. Contemporary theater frequently employs both narrative form and the onstage actor/audience—*Nicholas Nickleby* (1980), for instance—thus constantly reminding us that the work is intended for an audience.[13] (These devices, I should say, are quite different in effect from the more conventional means of calling attention to the existence of the play as play—a curtain, an overture, intermissions, a curtain call [none of which *A Chorus Line* has]—which indicate just the opposite: that the play exists wholly separate in time and place from the audience.) The audience is explicitly included in *A Chorus Line* as well by the use of the mirrors at the back of the stage, which reflect the house. These, Zach's presence in the house, and the onstage actor/audience confuse the distinction between the spatial and temporal location of subject and object, between the viewer and the viewed, and between life and art.

Although *A Chorus Line* is performed for the benefit of the audience, the audience takes on various roles in relation to the play and in that way is assimilated into it. We begin in the role of judge as, along with Zach, we try to discriminate between the aspirants on the basis of their dancing and personalities. In the final section we are cast in another role, that of the audience for the play-within-a-play.

The only learning—or, in an Aristotelian sense, recognition—in *A Chorus Line* is on the part of the audience. Whereas at first we assume the role of judge along with Zach, we soon find ourselves identifying with the dancers instead. Along with Cassie, the audience comes to feel that each of the dancers is special and that the judging process will be largely arbitrary, or at least chancy, and regrettable. With this realization, then, we cast off the role of judge.

In theme, the work, far from being anti-reality, embraces all the dancers as equally acceptable manifestations of human existence. The auditioning dancers are urged into very personal talk about themselves; anxious to please, they proceed to reveal old anxieties about, among other things, their first wet dream, uncontrollable erections, breast size, and height. According to Bennett, such discussion had the effect of sanctioning the audience's own discussion of these embarrassing and usually private matters; they go home, he said, talking not about the play, but about themselves.[14] To the extent that their identification with the characters prompts them to talk about their own otherwise private anxieties, perhaps they come to accept these anxieties, and to some extent even their own height, breast size, and sexual identity, as valid parts of reality.

Whether the ending of *A Chorus Line* is happy or pathetic depends on the interpretation of audience members, their participation in the work. The genre or tone of contemporary theater works is often no more distinct than that of life outside the theater. Bennett said that people are to get whatever they can out of it; his mother, he commented, felt that the show had a happy ending because all the dancers reappeared in the finale.[15] Others observe that the selection process is without evident logic and that the dancers wholly lose their individuality in the chorus line. *Village Voice* critic Julius Novick observes:

> The whole cast comes out, men and women, in preposterously spangly gold costumes, with gold top hats, singing and dancing, as if their lives depended on it, a song as outmoded, vulgar, and stupid as their costumes. Perhaps this is meant to make us feel all warm and delighted and enthusiastic: good old-fashioned show-biz, glitzy and trashy as it may be, makes all the suffering worthwhile. But to me it is a moment of savage irony, only deepened by the rousing energy of the dancing: all that effort, all that yearning, all that pain, were for *this*, this number, this orgy of vapidity and crassness? This, *this*, is what show-biz is?[16]

Not only does the relationship between audience and stage become intimate as the audience is brought into the play, but performer and role are also identified and made interactive. This is most obvious when the characters show their audition photos, which are, of course, photos of the performers themselves.[17] Yet there are many other ways in which performer and role are brought close together and made interactive. Far from claiming that any similarity to persons living or dead is purely coincidental, the program notes for *A Chorus Line* emphasize the similarities between the performers and the characters they play. On stage the dancers recall dance classes taken and previous auditions and professional experience. In the course of the audition, one of the dancers is injured and cannot continue. The program note informs us that

•••••••••••• prior to the first performance of *A Chorus Line* at the Public Theater, the original company had collectively appeared in 72 B'way shows, 17 national companies and 9 bus and truck tours in which they gave a total of 37,095 performances. Collectively, they had 612 years of dance training with 748 teachers—counting duplications. They spent approximately $894 a month on dance lessons. While performing they sustained 30 back, 26 knee and 36 ankle injuries. . . . The characters portrayed in *A Chorus Line* are, for the most part, based upon the lives and experiences of Broadway dancers.

Indeed, Bennett made no secret of the fact that *A Chorus Line* was based on the biographical material provided by the group of eighteen dancers in the first all-night group discussion he conducted very early in the preparation for the show, a number of whom appeared in the original cast. Nicholas Dante, for instance, who subsequently became co-author of *A Chorus Line*, revealed during the interviews that he had begun his dancing career as a female impersonator; this revelation became the "Paul monologue,"[18] even including his decision to change his name from a Puerto Rican to an Italian one for the stage.

Watching the performance, we are conscious of the fact that these dancers themselves auditioned before a director. We assume that the cast members have had anxieties similar to those of the characters in the play. They, like the characters, have to face the issue of what they will do when they cannot dance anymore. Some have surely had questions about their sexual identity. Quite specific parallels come to our attention as well. The woman playing the short, flat-chested Asian dancer is in fact short, flat-chested, and Asian, and perhaps on that account has had the same difficulties being cast in other chorus lines as the character expresses. The Latino girl is played by a performer with a Spanish surname. Thus, the ethnicity of both performers and characters is specifically called to attention. We wonder, then, whether the homosexual is played by a homosexual and whether the performer playing Val, the dancer who got work only after she had her breasts and buttocks surgically enlarged, also achieved success by such means. She gets a laugh by remarking that we must be looking at her "tits," as indeed we are—we are necessarily observing not just the character's breasts but the performer's, and we are caught at it. The characters' clothing, although carefully designed, appears to be what the dancers themselves might have selected to wear to an audition. The few props, like the costumes, serve as symbols but are also objects in the real world. Both clothing and props bring actor and role together and make them interpenetrating.

The distance between actual space and that of the play is also minimized: the play is set "here" in the theater in 1975, the year that *A Chorus Line* opened.[19] The mirrors, which in fact constitute a carefully designed set, hardly call attention to themselves as a set. We see the set as the actual environment of the actors—the stage. The two exceptions to this stage-set naturalness are the finale background, which replaces the mirrors, and the semicircle of mirrors that come down around Cassie for part of her dance, providing her with an intimate space where she can dance for herself. The characters in *A Chorus Line* are self-reflecting: Cassie sees herself as she is reflected in the mirrors.

The play is about what it is really about: performers trying to please their audience—or, in the play, the director. To a considerable extent, *A Chorus Line* recreates its actual inception. When Bennett held the original all-night interview session, the dancers began the evening by performing combinations provided them. (Just so, *A Chorus Line* begins with the auditioners dancing combinations provided them.) Then Bennett asked the dancers to talk about Broadway and their lives. Bennett was by then already an established Broadway director-choreographer, with *Promises, Promises, Company, Follies,* and *Seesaw,* among other works, to his credit; accordingly, Bennett said, they regarded the interview session as a form of audition. As they spoke, one person's thoughts triggered another's, a montage effect that is reflected in the structure of the play. Hence, not only the stories the dancers told but also the event of their dancing and telling is recreated—a self-reflexivity that bears a certain integrity.[20]

Neither the action nor the characters possess great magnitude. The action itself might take place any day in the theater and in roughly the same amount of time as the play takes, except of course that the actual performance could not immediately follow the audition. The characters' lives are plausibly the lives of dancers, even those of the particular dancers in *A Chorus Line.* The characters' goals are small and very personal; the consequences of their being cast or not affect very few. Nothing happens that cannot happen again. No war is concluded, no love consummated, no rite of passage completed. Nobody dies, grows old, or learns any great truth. Some of the dancers are cast and some not; each can try again. Since most of the speeches are essentially monologues, they hardly provide action in the sense of conflict. What interaction there is, is primarily with an offstage character, Zach.

The very ordinariness of the characters and the smallness and intimacy of the material suggest the appropriateness of any material, even the most mundane, to a theatrical work. Again, the idea is not anti-reality but the suggestion that all subjects are appropriate to our interest, even our own secret obsessions about the configuration of our body. Like *Rumstick Road, A Chorus Line* has a seeming artlessness that makes it close to life, suggesting that it is not an autonomous object heightening or epitomizing life but an event continuous with life. The apparent artlessness intensifies the relationship between actor and role. Much of the time the dancers stand in a line across the front of the stage in various informal, seemingly unposed, stances. Only the ad for *A Chorus Line* or repeated viewings of the play make clear that the informal look is set—the same for each cast and performance.

Dance critic Deborah Jowitt has observed that the choreography in *A Chorus Line* is suitably undistinguished: "The audition material doled out by the show-within-a-show's director, Zach, . . . is the usual unremarkable stuff: a little ballet, a little tap, a little jazz. . . . The big number for Cassie (Donna McKechnie)—the soloist trying out for a chorus job in order simply to keep dancing—is a skillfully built pastiche of everything that a splendid and glamorous dancer like Cassie/McKechnie may have been asked to do in a musical comedy."[21] The dances, in other words, look as if they might be no more than actual audition material or the kind of routine that a performer could probably have put together herself on the basis of previous work experience. They do not call attention to themselves as works of an artist outside the group of performers. The distinction between art and reality is deliberately narrowed and blurred.

The seeming artlessness is reinforced by the fact that the chorus-line dancers were not in the first instance singers and actors: most of the original cast members had never sung or spoken a line on stage before. Ironically, three of them—found objects, as it were—won Tony Awards for their acting, as if to verify that each one *is* special, and as if the critics were intent on further blurring the distinction between art and non-art.

The audience-stage relationship and the actor-role relationship are made intense. To what end? What is the interest of the "hot" musical? Why did Bennett "like making plays about how plays are made"?[22] After all, the world is full of things for theater to concern itself with other than itself—even Michael Bennett, who spent his own youth taking dance classes and dancing in a chorus line, knew this. I do not think that the interest of the backstage musical can be explained in terms of any message it may provide about the nature of reality ("all the world's a stage and life is a dream"), as Lionel Abel suggests for the interest of theater about theater, or "metatheatre."[23] Bennett's use of the term *hot* suggests that the form's fascination lies in the intensity or immediacy of the relationship between actor and audience. That's part of it. But what, then, is the function of the play? For presumably the relationship of performer and spectator would be even hotter if it were direct and unmediated. In an important sense, of course, so long as the performers are doing something for an audience, in this case an audience that has moreover left home, come to a theater, and paid to see them, they are framed as a work of art. As such, they are not unmediated. And Bennett never considered doing without the complex mediation that a play provides.

The primary interest of *A Chorus Line* arises from its layering or nesting of isomorphic elements. The word *isomorphism* applies when two complex structures can be mapped onto each other, such that each part of one structure has a corresponding part in the other, where "corresponding" means that the two parts play similar roles in their respective structures. *Hamlet*, with its play-within-a-play in which elements in the lower layer match those in the upper layer, exemplifies the layering of isomorphic elements. In *A Chorus Line* such layering can be seen in the performers who assume the role of performers; the audience that assumes the role of audience; the mirror set that reflects the actual theater; the theater that symbolizes the theater in the play; a dancer's remark, one hour and forty-five minutes into the play—without intermission—that the audition is getting long.[24] We jump back and forth between cognitive levels, and this jumping increases our sense of the work's juxtapositional structure. The actor as background oscillates with the character as foreground. The two layers come to seem—or actually are—interactive.

Movement and objects take on an interest in themselves, enhanced by and not subordinate to our interest in the story they tell and the images they stand for. The T-shirt with the *tkts* logo, the dance bag, and the mirrors stand out as real. Our attention shifts between the two levels on which they function, literal and symbolic. Indeed, one important use of documentary material in contemporary theater is in just this kind of layering, like newsprint in a collage. In a realistic play, by contrast, where a telephone, for instance, is indicated by a real telephone, no layering is achieved. Not only is the use of telephones on the stage a commonplace, but the apparatus does not even function as a real telephone; when it rings we know it is not really ringing and that no one from somewhere else is calling.

In *A Chorus Line* the relationship of layers is intensified by their affinities, particularly by their isomorphisms, which push the seeming or actual interplay between layers to the limit. Our attention oscillates between the actor as background and the character as foreground. We have no word for the kind of aesthetic experience provided by this layering of isomorphic elements: a kind of shimmering, density, or multitude, often suggestive of an infinite loop or akin to a religious experience, a mystery. Something of the same effect is provided by any play-within-a-play, where the inner play is isomorphic to the frame play; by imagery; and by disguisings or other mistaken identities that the audience is in on—all common theatrical devices. But the effect is greater when the isomorphism is between qualitatively different layers—between actor and role, for instance, as opposed to between two related roles, one within the framing play and the other within the play-within-a-play. Similarly, object-symbol isomorphisms are more powerful than those between two symbols. The backstage musical provides a context for this sameness-in-difference, a layering or nesting in which upper and lower or inner and outer in different realms are isomorphic. The exceptions to this layering effect in *A Chorus Line* are the use of lighting too elaborate for an audition, the use of an orchestra rather than merely a piano, the dancers' singing, and our presence at the audition—all of which work to counteract the interpenetration of realms and make the play steadfastly a play.

This analysis, incidentally, explains the principal interest of Jerzy Grotowski's theater as something more than he understood it to be. Grotowski favored "poor theater" because it put emphasis on the live actor, the one thing he thought theater could provide that film could not better provide. His "poverty" entailed the use of actors, props, and sets that were obviously those things, transformed only by their use. But the presence of both layers—object and symbol—provided a richness, a complexity more interesting than the mere meagerness of Grotowski's means. A single object usually had multiple symbolic uses, which were in turn related to one another via their common object. We jumped back and forth between the levels and symbolic meanings. And this jumping increased our sense that the work's structure, like that of so much new theater performance, was juxtapositional. Grotowski's environmental theater space worked to the same effect: it not only called attention to the presence of the audience but also made clear that the audience was cast in a role. The audience, like the actor, was at once both inside and outside the performance.

In *A Chorus Line*, the information-preserving transformations are not always exact, and sometimes the differences in the sameness-in-difference reverberate. Cassie, the only dancer in *A Chorus Line* who can be said to have an outstanding role, claims that she cannot act and that when she and Zach were living together he pushed her into principal roles merely to satisfy his own ambitions, in which he sought to carry her along. But the seeming isomorphism of actor and role causes us to ask whether Cassie perceives her acting ability appropriately.[25] Another example of the "strange loopiness"[26] of inner and outer, of the actor in the role, is that those not cast in the play-within-the-play are, of course, all cast in the play *A Chorus Line* and therefore appear in the finale, which is presumably part of the play-within-the-play.

The reverberations provided by the nestings of life and art in *A Chorus Line* are enhanced by several other kinds of nestings in the play. Concomitant with the oscillation of life and art as foreground and background are foreground and background switchings within the play itself. For instance, one of the characters begins to tell about himself with the rest of the chorus line as his audience. In the midst of his narration he becomes background, performing only in pantomime, as meanwhile the focus shifts to the chorus line as a group expressing their inner anxieties about what they will say when individually they are called on to describe themselves. The very story of *A Chorus Line*, with its focus on chorus-line dancers, not only gives a face to the faceless, thus suggesting the centrality of each person, but also serves to shift those who otherwise function as background to the foreground. As a backstage musical *A Chorus Line* also shifts background to foreground, providing a kind of nesting. The past, too, is nested in the present, as indeed it is in our lives; and internal and external, although they are differentiated at the beginning by light changes, are eventually freely juxtaposed as gradually we become used to public and private thought coexisting. Because the set is patently a set, it allows movement readily from external to internal and from present to past. It lets us be both in the theater and inside someone's head in a dance studio. This juxtaposition of internal and external and of past and present makes the structure of the work nonlinear, discontinuous.

Several times we are in the minds of one and many simultaneously. The song "At the Ballet" is internal to three people at once; at the same time, another group of dancers, presumably inside the heads of these three, demonstrates at the ballet barre the exercises they recall. We get a composite look at the dancers' development from ages four to eighteen. Because of this interpenetration of one and many, it was appropriate that for the 28 September 1983 performance celebrating *A Chorus Line* as the longest-running show on Broadway Bennett used 332 past and present performers. For their respective numbers there were, simultaneously, eleven Pauls, three Vals, and eight Cassies (the additional Cassies replacing the circle of mirrors in which Cassie sees herself reflected from various perspectives), as well as dancers variously speaking French, German, Swedish, Japanese, Italian, Arabic, and other languages who wondered what they would do when they could no longer dance. The idea that *A Chorus Line* is not framed in space was thus reinforced.

In itself, *A Chorus Line's* popular success would seem to suggest its conventionality. Yet examination of the work and the means of its creation makes clear that the work is based on a perception of reality radically different from that inherent in conventional theater. The materials out of which *A Chorus Line* is made—primarily performers, but also the theater itself, set and lights, and real time—are specifically called to our attention and attract us for themselves, not only for the images they serve. The use of and interest in advanced technology are overt.

Some of the autobiographical narratives are essentially non-art material; the characters are ordinary; the dramatic action of the play as a whole is minimal and has little magnitude. Any material, it is suggested, is appropriate to an artistic creation. Art and life, past and present, internal and external, this place and that, this time and that, foreground and background, object and symbol, one and many interpenetrate in a way consistent with the more limited interpenetration of actor and role. The audience is explicitly acknowledged and conceptually included in the work of art. Things have no hard edges.

There is an emphasis on process, not only in the work itself but also in its development. The subject matter of *A Chorus Line* is the process by which a musical is made; it was developed by a group; the performers are co-creators with the directors, designers, and composer. The work suggests to the audience the present-tense participation of the performers in it. One may also think of the performers as the principal material out of which the piece is made, in a process of interaction with them over a long period of time. Materials and creators are in a sense equal. The work itself conveys the idea of equality by being essentially nonjudgmental.

An emphasis on process means less definition of the rehearsal work in terms of a preconceived end. It invites greater risk-taking, more attention to personal responses than to those that are believable, to personal materials as opposed to the conventionally dramatic. Chance becomes a creative element in the work; there is less preselection, fewer presuppositions about what "belongs" in an artwork. The work is self-reflexive; it is about its own making. These facts reflect a certain integrity. The work calls attention to, by heightening, the interaction of the creator and that created, performer and that performed, perceiver and that perceived.

The work has less central focus in space and time than a conventional work. Each person, each story, tends to be the center. Just as there are no really central characters, neither are there subordinate characters: no person in the work exists to serve another. Multifocus is employed, giving the piece a structure that is less linear than in traditional drama, more discontinuous. Interest tends to be in the moments and not in the end they serve. Events are juxtaposed and simultaneous. There is a sense of potential extension outside the frame in time and space, possibly even to include 332 performers.

A Chorus Line's popularity does not, of course, suggest a widescale abandonment of Aristotelian aesthetic principles, or even an awareness that the work challenges those principles; nevertheless, the implications for theater of the popularity of performance based on a radically new aesthetic are enormous. The aesthetic pays.[27]

4 .... *Stanislavski's Nature; Stanislavski's Art*

In *A Chorus Line*, Morales, one of the auditioning "girls," sings about an acting class in which the teacher, Carp, asked her to experience various sensations. When she confessed to feeling "nothing," he allowed the class to humiliate her. So she went to a different acting class where she was well regarded. Six months later Carp died and Morales cried because she felt "nothing." The song, which is a send-up of Stanislavski's sense-memory and emotion-memory exercises, assumes the audience's passing familiarity with Stanislavski's ideas, if not their originator.[1]

Constantin Stanislavski (1863–1938) is credited with having "exerted a greater influence on modern practice and thought about acting than any other individual in Western theatre."[2] In this country Stanislavski's ideas have also influenced at least a generation of playwrights and directors. By 1936, when Stanislavski's first and most influential book, *An Actor Prepares*, appeared in English, his work as understood and taught by various devotees had already had a significant impact. By 1945 "the Method," as Stanislavski's system of acting was known in the United States, was triumphant, and remained so into the mid-sixties, by which time *An Actor Prepares* was in its twentieth printing. In 1958 Robert Lewis, a co-founder of the Actor's Studio, could confidently refer to *An Actor Prepares* and its 1949 sequel, *Building a Character*, as "the Bible."[3]

The increased emphasis in contemporary theater on performance elements, like the contemporary analytic shift from dramatic text to performance, suggests that the ideas about nature inherent in performance practices may be as important as those in the works. As we shall see, such examination shows that Stanislavski's acting techniques depend on a world view comparable to that in the traditional theater—for which they were in fact designed—but that these techniques and new theater are essentially antithetical.

The confidence with which the Method was taught, and in some cases still is taught, follows from Stanislavski's own confidence, which in turn followed from the relationship Stanislavski himself proclaimed between his system and nature: "There is no Stanislavski System. There is only the authentic incontestable one—the system of nature itself." As Stanislavski saw it, he was a discoverer of the natural laws of the actor's creativity: "What I write does not refer to one epoch and its people, but to the organic nature of artists of all nationalities and of all epochs."[4] These pronouncements reflect not so much vainglory as the assuredness and enthusiasm that turn-of-the-century scientists felt as they rapidly discovered what they believed were the laws of nature's single unified system. Stanislavski wrote that "in the expectation of these new triumphs of science" there was nothing for him to do except devote his labors and energy "almost exclusively to the study of Creative Nature."[5] Even as recently as 1973, Sonia Moore, president of the American Center for Stanislavski Art, reiterated Stanislavski's scientific claims for his work: "Since the rules developed by Stanislavski are based on objective natural laws, they can never be outdated. It is also obvious that the System is not a Russian phenomenon. The laws of nature are universal—the same for all people, in all countries, and in all times. Therefore, the rules developed by Stanislavski are obligatory for all actors."[6]

Stanislavski's "science" of acting is based on a perception of nature very like Aristotle's, which indeed largely accounts for its success, since his system therefore necessarily shares principles with traditional Western drama. Yet despite the many similarities between Stanislavski's and Aristotle's views, there is no indication that Stanislavski recognized these similarities or even that he had read Aristotle. Rather, he seems to have deduced his system from the plays on which he worked, which in turn, of course, relied on Aristotelian precepts. In Stanislavski's writing, the idea that human behavior can be understood in terms of action toward an end always has something of the excitement of an original discovery.[7]

Stanislavski's theatrical career, first as an actor and then as a director and teacher of acting, was a long one. At the age of fourteen he began making notes observing and criticizing his own acting technique. At forty-three he began to formulate his system of acting, which he continued to change and refine throughout the remaining thirty-two years of his life. The most original part of the system was the "psycho-technique," by means of which Stanislavski thought the actor could gain access to the unconscious—that is, to what he regarded as creative nature itself. Whereas his system was continually evolving, his ideas about nature, the very thing that the system was designed to replicate and release, were unvarying. It is these ideas and his theories about the relationship to nature of art, artist, and audience that I examine here, in order to suggest why the system no longer has, and can no longer have, the authority it once did.[8]

Stanislavski was first of all a man of the theater. His writing, as he himself seems to have sensed, lacks intellectual rigor.[9] He had a great deal of trouble committing his ideas to paper: he subjected his writing to endless revision and was never able to arrive at a form that pleased him. The final two books in his trilogy on acting were left in draft form, and the first, *An Actor Prepares*, which Stanislavski did see through the press, he continued to revise even after he had delivered the manuscript to the Russian publishers in 1937. Consequently, the Russian edition (which appeared two years after the American) contains a supplement, written by Stanislavski while the book was in press, showing how he would have modified the text to give his total scheme more coherence.[10] In any case, the fact that Stanislavski never succeeded in making his system fully systematic does not mean that we cannot or should not examine his view of nature and the corresponding theory of art on which his still very influential techniques are based.

Nature

Stanislavski's lifelong appeal was to the natural. Nature was for him the creator and measure of art. The aim of his art was to present nature truthfully by natural means. The idea that "nothing in life is more beautiful than nature" is one that Stanislavski often repeated, and the part of nature on which Stanislavski thought theater should focus its attention is "the life of the human spirit." "Our aim," he wrote, "is to create the life of the human spirit . . . 'in a beautiful, artistic form.' "[11] Stanislavski did not say whether other arts should represent other aspects of nature or whether they too should concentrate on the life of the human spirit. When writing about art, life, and nature, Stanislavski had theater art, human life, and human nature in mind. But because he assumed that the principles underlying all art, nature, and life are the same, he rarely delimited his remarks. He seemed to take for granted that nature constitutes a single, unified system and that art is its faithful representative. Human life is central to life, and human nature central to nature.

Nature, including human nature, has laws—eternally fixed principles of operation—and can be understood in terms of actions that are logical, consecutive, gradual, and, in some sense, purposeful. The view is similar to Aristotle's that "a thing is due to nature, if it arrives, by a continuous process of change, starting from some principle in itself, at some end."[12] Nature's principles of operation are also universal. To be sure, there is that in nature which is "conditional and fortuitous," but these elements are not characteristic of nature.[13] To understand nature, one must look at what is characteristic: the norm represents nature in its essence. Stanislavski assumed, as did Aristotle, that although nature is separate from the observer, there are correspondences between human faculties and nature, and between the purposes and values of humans and of nature, that render nature intelligible. In part for this reason, in Stanislavski's view, there is a correspondence between truth and what we already believe.

A human being is a single discrete coherent entity to be understood in terms of an action toward an end. For Aristotle, "the 'nature' or *physis* of living bodies to act in specific ways is their *psyche*, their 'life' their tendency to act and function in a determinate manner."[14] Stanislavski expressed the same idea: "The superobjective and through action are the inborn vital purpose and aspiration rooted in our being, in our mysterious 'I.' "[15] Stanislavski's "superobjective" is the same as Aristotle's "final cause." By "through action" he meant a logical consecutive action; like Aristotle, he meant not physical activity but a movement of the spirit. I do not know that Stanislavski would have wished to define human identity in terms of one overriding lifelong action toward a fixed goal, as the above quotation suggests, but he did regard human identity as a relatively fixed and recognizable constant, capable of being defined in terms of some limited number of subsuming desires and choices.

The centrality of action in Stanislavski's definition of the life of the human spirit helps to explain his insistence that the actor must attend to the character's actions rather than emotions. The character's emotions neither define the life of the character nor give the actor anything to do, whereas the character is always doing, because always wanting. Stanislavski's emphasis on action results also, I believe, in his coming in later years to downplay emotion-memory (the actor's recollection of an experience in his or her own life that evokes emotions like those of the character) because the actor's memory is irrelevant to the character's action.

Like Aristotle, Stanislavski understood the action that defines the life of the human spirit to be single and linear, "*one whole unbroken line that flows from the past, through the present, into the future.*"[16] The present, moreover, is defined strictly in terms of the past and future: "The present flows naturally out of the past. . . . Neither is there a present without a *prospect of the future*. . . . The present deprived of past and future is like a middle without beginning or end, one chapter of a book, accidentally torn out and read. The past and dreams about the future make up the present."[17] The action, then, can be conceived of as a series of sequential images. Human nature, defined in terms of action, is clearcut, coherent, logical, and sustained, developing gradually over time. Although "it sometimes happens that in the logic of human feelings one will find something illogical," that is not characteristic.[18] Too, in Stanislavski's view there are certain parallels between the life of the individual, the history of human culture, and evolution. He seems to have regarded all these "histories" as developmental and the development in them all as gradual, unilinear, and finite. He apparently did not seriously consider the possibility that theater art could be radically different from what he knew. For Stanislavski as for Aristotle, it had essentially reached its final form.[19]

Stanislavski saw human action as a movement against obstacles. "One runs inevitably into the counter-movements and strivings of other people, or into conflicting events, or into obstacles caused by the elements or other hindrances. Life is an unremitting *struggle*, one overcomes or one is defeated."[20] He defined the self in opposition to the world, relating the idea of individuality (and consequently psychology as a whole) to this separateness of the self from the rest of the world and from other persons. The context in which the self operates he called the "given circumstances." In Stanislavski's view, the human environment and human identity do not interact, and certainly they are not interpenetrating; instead the self is a largely autonomous constant, identifiably the same entity from beginning to end.

In Stanislavski's nature, as in Aristotle's, there is a hierarchy from parts to wholes. Thus actions can be analyzed in terms of their discrete parts, each smaller action with its lesser objective being subsumed by the larger action and superobjective. There is also a hierarchy from particular and temporary to universal and enduring aspects of nature. Accordingly, the actor must see

> the organic as well as the accidental traits in human passions, and . . . split them up into those which are less important, that is to say, those that apply only to the character he is representing at the moment, and those permanent ones that are inherent in the very nature of the feelings; [he must] discover the true nature of each quality, the organic nature of each passion, and not by any means only the accidental shade given to one or another feeling and the action arising from it, [and represent] what exists everywhere and at all times and in all passions and is common to every human heart and mind.[21]

Like everything else of nature's essence, the important human traits and passions are universal and timeless. There is a fundamental and unchangeable nature to things and persons, a general human nature, eternal and universal.

Although Stanislavski analyzed human behavior in terms of individual wants, he did not assume that objectives are always conscious. "Often, in life and also on the stage, the through line [of action] will manifest itself unconsciously. It will become defined only after the fact, and its ultimate goal, the superobjective, will have been secretly, unconsciously, exercising a pull, drawing to itself our human aspirations."[22] Stanislavski understood the unconscious in terms of its objectives; he was not concerned with the unconscious as a source of these objectives.[23] In many regards his views are comparable to those brought together by Eduard von Hartmann in the then well-known *Philosophy of the Unconscious* (1868).[24] For von Hartmann the unconscious is the fundamental active principle in the universe, the creative force on which the meaning of all creation depends. In this view teleology is fundamental, and instinct is action that embodies a purpose, though without knowledge of that purpose. This mysterious and hidden power guides to a definite end and goal all the phenomena both of the external world and of the mind. In the unconscious mind lies the contact of the individual with the universal powers of nature.[25] "Nature," writes Stanislavski, "is clear, intelligible and intelligent."[26] Here Stanislavski probably meant nature manifest as the human unconscious, but he did not bother to specify, I think because he also had a more general view of nature in mind. "Nature cannot be outwitted," he wrote, this time clearly referring to nature at large;[27] and: "How can we teach unobservant people to notice what nature and life are trying to show them?"[28] Nature and life, he wrote, are trying to show us that they are beautiful. I gather, then, that nature is also purposeful—as it is for Aristotle. Whether nature is also ethical Stanislavski did not say, though he did remark that "without love of man there is no way of being successful in art."[29] It would seem that all human beings, at least in essence, are lovable.

The life of the human spirit—the movement of the soul, action toward a specific objective—has its correlate, in Stanislavski's view, in external—bodily—movement. Although bodily and spiritual movement are separate, they are integrally related and exhibit the same characteristics. "Both physical and psychological objectives must be bound together by a certain inner tie, by consecutiveness, gradualness, and logic of feeling."[30] Because of the close bond between the physical and psychological, one can infer intention from external movement. Stanislavski insisted that the actor must work in a three-dimensional setting rather than in front of a two-dimensional painted set, not so much for the sake of the audience, but because such a setting helps the actor "to give a plastic outward form to [an] inner mood."[31]

While Stanislavski observed the Cartesian dualism of mind and matter, soul and body, his belief in the unconscious and in the intimate relationship between the psychical and physical works ultimately against this distinction. (Descartes thought that all that was not conscious in man was material and physiological, and therefore not mental.) Stanislavski's perception that subject and object are essentially static rather than interacting is closely related to this dualism, and is hardly altered by his reference to evolution, since he viewed evolution as finite.

Artistic Form

"The theatre is . . . the art of reflecting life," human life, understood in terms of forces: it is "created by human forces and reflects human forces through itself."[32] It consists of the deliberate imaginative re-creation of human life, a re-creation wholly separate from actual life. Stanislavski regarded the stage as a special and separate place where the life of the human spirit is to be created. But that is not enough: theater art must transform *"simple everyday human realties into crystals of artistic truth."*[33]

The play is the basis of theater. Stanislavski analogized the play to a living organism: to be like life, it too should be structured as a discrete consecutive linear action. "Art itself originates in the moment when that unbroken line is established, be it that of sound, voice, drawing or movement. As long as there exist only separate sounds, ejaculations, notes, exclamations instead of music, or separate lines, dots instead of a design, or separate spasmodic jerks instead of coordinated movement—there can be no question of music, singing, design or painting, dancing, architecture, sculpture nor, finally, of dramatic art."[34] Action is the basis of dramatic art. That being the case, time—conceived of as linear—is of the essence, as it is in life. Like human action, the action of the play is structured as a set of conflicts and, further, as a system of subordination, parts to a whole, smaller actions to one large encompassing one.

Like human action, the play should be understood in terms of its purpose. Just as the superobjective, or purpose of the play, must serve the intention of the playwright, which is always to express an idea, so must the art of the stage serve this "ruling idea." (In this analysis, what is earlier in time must be served by, or cause, that which follows.) Exactitude in representation cannot be an end in itself but must further the purpose of the play. "Now in Hauptman's play *Hannele*, naturalism has its place," remarked Stanislavski. "It is used for the purpose of throwing the fundamental spiritual theme of the play into high relief. As a means to an end, we can accept that. Otherwise there is no need of dragging things out of real life onto the stage."[35]

The playwright's intention must serve nature, true, but only by expressing its eternal and universal and therefore beautiful aspect.

.... Only that which remains in the play as the grain of eternally pure human feelings and thoughts, only that which does not depend on the mounting of the play and is understood by everybody in every age and in every language, only that which unites the Turk and the Russian, the Persian and the Frenchman, only that which can never under any circumstances lose its sense of beauty . . . it is that, and only that, which a theatre must look for in a play. . . . [The theater] seeks, as it were, to be a magic lantern which reflects life—vibrant and happy.[36]

Stanislavski, like his contemporaries, distinguished naturalism from *realism*: naturalism shows particular details; realism shows essential characteristics.[37] For him then, realism is a more significant art form than naturalism because, as for Aristotle, creation meant the uncovering of a true relation already existent in the scheme of things. In that sense art is better than life, for art shows life in its essence. The great classics express truth eternal and universal and are therefore eternally and universally beautiful themselves. The happy life is not a search for truth but a contemplation of truth already attained.

The character serves the play. Here, as in nature, a hierarchical relationship of parts to a whole obtains. The character must be understood as a real human being who, in a gradually developing linear action, struggles against obstacles toward a conscious or unconscious objective. That struggle consists of little actions toward small objectives subsumed by an overriding action and by the play's superobjective. The character possesses a past, a future, and a life that continues throughout the time periods not written into scenes. The assumption is that the structure of the play is linear and that one can reconstruct a linear real-time arrangement from it. To create a real human being the actor must supply what the playwright does not, by way of life history, physical characteristics, relationships, habits, and so forth. So strongly did Stanislavski believe in the actual life of the character to be "re-created" that he wrote:

•••••••••••• The main factor in any form of creativeness is the life of a human spirit, that of the actor and his part, their *joint* feelings and subconscious creation.... The playwright gives us only a few minutes out of the whole life of his characters. He omits much of what happens off the stage. He often says nothing at all about what has happened to his characters while they have been in the wings, and what makes them act as they do when they return to the stage. We have to fill out what he leaves unsaid. Otherwise we would have only scraps and bits to offer out of the life of the persons we portray. (emphasis added)[38]

The motto "There are no small parts, only small actors" rests on the assumption that even a one-line character has a fully reconstructible life, the sense of which must be provided for the audience.[39] "Every play, every role, has concealed in it a superobjective and a line of through action which constitute the essential life of the individual roles and of the whole work."[40]

While the character is to be conceived of as really living (with all that that entails in the way of an action, objective, and so on), the presentation of that character should be in beautiful artistic form. "*Truth* [must be] *transformed into a poetical equivalent*":[41] the actor must select that in the role which is representative of all human life, must provide "a clear-cut and truthful embodiment of life as a whole" in terms of "a whole world of poetic images and ideas which will live forever."[42] Truth, because it is in its essence eternal and universal, can be measured by our belief in it.[43] In insisting that the embodiment be precise, Stanislavski meant not only that the parts should be clearly articulated but also that their function in relation to the whole should be made clear.

Everything in the portrayal should be heightened and made as vivid as possible while yet giving the appearance of lifelikeness. "Creative objectives must call up not simple interest but passionate excitement, desires, aspirations, and action."[44] Even "a bent or outstretched arm or leg must be bent or outstretched to the utmost limit. . . . Everything on the stage—posture, movement, word—must be distinct and explicit. . . must be expressed in full tones and not in semi-tones."[45]

Stanislavski called the utmost heightening and clarity of effect consonant with faithfulness to appearances "heroic tension." "Just as the outward form of the body conveys a certain meaning to an audience only if the full extent of the plastic significance is realised, so does the inward meaning of a character get across to an audience. . . only if your life on the stage bears no resemblance, however true or subtle, to ordinary life, but if your thought and feeling have. . . risen to an act of heroic tension."[46] As for Aristotle, dramatic art, while seeming to resemble nature outwardly, mirrors the world not in appearance but in essence, revealing its underlying form and purpose. The theater "must reflect everything in life in its inner heroic tension, in the seemingly simple forms of the ordinary day, but in reality in precise and luminous images in which all feelings are alive and in which all passions have been ennobled."[47]

Stanislavski wanted art to include as subject matter a broader spectrum of humanity than did Aristotle, but all of it was to be ennobled. "People, and consequently also the stage as a reflection of life, are engaged in the pursuit of the most ordinary occupations and not in the performance of deeds that could be performed only by heroes"; in its heroic tension, though, the art of the stage must "rise above the beaten track of everyday life."[48] Thus, Stanislavski wrote not about the magnitude of the play—he was not primarily concerned with playwriting—but about the nobility of the character.

Although the representation of a character should give the impression of fidelity to natural appearances, this impression must be provided as economically as possible lest focus be drawn from the action and its intensity. Whereas Aristotle believed that nature "always succeeds in attaining maximum achievement by minimum effort," Stanislavski allowed that there is some illogic and lack of direction in nature. In art, however, because it represents nature in its essence, everything must be necessary, consecutive, and logical. "*So in the score of a role there should not be a single superfluous feeling, only what is needed for the purpose of a through line of action*."[49]

At the same time, there must be no empty time, no absence of meaningfulness on the stage. If the character "happens just to be sitting without uttering a word, his pose on the stage is brought to the utmost point of relaxation, clarity and plastic significance."[50] Even just sitting must clearly signify intention: the characterization must be sustained unbroken.

The character's action must develop gradually; there must be a regular trajectory of the passions. "If your suspicion has aroused jealousy in you, you will not of course betray it at once by proclaiming it aloud with all the intensity of your being; you will unfold the whole range of your emotion gradually, beginning with pianissimo and ending with the most ferocious storm of your heart—fortissimo."[51] The role should build in intensity.

Although the actor's art is by nature transitory, it must reveal passions, images, and ideas that will live forever. The actor must act as if his creation were for eternity[52]—more like an object than a process. At the same time, the actor must provide the illusion of presenting behavior for the first time. The creation must seem spontaneous.

The work must never seem forced. That which is believable—truth already known—comes into its own easily. Indeed, forced emotion does not arise from the actor's experience and feeling as the character, whose own feelings of course do not have to be forced. Further, forced emotion calls attention to the actor, the person making the effort, whereas neither the effort nor the actor is to be considered a part of the work.

Finally, at the same time that the work is replete with heroic tension, it must be delicate, charming, and restrained—like a classical dancer's leap. It should give a sense of completeness and look finished. Stanislavski's idea of beauty was, in a word, classical.

Actor and Role

Stanislavski wrote about the art of the actor, which he believed to be the preeminent art of the stage. The job of the actor, he believed, and the actor's greatest excitement, is that of "speaking the thoughts of another man on the stage, of putting [him]self entirely at the service of someone else's passions, and of reproducing [his] actions as if they were [his] own."[53] The actor should undergo a kind of renunciation of "self"; his entire attention is to be focused on the conditions for the character as supplied by the author.[54] One measure of truthfulness in playing is the extent to which an actor on stage can accommodate a chance happening, a mishap—a missed cue, a fallen prop—in character. The actor must be no more evident in his presentation than the scientist in nature.

Stanislavski insisted that for the actor to represent actions as his own he must experience them as his own, for "without experiencing a role there can be no art in it."[55] On this matter Stanislavski rejoined the long and heated debate that followed the publication in 1830 of Denis Diderot's famous treatise on acting, *Paradoxe sur le comédien* (actually written in 1773). Diderot maintained that great actors do not give themselves up to emotion but, rather, carefully imitate the exterior signs of feeling so perfectly that the audience is deceived. Stanislavski, however, argued that, to the contrary, the actor must actually live the part every moment, that only by relying on his own feelings and experiences in the creation of the character can an actor find truth. Departure from this personal involvement and sense of the truthfulness of one's undertaking, he said, leads only to artificial acting.

In order to experience what the character is feeling, the actor must believe fully and sincerely in the reality of what he, as the character, does and feels. He must think of himself in the role in the first person. It is because passions are universal that an actor can portray them; they lie hidden in his own heart.

By experiencing the role, Stanislavski's actor brings the playwright's character to life. In that sense the actor is creative. But to create the character, to support the assumption that the character is real and, further, to clarify the logic and meaning of that life, the actor's work must be creative in another sense: it must make an original contribution to the artwork. Aristotle assumed that the interest of a play arises principally from the plot and that whatever is can be expressed in words and discourse. Stanislavski, in contrast, did not assume the text to be self-sufficient. There is also the subtext, the inwardly felt expression of a human being, which flows uninterruptedly beneath the words of the text, giving them life and a basis for existing. Character, he insisted, exists beyond what the playwright has provided by way of words: as the tip is to the iceberg, so words are to the character. And it is for the revelation of this inner continuity and meaning, this living spirit, that the audience comes to the theater.[56]

The fact that this subtext is provided by the actor where he chooses to go beyond what the author supplies has two important repercussions. For one thing, emphasis is unavoidably shifted from the denotative value of words to their connotative values and to the visual aspects of performance. For another, the idea that the artistic interest lies beneath the text urges the actor to seek the character's unconscious intentions, as opposed merely to revealing those motivations that the character explicitly voices.[57] Inevitably, the importance of the subtext and of the unconscious puts emphasis on the character, thereby increasing the importance of the actor. The full effect of the play, then, can be obtained only from performance. As Timothy Wiles observes, Stanislavski apparently never considered the possibility of taking at face value Chekhov's repeated admonition, "Listen, I wrote it down, it is all there."[58] Instead he seems to have assumed that Chekhov's pauses are meant to be filled, and where no fill can be directly inferred from the text, it is to be invented by the actor. The actor, then, is not wholly subordinate to the text. In providing a subtext, the actor does not strictly renounce himself; he adds himself as a creator along with the playwright. In one passage, Stanislavski even wrote that because what is needed is a superobjective in harmony with the intentions of the playwright that at the same time arouses the souls of the actors, that superobjective must be sought "*not only in the play but in the actors themselves.*"[59]

It would appear that by insisting that actors are creative artists who use themselves as material, Stanislavski departed radically from Aristotle, for whom the only difference between nature and the human artist is that nature makes something out of its own materials, whereas the human artist makes something out of something else, some materials outside himself.[60] In point of fact, however, actors cannot make something from materials wholly outside themselves. And Stanislavski insisted not only that actors are creative artists who (at least in the one radical statement quoted above) should use themselves as material, but that they must also live the lives of the characters. Creator and created, it would seem, interact. But having thus raised the issue of the interrelationship of subject and object in performance, Stanislavski quickly circumvented it.

From the point of view of the audience, he said, the character should be regarded as an art object in which the actor is not evident as such. Moreover, he retained the traditional subject-object distinction by explaining that the actor is experientially divided into two persons, one the character, the other the actor-observer who never loses his self-possession—in the strongest sense, never becomes deluded that he is really the character. Kostya, the student-narrator of Stanislavski's acting texts, explains:

> While I was playing the part of the Critic I still did not lose the sense of being myself. The reason, I concluded, was that while I was acting I felt exceptionally pleased as I followed my own transformation. Actually I was my own observer at the same time that another part of me was being a fault-finding, critical creature.
>
> Yet can I really say that that creature is not a part of me? I derived him from my own nature. I divided myself, as it were, into two personalities. One continued as an actor, the other was an observer.[61]

Stanislavski thought in terms of an analogy that strengthens the idea of the actor as divided in two: "*Our type of creativeness is the conception and birth of a new being—the person in the part. It is a natural act similar to the birth of a human being.*"[62] Thus, by "naturally" dividing the actor in two, Stanislavski salvages the subject-object opposition.

His conception of the "person in the part" as a new being distinct from that portion of the actor which remains as observer is reinforced by his idea of the role of the unconscious in creativity. The unconscious, he said, is a separate realm, "that realm where nine tenths of any genuine creative process takes place."[63] The notion of the discrete unconscious rests comfortably alongside the faculty psychology to which Stanislavski adhered: not only are individuals divided into internal and external, soul and body, but the soul is further divided into mind or intellect, will, and feeling. Such divisions he thought to be comparable to those existing everywhere else in nature. The realm of the unconscious is not under the control of our conscious selves; it is creative nature itself as housed inside the human body, more closely related to will and feeling than to mind. "What is beyond our powers is done in our stead by nature itself."[64] In highest praise, Stanislavski sometimes referred to creative nature, the unconscious, as "the superconscious," the universal purpose in nature. "Nature is the great artist," "the only creator in the world that has the capacity to bring forth life."[65] In this view, then, Aristotle's distinction between nature and the human artist remains in force: with respect to acting, nature is the creator making something out of itself.

In 1906, Théodule Armand Ribot, who is the only psychologist Stanislavski refers to in his work, wrote, "it seems to be accepted that genius, or at least richness, in invention depends on the subliminal imagination, not on the other, which is superficial in nature and soon exhausted. The one is spontaneous, true; the other, artificial, feigned."[66] This view, that the unconscious was true because natural, was, of course, also Stanislavski's.

By and large Stanislavski seems to have thought of the unconscious as logical and consistent, clear and intelligent. "Technique follows logically, admiringly on the heels of nature," he wrote at one point; "everything is [therefore] clear, intelligible, and intelligent."[67] It seems, then, that, in the words of the psychologist William Wundt (1832–1920), "this unconscious mind is for us like an unknown being who creates and produces for us, and finally throws the ripe fruits in our lap."[68] But at one point at least, Stanislavski seems to have had the idea that the fruits of the unconscious might need some sorting and selecting: "Unconscious objectives are engendered by the emotion and will of the actors themselves. They come into being intuitively; they are then weighed and determined consciously. Thus the emotions, will, and mind of the actor all participate in creativeness."[69]

In any case, Stanislavski's unconscious is certainly not the unconscious of the surrealists. Nonetheless, in one remarkably modern-sounding late passage Stanislavski discusses the role of surprise—the unexpected and illogical in acting—in a way that is seemingly as inconsistent with his view of nature as is Aristotle's own valuation of surprise in tragedy. This impulsive passage is outstanding enough to warrant quoting at length:

•••••••••••• There is still one lack in such [what one might otherwise regard as great] acting. I do not find in it that quality of the unexpected which startles, overwhelms, stuns me. . . . The actor himself is overwhelmed and enthralled by it. He is carried away to a point beyond his own consciousness. It can happen that such an inner tidal wave will pull an actor away from the main course of his part. That is regrettable, but nevertheless an outburst is an outburst and it stirs the deepest waters. . . . Such acting is stunning in the very audacity with which it brushes aside all ordinary canons of beauty. It is powerful, yet not because of the logic and coherence we admired in the first type of acting [which provides "wonderfully beautiful, esthetic, harmonious, delicate impressions of forms completely sustained and perfectly finished"]. It is magnificent in its bold illogicality, rhythmic in its unrhythmicness, full of psychologic understanding in its very rejection of ordinarily accepted psychology. It breaks through all the usual rules and that is what is good and powerful about it. It cannot be repeated.[70]

Even though the unconscious is beyond our direct control, Stanislavski wondered "how the actor may create the conditions that are favorable to true scenic inspiration, and in the same manner call it forth at the moments necessary for his art." "Are there no technical means," he asked, "for the creation of the creative mood, so that inspiration may appear oftener than is its wont?"[71]—a question that led Stanislavski to "search for some method of inner technique, ways leading from the conscious to the subconscious."[72]

While my focus in this essay is not on the requisite conditions for creativity as Stanislavski saw them, I discuss some of them here because they derive directly from his ideas about nature, art, and their relationship. Stanislavski was concerned about the difficulty of the actor's having to do his creative work before an audience, a difficulty necessitated, he believed, by the fact that in order to provide real emotion and the impression of spontaneity, the character has in some sense to be created in the course of each performance. In part, of course, this situation is salutary, for the audience provides a kind of energized space in which the actor can work. An atmosphere "heavily impregnated with the nervous excitement of the crowd, serves as the most effective channel of the actor's creativeness."[73] Nonetheless, the circumstance of having to create the life of the character in public is "abnormal."[74] A playwright is not called on to create in front of her audience; nor is the character that the actor is to play commonly, at the time, acting in a theater. "All we ask is that an actor on the stage live in accordance with natural laws.... [The] 'system' should restore the natural laws, which have been dislocated by the circumstances of an actor's having to work in public, it should return him to the creative state of a normal human being."[75] The actor must have the feeling of being, as it were, in public solitude.

In Stanislavski's view, only that solitude allows the actor to create out of the essential state of repose.

•••••••••••• The conventional [Romantic] conception of "creative agitation" must be abandoned. No such organic action exists. What does exist is *creative repose*, that is to say, a state of mind in which all personal perceptions of the passing moment have disappeared and in which life—the whole of life—is concentrated clearly, forcefully and definitely, on the circumstances given in [the] play and only on the given piece of the scene....

Both forces—heart and mind—acting in repose, can by the concentration of attention bring about so great a renunciation of the personal "I" that a state of complete harmony can be created in the mental make-up of a man.... The first thing an actor must do on entering the rehearsal room is to shed all the ties that bind him to his private life.[76]

There is for each performance the problem of how to create that which is living, not only in the sense of being lifelike, but also in the sense of having lasting value. Only when free of the pressures of personal life, Stanislavski said, can the actor create the life of the character. Repose—the removal of the self, particularly of the momentary and personal—thus allows the artist to express the eternal and universal; not only that, but it permits access to the clarity and vividness that Stanislavski believed events to have in memory. His idea of the importance of repose in creation is therefore related to his idea that the work must seem—indeed, be—effortless. Freedom from physical tension is akin to freedom from personal passions: both are related to the idea that action must be presented economically.

In later years, Stanislavski came to emphasize that correct physical actions could not only reveal the inner life of the character but also affect that life *in the actor*, an idea evidently encouraged by Pavlov's work on conditioned reflexes.[77] In other words, the actor's psyche could be persuaded to believe that it was experiencing the life of the character through the actor's realistic physical enactment. This idea, in Stanislavski's view, constituted a powerful argument for realism in art; the appearances are as much to get the actor as the audience involved in the psychic life of the character. "*The superconscious begins where reality, or rather, the ultranatural, ends....* The only approach to the superconscious...is through the real, the ultranatural."[78] In sum, this constituted an argument not only for realistic action but also for repose, relaxation, and control—the latter elements being ones that Stanislavski believed the actor's usual working conditions did not promote. He deplored what he saw as the disorder, fighting, and competition fostered, he thought, by the close and nervous atmosphere of the stage. He longed to promote peaceful and supportive conditions, conditions of "mutual responsibility" within which people might work on their roles—individually—under the authority of the director.[79]

He wanted conditions in which the characters could uninterruptedly exchange feelings, thoughts, and actions. He sought not group creation by actors but an ensemble of characters. Stanislavski's understanding of the relationship of actors to their roles is intimately related to his beliefs about the ideal relationship between actors. Each actor should relate directly only to his or her character, and through that character to other characters, and hence, indirectly, to other actors. When the actor is "infected" by a role, other actors will find the infection contagious.[80]

Audience and Performance

If the relationship between actor and role as Stanislavski saw it can be summed up as being "the same, only different," what then did he see as the ideal relationship between audience and actor or between audience and the performance as a whole?

In Stanislavski's view, the actor should accommodate the audience by moving where she can be seen and making her gestures large enough for viewers to perceive and clear enough in intent for them to understand. Her voice must be sufficiently loud for the audience to hear and her intonations clear and meaningful. Beyond that, though, the actor should conceive of herself as the character, someone who is not on that stage performing for that audience; she should not relate directly to the audience but only indirectly through the character. All told, the artwork is an object wholly separate in space and time from the audience.

At the same time, however, the performance should make the audience—which Stanislavski thought of as a single, undivided entity—feel that "the frontiers of space and time that separate the stage from the auditorium are abolished."[81] It should capture the audience's closest possible, unflagging attention, draw it in and make it believe in the play's reality. It should control the emotions of the audience by evoking feelings that Stanislavski assumed to be common to all human beings.

The audience's experience of the performance should be not only intense but also enriching and memorable. "Only our kind of art, soaked as it is in the living experience of human beings, can artistically reproduce the impalpable shadings and depths of life. Only such art can completely absorb the spectator and make him both understand and also inwardly experience the happenings on the stage, enriching his inner life, and leaving impressions that will not fade with time."[82] The happenings on stage should be made understandable because nature is ultimately comprehensible and meaningful. Presumably the performance should be made memorable because truth and beauty are eternal. While the actor is to work in true and precise detail, she must also select details that are typical so that the audience can complete in imagination that ongoing life and life history which the performance can only imply.[83]

The audience will be moved and involved to the extent that the performer is, Stanislavski said. Furthermore, it will be involved in the same way that the actor is, to "weep and suffer as well as rejoice and laugh" with the character.[84] The audience will be involuntarily drawn into the action by the intense involvement of the actor in her role and, he added, by the very beauty of the portrayal.[85]

At the same time that the audience is wholly involved in the artwork, of course, it is aware that the artwork is quite distinct from real life. This divided experience of being wholly involved but also distinctly separate is akin to that of the actor. Edward Bullough's still widely held idea, formulated in 1912, that aesthetic experience is a function of psychical distance is clearly consonant with the kind of art and art experience that Stanislavski describes.[86]

The purpose of the art experience, in Stanislavski's view, is to reaffirm the audience's knowledge of reality in its essence,[87] to awaken the audience's interest in beauty, and to ennoble the audience—that is, to show it that it too is a part of beauty. Society for Stanislavski, as for Aristotle, seems to be at one with nature. We have no evidence that Stanislavski's view of the function of theater and of the actor changed with the Revolution, some new turns of phrase notwithstanding;[88] to the contrary, the purpose of art is constant. And in this art "an actor is the priest of beauty and truth," superior to the spectator, standard-bearer even in everyday life of all that is fine, elevating, and noble.[89]

In Stanislavski's system the work of actors is of central importance in the theater and in life. In its insistence that acting is both a creative art and an art that can be taught, the system is a boon for actors and acting teachers. Despite its lack of rigor, it is still more systematic and thorough than any Western theory of acting before or since. It suited the hope of the times to make everything into a science, and it took up the excitement of the new science of psychology. Although the analysis it provides leans too heavily toward psychological realism to suit plays of previous centuries, it is, like realism itself, by and large consistent with the tenets of the Western dramatic tradition. Consequently, it provides a means for actors effectively to analyze and perform most existing Western plays.

Like the writing of Aristotle and Cage, that of Stanislavski is of a piece with the ideas he presents. His three texts on acting, *An Actor Prepares, Building a Character*, and (except for the first part) *Creating a Role*, all take a fictional form in which there is an acting teacher, Tortsov (whose name means "creative artist"), a student, Kostya (short for Stanislavski's own first name, Constantin), and other acting students. Kostya is ostensibly recording in detailed diary form his experiences in acting class with the master. The master never errs and never needs to hunt for a solution to the various acting problems the student actors have. Kostya obviously worships him: in no little excitement he reports that "Tortsov is coming himself to see them" and that he, Kostya, is in "a state of ecstasy over having thus been given a token of the director's [Tortsov's] approval."[90] "We did not dare to criticize him," he reports elsewhere.[91] Nevertheless, we are to understand that Kostya's account is objective.

This form enabled Stanislavski to present acting problems as lived experiences and to describe exercises in terms of actions. It further served to make the textbooks artworks in their own right. They have dialogue, a fixed cast of characters who act toward fixed objectives, a set—and the author is nowhere apparent.

The form provides a distance and authority consistent with Stanislavski's belief in his own rectitude. As Tortsov speaks, Stanislavski is, in fact, quoting himself.

Stanislavski's style seems less modest and (the Carps of the world notwithstanding) Tortsov's teaching more authoritarian than would be acceptable today.[92] Perhaps Stanislavski's enormous confidence in science and his belief that he had discovered a new science must excuse a great deal. Just as the natural scientist was nowhere found in what he observed, so Stanislavski is not present in his work. His student can extol his system because it is, after all, nature's.

Stanislavski refers repeatedly to his work as a system. It was his belief that his work constituted the discovery of a natural, and hence systematic, method for the teaching of acting. At the end of *Creating a Role*, Tortsov has his students put a chart on the wall showing the system and all its parts. But although both Robert Lewis and Jean Benedetti have tried to reconstruct the chart as described, Stanislavski himself did not provide it.[93] In fact, he never actually achieved the fully systematic system he sought. At one point Torstov remarks, "It will be necessary to interrupt the strictly systematic development of our program, and to explain to you, somewhat ahead of the usual order, an important step which we call 'Freeing our Muscles.' The natural point at which I should tell you about this is when we come to the external side of our training. But Kostya's situation [an injury] leads to our discussing this question now."[94] In other words, in order to make his presentation of the material lifelike, Stanislavski felt the need to depart from the natural, systematic order—a baffling state of affairs. The moment cuts through Stanislavski's system and his view of nature as surely as the object clutched too tightly in Kostya's hand cuts his artery.

In the next chapter I examine acting methods (and writing styles) which incorporate freely the idea that chance and discontinuity are as much a part of nature as Stanislavski's impulsive digression hints. They also incorporate as natural his endless process and lack of hierarchical system.

5 .... *Improvising Ensembles*

An important measure of the value of the Stanislavski system is the extent to which it is correlated with the view of nature represented in the plays it seeks to serve. New plays reflecting Cagean views of nature, like Pinter's and Beckett's, have necessitated new acting techniques consistent with such views.[1] But often the relationship of new theater to performance techniques has been even more intimate: many influential new theater works were developed in workshops along with or, indeed, by means of the new acting techniques and often to serve them, thus challenging Stanislavski's idea of the hierarchical relationship between actor and play. The relationship between new theater works, including radical re-presentations of traditional plays, and contemporary acting techniques is best seen as one of interprenetration: the works exist in their performance. Not surprisingly, a view of nature consistent with that implicit in such works is also entailed in the acting techniques. Hence, an important measure of these techniques might be not only the extent to which they serve contemporary plays but also the extent to which they make performance, even of older plays, consistent with contemporary views of nature.

In 1964, the *Tulane Drama Review* (*TDR*; later, *The Drama Review*) published two issues on Stanislavski in America. In his editorial comments introducing the first issue, Theodore Hoffman complained that "too many of our teachers and practitioners have had only a smattering of Stanislavski." The second issue ended with Richard Schechner's assertion that "a careful working through of the starts Stanislavski has given us" is needed, including a consistent method for teaching acting in universities based on the vocabulary and system of Stanislavski.[2] In retrospect, the editorial statements notwithstanding, it is apparent that the two issues marked the end of Stanislavski's hegemony as much as they celebrated it.

The first special issue began with a report that the newly formed theater at Lincoln Center had received an anti–Obie Award from the *Village Voice*. The theater's leaders, Harold Clurman, Elia Kazan, and Robert Whitehead, distinguished members of the Group Theatre in the thirties and strong proponents of

Stanislavski's methods, were peddling something too old-fashioned for *Voice* critics. The latter half of the second special issue comprised pieces by Bertolt Brecht, Paul Sills, and Joseph Chaikin, whose own ideas about acting have played an influential role in the diminution of the Method's importance.[3] *TDR* itself, under the editorship of Richard Schechner, soon became the champion of all that was new in theater and the most influential theater journal in America.[4]

The most significant recent changes in acting methods, and in the very idea of what acting is, arose from the improvisational work begun in the 1960s. Viola Spolin's seminal *Improvisation for the Theater* was first published in 1963.[5] Joseph Chaikin began work with his improvisational group, the Open Theater, in 1964. Also in 1964, Charles Marowitz and Peter Brook invited the public to see the improvisational exercises they had developed with their new Royal Shakespeare Experimental Group, and the Living Theatre presented *Mysteries and Smaller Pieces*, a collection of nonrepresentational acting exercises developed through group improvisation. In 1966, the kind of improvisational work Jerzy Grotowski had been doing with his Polish Theatre Laboratory group since 1962 was first seen outside Poland, making a profound impression.

The improvisational workshops that flourished in the sixties and early seventies grew out of the same spirit that somewhat earlier had produced improvisational dance and action painting. Improvisational theater was also closely related to the human potential movement and, in Spolin's case, to progressive education: improvisation could, it was believed, free actors to explore their full potential and experience the world. The emphasis on group work arose as well in a period of anti-authoritarianism, in this country an anti-authoritarianism fueled by anger over the Vietnam War and the draft. There was admiration for those who chose to work communally outside the establishment for other than money, their idealism enhanced by the period's economic prosperity.

Although few of the improvisational ensembles have continued and far less concerted experimentation is done today with acting techniques, many of the principles on which that experimentation was based have been unobtrusively incorporated into contemporary performance works and practices. Eileen Blumenthal proposes that "the most central, lasting, and nourishing energy of the contemporary theater" is Joseph Chaikin's and that "if many of his approaches seem familiar now, it is precisely because they have become absorbed into the fabric of modern theater."[6] To Chaikin's energy I would add Viola Spolin's; her *Improvisation for the Theater*, which has been translated into Portuguese, Dutch, and German, has sold well over one hundred thousand copies in the English edition and continues to sell well. Chaikin studied with Viola Spolin among others, and many of his ideas are expressed more resolutely by her.

Of nature and its relationship to acting, the proponents of contemporary improvisation have had little to say explicitly except that nature is a discontinuous and not altogether orderly process of which we are a part. Everywhere implicit in the writings of those who led the improvisational work and in the exercises they devised, however, is a view of nature antithetical to Stanislavski's. The inconsistency in the fact that much contemporary teaching of acting consists of some amalgam of Stanislavski and contemporary improvisational techniques goes unmarked; nonetheless, and however inadvertently, the view of nature implicit in the work of contemporary acting teachers following the likes of Chaikin and Spolin has greatly affected contemporary theater in general and performance technique in particular.

In what follows I piece together the theoretical premises of those who have elaborated the techniques of contemporary improvisation, relying most heavily on the writings of Spolin and Chaikin but also including the ideas of other influential experimenters. I first describe the purpose of this improvisational work and then analyze it in terms of the characteristics that make it attractive to those who employ it: the idea of improvisation as a game; the importance of the ideas of presence and the now-moment, of process and transformation, and of interpenetration. Implicit in the categories under which I analyze these ideas are the assumptions that we exist in a field situation, that we are an interpenetrating part of nature, and that nature has no essence, meaning, or ultimate purpose—all Cagean assumptions.

Grotowski is certainly the best known of those who conducted acting workshops in the last quarter century. Although his work was important in shifting emphasis away from the text to both the performance and the actor as creator, its purpose was traditional. Grotowski's actor was the contemporary equivalent of the tragic hero: he expressed the special role of man in the mystery of life. The actor's radical self-expression was to reveal man's essence, his transcendent self. The actor/priest committed, in Grotowski's phrase, a "total act," one for which he mobilized his body and voice in order to exteriorize his deep inner being. Richard Schechner, then a proponent of Grotowski, explained that the actor was to "*show himself as he is in the extreme situation of the action he is playing*" so that the "essential human truth" could be revealed. "The act of spiritual nakedness," Schechner declared, "is all there is to performing."[7]

The revelation of "essential man" beyond the bounds of societal constraints constituted a kind of spiritual healing not only for the actor but also for the audience. The theater experience was to be searingly intense and memorable, the actors, in an image Grotowski borrowed from Artaud, "burnt alive. . . signalling to us from their stakes."[8] So compelling was this view of the actor's centrality to society that David Cole, responding to it, wrote a book analogizing the actor to a shaman, and E. T. Kirby wrote one arguing that the historical root of acting was, in fact, shamanism.[9] In effect, the actor in this view took on the writer's traditional role as described by Robbe-Grillet:

.... [it] consisted in excavating Nature, in burrowing deeper and deeper to reach some ever more intimate strata, in finally unearthing some fragment of a disconcerting secret. Having descended into the abyss of human passions, he would send to the seemingly tranquil world (the world on the surface) triumphant messages describing the mysteries he had actually touched with his own hands. And the sacred vertigo the reader suffered then, far from causing him anguish or nausea, reassured him as to his power of domination over the world. There were chasms, certainly, but thanks to such valiant speleologists, their depths could be sounded.[10]

The actor expressed or represented ultimate knowledge, which he was privileged to have by virtue of his intense experience. Truth was more inward than it had previously been understood to be, but the artist assured us that it was locatable, that he was central to it and could express it.

At one point Chaikin was influenced by Grotowski, and his writing is occasionally "speleological." But Spolin's and Chaikin's purpose is essentially different from that of those who sought what Christopher Innes has appropriately called "Holy Theater."[11] Both Chaikin and Spolin are motivated by the idea that theater can explore and expand experience, rather than present its supposed essence.[12] "We live," writes Chaikin, "in a constant state of astonishment, which we ward off by screening out so much of what bombards us."[13] The name of Chaikin's group, the Open Theater, implied that the actors were to be open to all their experiences. Further, they were not to portray anything inconsistent with actual experience, which in Chaikin's view actors in most commercial theater are required to do. "Open" implied honest. It also suggested a frame of mind quite different from Grotowski's dark and intense sensibility. "The joy in theater," Chaikin declares, "comes through discovery and the capacity to discover. . . . 'Reality' [he writes, recalling Frank Stella's dictum that what you see is what you see] is not a fixed state, . . . [it] means 'that which we can fathom' "; and he would have us widen our embrace.[14] Spolin's purpose, as she repeatedly asserts, is to help actors and audiences "make direct and fresh contact with the created environment and the objects and people within it. When this is learned inside the theater world, it simultaneously produces recognition, direct and fresh contact with the outside world as well. . . . We seek the experience of going beyond what we already know." Improvisation, she believes, can enable us "to receive the phenomenal world."[15]

Spolin, who defines improvisational acting as "openness to contact with the environment and each other and willingness to play," holds that anyone can act, that talent is nothing but the capacity for experiencing.[16] Indeed, many improvisational groups of the sixties and seventies consisted of people with no formal training in acting, it having been assumed, at least in part, that such training only supplanted the capacity for actual experience, substituting instead responses of a predetermined nature.

Improvisation as a Game

Spolin conceives of her improvisational acting projects as games and in fact devised them as acting exercises for children, not as material for performance or even as means for developing a performance. The idea of improvisations as games makes them very different from story-telling *commedia dell'arte* improvisations and from the skits improvised by Second City under the direction of Viola Spolin's son Paul Sills.[17] "The game," Spolin explains, "is a set of rules to keep the player playing."[18] Joseph Chaikin borrowed Spolin's exercises, devised others like them, and performed them. They made for unconventional performance material, providing no assumption that human life is central or that identity is constant, single, or discrete—hence the importance of the ensemble. For instance, in the "Machine" exercise, one actor starts by doing a sound or movement representing a moving machine part. Another actor may join in representing another part of the machine. Yet another may join in changing the nature of the machine.[19]

The analogy of life to theater games suggests that there is no right way of playing it. In *As You Like It*, Jaques's "All the world's a stage" speech employs the image of the theater to suggest the inevitability of the progression of life's stages. In *Waiting for Godot* the world-as-stage image is used quite differently: the characters are simply set out on a stage (the road of life) and left to their own devices. They speak about their role in some larger plot, but we see their lives as a compilation of moment-to-moment improvisations. As Tom Driver observes, Beckett makes clear that "as theater is for the passage of an evening, so life is for the passage of—life."[20] The idea of life as an improvisational game has become an important one in the theater.

Spolin's games tend to be quite physical, relying little on the verbal, she says, because they were designed for children. They begin with the body in motion, with the participants merely task-oriented. Spolin wants the performers to have no preconceptions about a right way to accomplish the tasks—by striving for heroic tension or gradualness, for instance. On the contrary, the tasks emphasize the immediacy of physical response, ideally obliterating the distinction between mind and body and thus facilitating the intuitive response: "When response to experience takes place at this intuitive level," Spolin says, "when a person functions beyond a constricted intellectual plane, he is truly open for learning."[21] Chaikin remarks that "because the theater involves behavior and language, it can't be completely separate from the situational world, as music can. But much passes between people in the theater which is intuitive and not at all concrete, having nothing to do with data."[22] Improvisation is, in Spolin's word, "communion," a response to one another's rhythms, movements, and sounds, a transmission of energy and a passing of bodily and vocal energy. Spolin's desire for actors' communion of rhythms, movements, and sounds is quite different from Stanislavski's desire for the characters' exchange of feelings, thoughts, and actions. In Spolin's view, actors should communicate directly, not through character. Energies, movements, and sounds are neither as sustained and coherent as feelings, thoughts, and actions nor as memorable, and the word *communion* does not imply the communication of concepts.

The analogy of actors to game-players suggests that those who make theater have no obligation to provide an intense, meaningful, memorable experience for the audience. Few of Spolin's exercises are based on conflict, the chief source of intensity in traditional drama, for such exercises, she believes, generate "emotionalism and verbal battles," not intuitive responses.[23] Her improvisational games focus instead on the immediacy of the actual materials: the game and the actors in present time and space. The "drama" in this sense becomes the operations performed on stage, operations that serve as opportunities for participants and observers to perceive. The performers' only obligation is to "share" their games with the audience.

When the idea of acting as game-playing is applied to a text, it suggests that the actors and director should play with the text as they might with a prop. A theater game, like one of Cage's "mesostics," is intended as a way of experiencing the material rather than of serving the author's intention and representing the text. "It's all a game anyway," Peter Brook said, justifying his and the actors' play with *A Midsummer Night's Dream* (1970).[24]

In Peter Sellars's production of *The Count of Monte Cristo* (1985), some servile figures in the corrupt judge's chambers made appearances from beneath the judge's desk by sticking their heads through a hole in it, entrances that played on the idea that the figures were lowly and evil was lurking all about. The desk (or judge's bench?) not only had traps in it but also spun around subject to the judge's manipulations. At one point a factotum's head appeared in the wall of the judge's chambers, suggesting perhaps that the walls had ears. In Robert Falls's production of *The Tempest* (1986), Ferdinand first appeared centered nude on a platform inside a large ring in the pose of da Vinci's Man. Ariel "flew" by means of a hydraulic lift with the manufacturer's name, "Genie," clearly visible. Such play with the text deemphasizes its linear structure and literal meaning in favor of the actors', director's, and designers' more freely associative responses to the moments. A punning relationship may obtain between the text and the performance. In the case of the Genie lift, I was told that the pun was purely accidental; the lift was borrowed and the name could not be effaced.[25] Chance, like free association, can perform an important role in the game.

The German director Heiner Müller explains the idea of the text as an object in the game: "A good text has to be like a thing, like a stone. Theater people in Germany always try to find something inside the text, but [Robert] Wilson just takes it, like a kid playing marbles."[26] The actor or director, like the critic in reader-response theory, takes the text for what he can get out of it at that time, not to reveal its "real" meaning. The play, then, exists overtly as a play; it is not so much represented as played with, like an object in a theater game.

C. H. Waddington makes an observation about contemporary painting that can be usefully applied to contemporary theater performance as well: "In the painting of the last twenty years...the presentational immediacy that has been insisted on is the immediacy of the actual material presence of the painting itself, its colored and textured pigments, while the causal efficacy has been in the more or less deeply buried symbolic and emotional reverberation of these same physical materials."[27] The materials out of which theater performance is made, including the performers and the text, are there, like stones; ratiocination is bypassed; they play or are played with to provide symbolic and emotional reverberations.

Presence and the Now-Moment

Charles McGaw's long-popular acting text, based on Stanislavskian principles, is called *Acting Is Believing*.[28] Spolin's sharply different idea is that as an actor you should "reflect what you see, not what you think you see."[29] This shift from pretend to actual is also evident in the titles of such books on acting as Charles Marowitz's *The Act of Being* and Joseph Chaikin's *The Presence of the Actor*.[30]

Chaikin's use of the word *presence* recalls Robbe-Grillet's insistence that objects and gestures must first of all establish themselves by their presence. Like Cage, who says he finds more interest in the horn player cleaning spit out of his horn than in what the horn player plays, Chaikin observes that when he goes uptown to see a Broadway play, he goes primarily to see the ushers, the box office, and the theater itself. The actuality of the theater event is more interesting for him than the fiction presented. Accordingly, Chaikin wants his actors to acknowledge the presence of the other actors, the theater, the set, the lights and lighting, the props, and the text. The audience is encouraged to acknowledge the actors' presence and the effort their work entails. Reality is not elsewhere in an idea but here and now, and it includes the means by which the work is presented or created. This is a matter of integrity. The work takes place in life, on the stage, not in a supposititious place. Holding this same view, Spolin asserts that "there is no such thing as a break on stage;"[31] if an actor laughs at what he is doing on stage, she explains, he should use the laugh as part of what he is doing.

Presence demystifies art and de-deifies artists. The revealed creator/observer is less omnipotent; by implication, anyone can perform. In *Nicholas Nickleby*, for example, the actors were intent on showing the public "that we're not magicians," that the act of creation is not special.[32] At the same time, though, presence calls attention to the wonders of the acting process. Peter Brook says of his production of *A Midsummer Night's Dream* that he "wanted everybody to understand that it was actors always playing and improvising" and the stunts he had them perform heightened the audience's awareness of their presence.[33]

The stunts in *A Midsummer Night's Dream* emphasized not only the actors' presence but their present-time activity as well. The actors playing the fairies tossed plates spinning on sticks among themselves; similarly, actors were instructed to speak the verse as if it were like juggled objects "thrown across the room" from one group to another.[34] This emphasis on present-time activity enhances the dramatic quality of the moment. "I want to be seized," exclaims Richard Foreman, "by the elusive, unexpected aliveness of the moment."[35] Benedetti claims that "the actor's truth is in the act of unfolding the present, in showing the inherent drama of our existence," and that theater celebrates "the unending flow of the present moment."[36] In this view, the dramatic interest is not in the plot's unraveling but in the moment-to-moment occurrences. In a production like *A Midsummer Night's Dream*, the present moments include the interactions between plot and present activity and between character and actor. The actors' plate-tossing is an inspired choice because the characters they play are magicians—who, in this case, can perform real, not make-believe, tricks.

The view that the interest of theater is not in the stories told—or at least not in them alone—but rather in the moments they facilitate has had a profound effect on theater history, allowing works not highly regarded as literature to be reclaimed for the (redefined) canon. (With this view, for instance, J. L. Styan has wholly reevaluated Restoration comedy, the meaning and plots of which he grants are negligible.)[37] If the moments are significant in themselves, the structure of the work cannot be hierarchical in time, developing to certain moments. Accordingly, the actor's and director's examination of the material tends to become spatial rather than linear, providing a series of extended moments. This interest in the extended moment explains the often-remarked-upon eclecticism of postmodernism: the present moment includes all associations extending in time and space without bounds, without any preconception of what things belong together or of one thing's being subordinate to another.

The emphasis on the moment suggests that human existence is potentially redefinable at any moment: it consists in the shifting currents of our most immediate consciousness. In improvisation, actors do not reveal characters or move through predetermined actions; rather, they make choices to get from moment to moment. The actors play the moments, providing momentary personal perspectives, not a final order to the world. There is no sense, as in Stanislavski, that what is remembered is truer.[38] Presence and the now-moment are intimately related because (we are to understand) presence is not a constant but something that changes and because we are to see the possibility for choice where otherwise we are unaware that our presence counts for anything in making our situation. We are to view the world as something that we make at each moment, as we make ourselves. From these interrelated concepts of presence and the now-moment follows Spolin's and Chaikin's interest in goallessness, no-mindedness (experience without valuation), or examination of the role that valuation plays in our experience, and complexity.

Chaikin objects that "we are trained and conditioned to be 'present' only in relation to the goal. When I go from my house to the grocer, I'm not present. Once I arrive at the grocer, I'm not present until I'm back at the house. Going from point A to B we are in a kind of nonlife, and from B to C the same. This is one of our earliest lessons . . . to be in relation to the goal. This teaches us to live in absent time."[39] Jack Poggi sums up the belief behind the effort to conceive of acting as goalless: "When we are most alive it is the present doing, not the distant goal, that occupies and absorbs our energies."[40]

Unlike most games, theater games are not designed to have winners; they are not defined in terms of their ends. And so they suggest that life ought not to be either.[41] They accord with Cage's idea that art should teach us to live in the present.

Spolin and Chaikin are interested in working without specific performance goals. The Open Theater was devoted merely to exploring acting as such until the critic Richard Gilman persuaded the group to perform, and then they performed their acting exercises. The process became the performance. Under the direction of Andre Gregory, the theater ensemble ironically called the Manhattan Project worked for two years on their version of *Alice in Wonderland* without knowing where it might lead; they set out "to just keep working until something resulted and then see what it was."[42] "The path and the detour, which is which?" asks Chaikin.[43] He is willing to tolerate a considerable amount of indirection, confusion, and chance.

Related to goallessness is the idea of no-mindedness, which for actors means giving up assumptions about the nature of reality and being in touch with their "continual astonishment and bewilderment. . . . We can't be informed," remarks Chaikin, "if we already know what the character of an experience is to be. [Presence] is a deep libidinal surrender."[44] Similarly, Spolin suggests that the actor "get rid of himself and be totally in response to another"; to this end she devised an exercise that she calls "Following the Follower."[45] And Meredith Monk explains that in preparation for performances she puts herself "in a state of receptivity to whatever will happen."[46]

Spolin objects that our intense need for approval prevents our being open to whatever will happen and thus keeps us from our actual experience: "Our simplest move out into the environment is interrupted by our need for favorable comment or interpretation by established authority. . . . In a culture where approval/disapproval has become the predominant regulator of effort and position, and often the substitute for love, our personal freedoms are dissipated.... Having thus to look to others to tell us where we are, who we are, and what is happening results in a serious (almost total) loss of experiencing."[47] For Spolin, the importance of the impulse, of the experience in the moment, is that it is without valuation.

Chaikin's work with the Open Theater was in large part an examination of the myths and values that shape our perceptions. Like Spolin, he is interested in expanding perception; but unlike her, he aims to do so by examining the assumptions that are so much part of our daily life we do not see them for what they are. He wishes to highlight the relationship between ideas and perceptions. Chaikin comments on his early life: "I wasn't aware until much later about the point system. It's something which moves you and controls you all the more when you're not aware of it. I was Jewish and poor and homosexual in Des Moines, Iowa, where I lost so many points that I was among the subtractions."[48] The actor, he insists, must not cling to the idea that some internal conditions are more human, more theatrical, or more appealing. There is no hierarchy of more universal and enduring aspects of nature over those less so. What we take to be given circumstances are often humanmade values and roles. Chaikin regards his theatrical examination of given circumstances—of, for example, our society's unspoken attitudes about death, guilt, and social misfits—as an expressly political act.

The Open Theater's *Mutation Show* was an examination of society's "aberrations," based on the assumption that the norm is not nature in its essence but, rather, that each human being is central. Increasingly this idea has had an effect on theater. Many plays are now being written that sympathetically examine the point of view of "abnormal" people: blacks, women, homosexuals with AIDS, a suicidal paraplegic, a lifelong criminal. Joseph Chaikin, now, after a stroke, aphasic himself, is playing the role of an aphasic. And older plays are being produced to provoke our questioning of the values imbedded in them. In 1984, for instance, Anne Bogard directed a production of *South Pacific* at New York University with student actors, ostensibly setting its performance in an institution for disturbed teen-agers. The young characters performed the play under doctors's supervision as a means of helping them to adjust to societal mores. By framing the play thus, Bogard called attention to the ideas of enforced heterosexuality and patriotism contained in it. Similarly, Lee Breuer cast *King Lear* (forthcoming) so that male characters are played by females and vice versa, to examine our assumptions about the "normal" relationship between gender and power and the consequent privileging of males.

Examining the premises on which we build our lives makes us aware of a complexity that, in Chaikin's view, the prevailing value system seeks to conceal.

Many of Chaikin's exercises with the Open Theater were designed to reveal the contradiction and confusion he thinks is present in much of human experience: "The actor must know the whole event in all its incongruities, seeing the chaos clearly. From that perspective we have a better view of the structures in which we live, these structures being arrangements we make to deal with chaos."[49] Spolin sees her games as opportunities for making the moment complex and then for acknowledging and coping with the complexity: "Players grow agile and alert, ready and eager for any unusual play as they respond to the many random happenings simultaneously."[50] The moment is necessarily complex when actor and role, and thus past and present, here and there, this one and that one, are both present and interpenetrating.

Process and Transformation

Few theater works are actually improvised in performance. Improvisation is used primarily as a means for constructing performance. Nonetheless, improvisation as a working technique affects the nature of the performance, for it shifts part of the interest from what is made to its making. A work developed by improvisation with materials or on a text is clearly as much made by its director and actors as it is presented; the act of creating or perceiving thus becomes central to what is created or perceived. As audience we regard the work as a process rather than a product, as a performance rather than a play.

Not only can new theater work be understood as a process, but its makers and perceivers may understand themselves as such as well. Benedetti insists that we should think of ourselves not as "being"—a fixed state—but as "becoming"—"a dynamic process of interaction between our organism and our environment through our actions and reactions."[51] Chaikin, too, wants us "to see ourselves, in the largest possible way, as part of the process of nature. . . . Everything we do changes us a little, even when we purport to be indifferent to what we've done. And what we witness, we also do."[52] The idea that we have a single clear fixed identity is regarded as a logical construct made when we transpose the data of experience into concepts extraneous to the data.

The name Open Theater, remarks Chaikin, was intended to remind the group of its commitment to process. Indeed, he conceived of the group itself as a process: "As a group, I'm never sure how long we will survive; endurance probably isn't the best criterion anyway."[53] He subsequently disbanded the group—as the Open Theater's work *Terminal* suggested, process includes death.

Central to the idea of process as Spolin and Chaikin conceive it is transformation. Death can come unexpectedly. Change in theater, as in nature, is neither necessarily gradual nor developmental. For Spolin, the heart of improvisation is transformation; and Chaikin's best-known acting exercises are what he calls "open transformations," in which anything can suddenly change: who, what, why, where, when, style, mood, the actor playing the role. For example, two actors play teen-age brothers arguing over who gets to sleep in the lower bunk of their new double-decker bed. There are claims and counterclaims, threats and entreaties. Abruptly, the actor playing the older brother starts acting like a wild animal, say a lion. He has effected a transformation, and his partner must do likewise, becoming perhaps a small animal trapped by the lion or, conversely, a hunter stalking the lion. His change in identity establishes a new set of circumstances, which he and his partner then elaborate improvisationally.[54] In such exercises, expositions and transitions have little place. The relationship between parts is not developmental but subliminal, metaphorical, tangential. The actor, it is assumed, can go from one emotion, one character, one style, to another in an instant. Objects, too, can transform. The suddenness with which the situation can change either by choice or by chance emphasizes the now-moment.

Surprise becomes a central interest in improvisational acting. The juxtapositional structure that results from transformations is nonhierarchical. "One of the main objects behind the work," remarks Marowitz about his exercises for the Royal Shakespeare Experimental Group, "was to create a discontinuous style of acting; that is, a style which corresponded to the broken and fragmentary way in which most people experience contemporary reality."[55] The acting style was intended to create the sense of a world subject to choice, change, and chance. If objects can transform, their solidity becomes doubtful; they, too, are in process. Character must likewise be understood as discontinuous. We are not tied by our past, by our future, or by definitions of our identity. "Through the working process," Chaikin says, "the actor recreates himself," thus testifying to the possibility of human change.[56]

The Royal Shakespeare Company brought their productions of *Cyrano de Bergerac* and *Much Ado About Nothing* to the United States in 1984 with the same actors playing the leads in both plays, sometimes performing both plays on the same day. As in traditional repertory theater, considerable interest arose from the actors' transformations. Epic stories like *Nicholas Nickleby* and *Candide* can also provide the opportunity to show off a few actors and set pieces in numerous roles and contexts and for this reason have been recently adapted for performance. And a number of literary works have been chosen for recent theatrical productions precisely because they both entail transformations and have transformation as their central subject matter—*The Bacchae, A Midsummer Night's Dream, The Tempest*, and *Alice in Wonderland* are all good examples. The Mabou Mines production about the discovery and uses of radiation, *Dead End Kids* (1980), examined our fascination with transformation, beginning with our effort to turn base metal into gold and ending with our success in turning atoms into bombs. Quite naturally, the play, like so much of contemporary theater, was also about our fascination with actor and object transformations.

Interpenetration

In the theater envisioned by Spolin and Chaikin, the actor is not only present but also openly interacting with the environment, with other actors, with the role, and often, with the audience. Spolin writes that improvisation means "acting upon [the] environment and allowing others to act upon present reality. . . . The actor is acted upon and is acting, thereby creating process and change within his stage life."[57] Interaction with particular actors and spaces necessarily results in work that is dependent on those particular actors and spaces.

Stanislavski's concept of "given circumstances" implies that we are distinct from our circumstances, which are in turn fixed. So, for that matter, does the concept of "the set." Improvisational theater, in contrast, assumes that space and bodies co-determine each other. In Spolin's terms, experiencing is "penetration into the environment, total organic involvement with it."[58]

Implicit in the game is the idea that human circumstances are to a considerable extent made by human beings. Spolin requires that her student actors make their own decisions and set up their own physical world around the problems given them. Exercises are devised to make the actors aware of their interaction with the actual space and to underscore that people are not separate from the world. In effect, Spolin's exercises are designed to change our long-standing Western perception of the environment as our adversary.

Spolin's idea that actors should set up their own physical circumstances and that they should increase their awareness of the actual space in which they are working is intimately related to some contemporary ideas about set design in the new theater. Leon Rubin, assistant director of the Royal Shakespeare Company's production of *Nicholas Nickleby*, believes that stage design should never come before rehearsal, that "it is so much more liberating to have a design that suits what has been discovered and explored in a rehearsal situation."[59] In *Nicholas Nickleby* the actors created part of the set design themselves out of found objects. For instance, they built a coach out of various boxes and chests; this "coach" was then used in performance, with the fact of its creation by the actors deliberately called to the audience's attention. Stage design, some directors and designers now feel, should be the result of an interaction between actors, materials, and space, something the actors help to create, not something in which they are merely situated.[60]

The idea of the interplay between actors and their environment, along with the ideas of presence, process, and transformation, is reinforced in many contemporary productions where actors visibly make the scene changes themselves and where these changes are an important part of the theatrical event. The use of the same set elements over and over in various contexts suggests that contexts can be transformed and that objects are defined by their use. In Chaikin's and Peter Brook's sets, as well as in the sets for Peter Sellars's *Count of Monte Cristo* and for *Nicholas Nickleby*, the set pieces represent nothing until the actors interact with them. This definition of the set pieces through interaction with them encourages the audience to pay attention, not only to the images made but also to the materials used, to the way the materials evoke images, and, finally, to the fact that the images are just that—images. The frequent use of anachronistic materials—of Mylar in *The Count of Monte Cristo*, for instance—calls attention to the fact that the play is crafted and that impressions arise from the actors' use of the materials.

The work of Spolin and Chaikin entails the actors' interaction with and interpenetration of both their actual environment and one another. In *Improvisation for the Theater*, Spolin writes that one of her games, to be played daily, "quiets the mind and frees players to enter a time, a space, a moment intertwined with one another";[61] it is a means of making a present-time interaction between actors. Chaikin also wishes for the actors to "work off" of one another, proceed from what is here and now rather than from conjecture about the characters' past or future. He objects that the Stanislavskian actor works off himself rather than off those around him.[62] For a *A Midsummer Night's Dream*, Peter Brook, like Spolin, devised many exercises to increase present-time actor interaction. For instance, he sought to have one actor play fear not by helping her to imagine more vividly the situation the text presented, but by making her interaction with the other actors actually frightening for her. According to David Selbourne's account of the matter, this fear of what the other actors were doing was "the goad which drives Hermia...to a 'genuinely' despairing impulse. 'Help me, Lysander,' as Brook had originally wanted, is audibly drawn from panic feeling rather than from girlish coyness; and now not out of fear of the director, but of the other actors."[63] Actors have surely always found some of their motivation in present-time situations and persons—but here techniques to find such motivations are given emphasis. Indeed, the relationship between present-time situations and persons on the one hand and the play on the other is a primary subject for examination in many contemporary performances.

Spolin's idea of the generally appropriate interaction between participants, including the group's leader, is appropriately described as following the follower. If one person dominates—even, or rather especially, if that person is the teacher—a true group relationship cannot exist.[64] Her assumption that nonhierarchical relationships must prevail if the participants are to have genuine firsthand experiences was shared by various improvising ensembles and explains, in concert with the political ethos of the time consistent with such a view, why such work was conducted by collectives. These groups were formed in the belief that perception is perspectival and that each person is central. While most collectives were, in fact, led by a single strong individual, in theory no one point of view informed the work of the group as a whole; creations were, rather, supposed to be truly collaborative. "It would be hard," says Chaikin "to overstress the importance of the group effort."[65] In *Nicholas Nickleby*—which told a story—the actors were inculcated with the idea that "they all had an obligation to continue the story, as narrators and observers"; the omnipresence of actor/observers on stage made clear to the audience that the work was a group process.[66] The group improvisations that preceded the writing of the dramatic text of *Nicholas Nickleby*, Leon Rubin reports, "proved how collective imaginations could achieve startling effects."[67] The groups devised more (and, in some cases, more interesting) solutions to problems of dramatizing the text than the director had thought of, solutions not constrained by any "directorial concept" and which enriched both the resulting text and its presentation.

In new theater the relationship between actor and role, like that between participants, is often regarded as one of interpenetration.[68] Just as the actor as participant-observer does not constitute a discrete whole, neither does the role. Says Chaikin: "Our memory is like an attic which stores all the people we've ever known and we become them. The study of character is the study of 'I' in relation to forces that join us. We are joined to each other by forces. . . . As frequently taught, characterization is an exploration of the limits of a person. The borders of the self, the outline, the silhouette, tend to be the actor's study. . . . It sustains the stereotyping of people, the stereotyping of ourselves."[69] Without the idea that the self has distinct boundaries, the study of character becomes a study of interactions, of which the character's or actor's identity is a function. It is not fixed. If character does not constitute a discrete whole, no aspect of the person being portrayed can be seen as subordinate to another. Moreover, individual character can be seen as central only if identity is understood as separate from both other people and the environment and fixed over time. The idea of interpenetration vitiates the central importance of character conflict in drama, of the opposition of fixed forces in opposition.

In Chaikin's view, the actor can play with or without disguises. The relationship of actor and role can be various and changing in the course of a performance; the boundaries between the two need not be fixed. The question of whether the role is a mask or a face, of whether the actor pretends to experience the role or actually does experience it, is dissolved in the view that actors and roles may have myriad interactions, not all consistent. A number of actors can simultaneously play one role, thus challenging the idea that an individual is an entity occupying bounded space. A familiar example of a group portrayal of one role is the Open Theater's many-tongued serpent, played by five actors simultaneously. That an actor may represent merely part of a person—an arm, for instance—further challenges the assumption of the inviolable integrity of the individual. At one point, the actors in *Nicholas Nickleby* collectively play inchoate fear, not a character or thing at all.

The interaction of actor and role means that no hierarchy obtains between playwright and actor. The actor who played Newman Noggs in *Nicholas Nickleby*, for example, successfully argued that his character needed to be written more fully into the script. Putting in the strongest possible terms the idea that *A Midsummer Night's Dream* was in process, a work made by the actors as well as by Shakespeare, Brook said: "I wanted a context in which the actor could continually come back remaking the play."[70]

Actor and environment, actor and other actors, actor and role are all interacting and interpenetrating in the theater envisioned by Chaikin and Spolin. So are audience and performance. Unlike Stanislavski, both Spolin and Chaikin consider work in front of the audience, for the audience, and with the audience to be a normal condition of performance, rather than an abnormal condition to be overcome. The ensemble includes the audience; the audience is part of the event, informed of the means of its making.

While Chaikin suggests that each actor should dedicate his or her performance to a particular actual or imagined person in the audience, he does not think of the audience as interacting with the work. Spolin, in contrast, is quite definite about the matter of audience participation:

> If there is agreement that all those involved in the theater would have personal freedom to experience, this must include the audience—each member of the audience must have a personal experience, not artificial stimulation, while viewing a play. If they are to be part of this group agreement, they cannot be thought of as a single mass to be pulled hither and yon by the nose, nor should they have to live someone else's life story (even for one hour) nor identify with the actors and play out tired, handed-down emotions through them. . . . When our theater training can enable the future playwrights, directors, and actors to think through the role of the audience as individuals and as part of the process called theater, each one with a right to a thoughtful and personal experience, is it not possible that a whole new form of theater presentation will emerge?[71]

This right of the audience to participate in its own way and, moreover, to become conscious of this participation (for the audience has always participated, and in its own way) is, along with the participation of the creator/presenters, one of the most important features of contemporary theater. Richard Foreman, an articulate spokesperson for contemporary theater, expresses the current morality of this "value-free" art: "Good (moral) art (and yes, I dare refer to those categories) in which—to make it be for himself—the spectator must use active, intentional perceptive modes, has as its end the exercising of those active perceptional modes which might then, someday, enter life itself. . . . and transform it."[72] Even Pinter, who declares that he has no values, not even of life, evidently values the possibility of the spectator's using active, intentional perceptual modes. Robbe-Grillet comments on the relationship of the reader to the new novel: "For, far from neglecting him, the author today proclaims his absolute need of the reader's cooperation, an active, conscious, *creative* assistance. What he asks of him is no longer to receive ready-made a world completed, full, closed upon itself, but on the contrary to participate in a creation, to invent in his turn the work—and the world—and thus to learn to invent his own life."[73] The creators of contemporary theater make the same request.

The desire for the creative assistance of the audience explains the overtly theatrical choices made in many works. David Selbourne comments on the wire springs used for trees in Brook's *Midsummer Night's Dream*: "To make of this *matériel* the snares of a dream-forest depends as much on us, as on the actors."[74] The widespread idealization of the audience's creative participation explains why Broadway works can now be fine-tuned in New York previews or workshop presentations rather than in out-of-town tryouts: it is assumed that the New York audience will willingly participate in a work in progress.

The recent interest in designing performance environments that encourage audience members to move about expresses a desire to have the audience witness events from different, changing, and unfamiliar points of view and thus actively, and with self-awareness, participate in the production. Performances arranged for stationary viewers all facing the same way now frequently have multiple foci. The relationship of the audience to the production may vary from work to work and may change rapidly in the course of a single work. Old conventions like the aside and the soliloquy take on renewed interest because they treat the audience as at one moment there and at the next moment not there. Robert Wilson, like Cage, even claims not to mind if the audience falls asleep.[75] The relationship of theatergoers to the work thus varies from person to person, from work to work, from moment to moment, and, ultimately free, the somnolent audience member may even ignore the work entirely.

Performance with a variable relationship to its audience, including, in the last analysis, the possibility of an audience sleeping, is a far cry from Stanislavski's actor as the priest of beauty and truth who bends his efforts to control the audience's attention. I have tried to show how that difference and others described in this chapter represent part of the conceptual revolution described and, to a degree, effected by Cage.

Not surprisingly, proponents of acting styles that accord with contemporary views of nature write in a manner consistent with their views. Much writing on contemporary acting is in the first person and explicitly makes use of autobiographical material, thus calling attention to the author as perceiver and creator. Chaikin explicitly relates his feelings about being Jewish, poor, and homosexual in Des Moines, Iowa, to his ideas about acting. Likewise, the account Leon Rubin provides of the development of the production of *Nicholas Nickleby* is, he says, "a very personal view of the work."[76] That he provides such an account at all, not to mention that he found a reputable publisher for it, presumes the readers' interest, not only in how the production was developed, but in his authorial process as well. David Selbourne, the chronicler of the rehearsals of *A Midsummer Night's Dream*, freely admits in his book that he was too weary or too depressed to attend some of the rehearsals; there is no suggestion, then, that what he provides is a definitive account of the rehearsal process. These men deliberately seek to make both their writing and what they write about a personal, perspectival process.

Chaikin's book has as its subtitle *Notes on the Open Theatre. . .*; Benedetti entitles an essay on acting "Notes to an Actor"—titles that are meant to imply a lack of authoritarian finality. The book containing Benedetti's essay is one of a three-volume series entitled *Actor Training*, published between 1972 and 1976. The books are oversized paperbacks of different sizes, produced by offset printing, and in various typefaces. Their form provides no sense of finality; like ensemble workshops, the books, with articles by various authors, were intended as a "free space" in which experiences could be shared.[77] Similarly, the books on the making of *Dionysus in 69* and of *Alice in Wonderland* are compilations of comments, occasionally contradictory, made by members of the ensembles that created and performed these works.[78] The pages of *Dionysus in 69* are not numbered, as if the book was not conceived as a permanent reference. Chaikin's and Benedetti's writings about acting are juxtapositional in form, consisting of other people's quotations interspersed with, rather than integrated into, their own gnomic writings. In this sense they, too, are communal works unbounded in space and time. Benedetti's *Seeming, Being, and Becoming* includes his squiggly nonrepresentational drawings: he seems to wish to capture not only the process of writing but also that thought which came to him in a form other than words. Like Cage's works, his book approaches performance.

Conclusion

In 1983 I was invited to speak about Cage's aesthetics at the Chicago Institute for Psychoanalysis. Afterward (and in that place, not surprisingly) I was asked about Cage's life, particularly about his relationship to his father. His ideas had angered the analysts; one declared that they were those of someone with a case of "arrested development," arrested at the stage of rebellious adolescence. Such an interpretation, from which no analyst there dissented, suggests that Cage's ideas are idiosyncratic, that they were generated merely in opposition to the "important" ideas, and that they will go away. Comparable views on the contemporary theater describe its interest as being in acts of transgression, hence anti-theater and anti-reality. I do not know why Cage in particular has the ideas he has, but I have tried to show that they are not peculiar to him and to explain why I do not think they will just go away and why theater consistent with his ideas is of considerably more interest and import than the term *anti-theater* suggests.

Christopher Lasch has argued that the "advanced" arts are a response not to individual psychic disturbances but to overwhelming general social problems: the escalating arms race, an increase in crime and terrorism, environmental deterioration, and the prospect of long-term economic decline.[1] Lasch sees the works of Merce Cunningham, Samuel Beckett, and Alain Robbe-Grillet, to name but a few of those he mentions, as survival mechanisms for our desperate situation. He quotes Robbe-Grillet as evidence for his view: " 'Not only do we no longer consider the world as our own, our private property, designed according to our needs and readily domesticated, but we no longer even believe in its "depth." ... The *surface* of things has ceased to be for us the mask of their heart, a sentiment that led to every kind of metaphysical transcendence.' " In Lasch's view, Robbe-Grillet's statement is evidence of the "flight from selfhood" characteristic of those faced with extreme situations, like that provided by the present-day sociopolitical and economic climate; the statement represents the diminishment of the self, of one's perspectives and feelings, a way merely to survive by turning away from the present horror.[2]

I do not belittle the seriousness of the arms race, environmental deterioration, or crime and terrorism, nor do I deny that art does and should respond to these concerns. I do suggest, however, that neither the existence of a discrete and constant self nor its link to a healthy society is self-evident. Robbe-Grillet's words can be understood as he would have them understood—not as a last-ditch effort to preserve the self, in whatever minimal condition that might be possible in the face of chaos and imminent annihilation, but as an expression of a contemporary understanding of the physical world and our relationship to it, a relationship not created by new politics or technology.

To deny the overweening importance of the self, as do Schrödinger, Cage, and Spolin, or to explore the self like any other interpenetrating aspect of reality, as do Heisenberg, the Wooster Group, and Chaikin, is to cease to take it for granted. The positive desire of artists to participate with their materials rather than use them to express themselves (or even profundities about themselves) can be understood as a way of embracing the world, not of withdrawing from it. Perceivers and makers are intertwined with what they see and make. Neither the self nor that seen is discrete, inviolable, and constant. Contemporary artists do not find this idea depressing. Its exploration has not led them to abandon interest in or feeling for the world. On the contrary, for them the exploration is exciting: it has become not only an aesthetic necessity but a moral and political one as well.

Notes

Introduction

1. Niels Bohr, *Atomic Theory and the Description of Nature* (Cambridge: Cambridge University Press, 1961), 119.

2. Albert Camus, *The Myth of Sisyphus*, translated by Justin O'Brien (New York: Vintage Books, 1959), 18.

3. Others have seen a relationship between the works of particular playwrights and contemporary science. Florence Falk ("Physics and the Theatre: Richard Foreman's *Particle Theory*," *Educational Theatre Journal* 29, no. 3 [1977]: 395–404) establishes such a relationship for the work of Richard Foreman; and John Lahr, in two articles ("Pinter the Spaceman," in *Up Against the Fourth Wall* [New York: Grove Press, 1970], 175–94; and "Pinter and Chekov: The Bond of Naturalism," in *Astonish Me* [New York: Viking Press, 1973], 67–82), has shown such a relationship for Harold Pinter's work. Edwin Schlossberg (*Einstein and Beckett* [New York: Links, 1973]), while he does not deal specifically with Samuel Beckett's plays, has whimsically constructed an imaginary conversation between Einstein and Beckett. Similarly, N. Katherine Hayles (*The Cosmic Web: Scientific Field Models and Literary Strategies in the Twentieth Century* [Ithaca, N.Y.: Cornell University Press, 1984]), Robert Nadeau (*Readings from the New Book on Nature* [Amherst: The University of Massachusetts Press, 1981]), and Wylie Sypher (*Loss of the Self in Modern Literature and Art* [New York: Vintage Books, 1962]), have shown relationships between contemporary literature and science, and C. H. Waddington (*Behind Appearance* [Cambridge, Mass.: MIT Press, 1970]) has shown such a relationship between contemporary painting and science.

4. See Marvin Carlson, *Theories of the Theatre* (Ithaca, N.Y.: Cornell University Press, 1984), 15.

5. For an elaboration of these views in relation to the *Poetics*, see my "Aristotle's *Poetics* and Aristotle's Nature," *Journal of Dramatic Theory and Criticism* 1, no. 2 (1987): 3–16.

6. Ronald Hayman, *Theatre and Anti-Theatre* (New York: Oxford University Press, 1979), 241, xi.

7. Robert Brustein, "The Classical Avant-Garde," *New Republic*, 18 November 1985, 30.

8. John Cage, *A Year from Monday* (Middletown, Conn.: Wesleyan University Press, 1969), 32.

9. Ibid., 31.

10. Charles Hamm, "John Cage," in *The New Grove Dictionary of American Music*, vol. 1, edited by H. Wiley Hitchcock and Stanley Sadie (London: Macmillan, 1986), 334.

11. Richard Kostelanetz, "Contemporary American Esthetics," in *Esthetics Contemporary*, edited by Richard Kostelanetz (Buffalo, N.Y.: Prometheus Books, 1978), 26–27.

12. Waddington, *Behind Appearance*, 1. In a symposium Waddington organized, entitled "Biology and the History of the Future," Cage was an invited principal participant. Thus Waddington, like Cage, not only recognized but directly sought to promote the reciprocity between contemporary art and science. The proceedings of this 1969 symposium, sponsored by the International Union of Biological Sciences, were published under the same title with Waddington as editor (Edinburgh: Edinburgh University Press, 1972).

13. The term *performance theater* is borrowed from Timothy Wiles, who defines it as works whose "meaning and being is in performance, not in literary encapsulation, the preservation of which has prompted the writing of so many poetics" (*The Theater Event* [Chicago: University of Chicago Press, 1980], 117).

14. Wiles (ibid., 18) observes that both Pinter and Beckett have incorporated their ideas about life-as-performance in new literary forms that have already become part of the canon of masterpieces. I would add, however, that the aesthetic of which I write tends to redefine the playwright's enterprise and that Beckett's stage directions render his works more akin to musical scores than to literary texts: directions for performance rather than art objects proper. Similarly, this aesthetic redefines theater of all periods. Verdel Kolve's innovative book on medieval theater, *The Play Called Corpus Christi* (Stanford: Stanford University Press, 1966), for instance, hinges on the use of the word *play* as both a verb and a noun.

15. See, for instance, Robert Benedetti's *The Actor at Work* (Englewood Cliffs, N.J.: Prentice-Hall, 1986), a mixture of exercises following from both Stanislavski and contemporary theory.

16. Bohr, *Atomic Theory*, 117. "Above all, my purpose has been to give expression to our enthusiasm for the prospects which have been opened up for the whole of science. In addition, it has been my desire to emphasize as strongly as possible how profoundly the new knowledge has shaken the foundations underlying the building up of concepts, on which not only the classical description of physics rest but also all our ordinary mode of thinking" (ibid., 101).

Chapter 1

1. I discuss Cage's theoretical writing after 1974 in "John Cage in a New Key," *Perspectives of New Music* 20, no. 1 (Fall–Winter 1981): 99–103. Even though the last essay in Cage's *Empty Words* (Middletown, Conn.: Wesleyan University Press, 1979), "The Future of Music," bears the same title as the first essay in his first book, *Silence* (Middletown, Conn.: Wesleyan University Press, 1961), the newer essay reveals a marked change in his thinking which puts it beyond the bounds of this book—for now the function of art is not simply to reveal nature but to change society. This shift is obscured by the fact that Cage's writings have gradually become more political and that heretofore nature, through art, has indirectly been the model for society. Moreover, although Cage does not discuss the role of technology in this essay, it has clearly become problematic for him; he fears its immediate potential for providing unlimited destruction rather than unlimited abundance. The rest of *Empty Words*, like *X* (Middletown, Conn.: Wesleyan University Press, 1983), serves as an example of his art rather than a discussion of his aesthetic. Thus, my references to Cage's aesthetic are to his ideas prior to the 1979 "Future of

Music," although I do use quotations from after that date where they exemplify ideas worked out earlier.

2. For instance, Michael Kirby (*The Art of Time* [New York: Dutton, 1969], 77) declares that Cage's work forms "the backbone of the new theatre," and both James Roose-Evans and Richard Schechner state that Cage is one of the two most important influences on contemporary theater, although they do not agree on who the other most important influence is. James Roose-Evans: America's theater "is perhaps the most avant-garde in the world, and its two most important influences would appear to be Antonin Artaud and John Cage" (*Experimental Theatre* [New York: Avon, 1973], 132); Richard Schechner: "It was from the direction of music and painting that theatre was revolutionized and no one has had more effect than Cage and Kaprow" (*Environmental Theatre* [New York: Hawthorne Books, 1973], 60–61). See also C. W. E. Bigsby, *A Critical Introduction to Twentieth-Century American Drama* (Cambridge: Cambridge University Press, 1985), vol. 3, passim, for acknowledgment of Cage's contribution.

3. Kirby, *The Art of Time*, 77–98.

4. Virgil Thomson, "Cage and the Collage of Noises," *New York Review of Books*, 23 April 1970, 14; and Donal Henahan, *New York Times*, 22 October 1976, C7.

5. John Cage, "Letter to Paul Henry Lang" in *John Cage*, edited by Richard Kostelanetz (New York: Praeger, 1970), 117–18.

6. Richard Kell, "The Great Repression," *British Journal of Aesthetics* 13 (Winter 1973): 44.

7. George Steiner, "The Retreat from the Word," *Kenyon Review* 23 (Spring 1961): 191. Steiner refers not to Cage specifically but to the general effort to see contemporary science expressed in art.

8. Percy Bridgman, *The Way Things Are* (Cambridge, Mass.: Harvard University Press, 1959), 8, 168. Bridgman was an operationalist. He held that a concept in physics is no more than the operations a physicist goes through. A play, by analogy, is what happens when a play is acted.

9. See for instance, Richard Foreman, "How to Write a Play," *Performing Arts Journal* 1, no. 2 (1976): 86; and Richard Foreman, *Plays and Manifestos*, edited by Kate Davy (New York: New York University Press, 1976), 138, for his use of the words *field* and *quanta*, and pp. 135 and 145 for his desire for us to "see small" and to become aware of perceptual acts.

10. Kate Davy, *Richard Foreman and the Ontological-Hysteric Theatre* (Ann Arbor: University of Michigan Research Press, 1981), 29.

11. John Herman Randall, Jr., *Aristotle* (New York: Columbia University Press, 1960), 7–8, 243. Only a small portion of Aristotle's work is concerned with what he called productive science, the art of making things like houses and plays. Aristotle was also interested in practical science, which is concerned with how people are to act in various circumstances, and with theoretical science, which includes mathematics, theology, and natural science. Indeed, the greatest part of Aristotle's life was devoted to the study of natural science, including areas we could now call meteorology, chemistry, physics, psychology, and biology. Fully a third of Aristotle's work was in biology.

12. See Aristotle, *Physics*, Book 3, and *Metaphysics*, Book Theta.

13. See Gerald F. Else, *Aristotle's Poetics: The Argument* (Cambridge, Mass.: Harvard University Press, 1967), 73.

14. Jacob Bronowski, *The Common Sense of Science* (New York: Vintage Books, 1960), 79.

15. John Cage, *A Year from Monday* (Middletown, Conn.: Wesleyan University Press, 1969), 91.

16. Henry Stapp, quoted in Fritjof Capra, *The Tao of Physics* (Boulder, Colo.: Shambala, 1975), 136.

17. Niels Bohr, quoted in Bruce Gregory, *Inventing Reality* (New York: Wiley, 1988), 95.

18. Bridgman, *The Way Things Are*, 3–4.

19. Cage, *Silence*, 53.

20. Bridgman, *The Way Things Are*, 45.

21. Percy Bridgman, *Reflections of a Physicist* (New York: Philosophical Library, 1950), 108.

22. For this idea see Percy Bridgman, "Science and Common Sense," *Great Essays by Nobel Prize Winners*, edited by Leo Hamalian and Edmond L. Volpe (New York: Noonday Press, 1960), 312–13.

23. Michael Kirby and Richard Schechner, "An Interview with John Cage," *Tulane Drama Review* 10, no. 2 (1965): 51, 55.

24. Cage, *A Year from Monday*, 159.

25. Cage, in Richard Kostelanetz, "Conversation with John Cage," in Kostelanetz, *John Cage*, 11.

26. Ibid.

27. Cage, *Silence*, 106, 134.

28. John Cage, *M* (Middletown, Conn.: Wesleyan University Press, 1974), 3.

29. Cage, *A Year from Monday*, 32.

30. Bronowski, *The Common Sense of Science*, 103. Thus, of the grand unified theories, Howard Georgi says, "unification is clearly fundamental, but it may not be physics if you can't see any of the effects" (quoted in Robert Crease and Charles Mann, *The Second Creation: Makers of the Revolution in 20th-Century Physics* [New York: Macmillan, 1986], 417).

31. Cage, *A Year from Monday*, 100.

32. Cage, "Letter to Paul Henry Lang," in Kostelanetz, *John Cage*, 117.

33. Cage, *A Year from Monday*, 97.

34. Cage, *Silence*, 95; Kirby and Schechner, "An Interview with John Cage," 70. Aristotle did not consider landscape and animals, lacking souls, as objects of aesthetic imitation; see Samuel H. Butcher, *Aristotle's Theory of Poetry and Fine Art* (New York: Dover, 1951), 124.

35. From Bruce Glaser, "Questions to Stella and Judd," *Art News* (September 1966), quoted by John Lahr, *Up Against the Fourth Wall* (New York: Grove Press, 1968), 191.

36. Cage, *Silence*, 95.

37. Cage in conversation with Richard Kostelanetz, *John Cage*, 191.

38. Cage, *Silence*, 32.

39. Cage, *M*, xiii.

40. Cage, quoted by Richard Teitelbaum, " 'Live' Electronic Music," in Kostelanetz, *John Cage*, 141 (ellipsis in original).

41. Cage, in Richard Kostelanetz, "Conversation with John Cage," in Kostelanetz, *John Cage*, 13.

42. Jerzy Grotowski, *Towards a Poor Theatre* (New York: Simon & Schuster, 1968); and Kristin Linklater, *Freeing the Natural Voice* (New York: Drama Book Specialists, 1976).

43. Cage is much influenced by his study of Zen. Physicist Fritjof Capra, in *The Tao of Physics*, explores the parallels between modern physics and Eastern mysticism. Cage has long been aware of these parallels.

44. Cage, "Memoir," in Kostelanetz, *John Cage*, 77.

45. Cage, *Silence*, 23.

46. Ibid., 195.

47. Ibid., 8.

48. Ibid., 195.

49. Cage, "Letter to Paul Henry Lang," in Kostelanetz, *John Cage*, 118.

50. Cage, *A Year from Monday*, 8.

51. Pascual Jordan, *Science and the Course of History*, translated by Ralph Mannheim (New Haven, Conn.: Yale University Press, 1955), x.

52. Jill Johnston, "There Is No Silence Now," in Kostelanetz, *John Cage*, 147.

53. Cage, *Silence*, 129. (Dashes Cage included in the text for rhythmic purposes have been omitted.)

54. Ibid., 17.

55. Cage, *M*, 213.

56. Cage, *Empty Words*, 181.

57. Ibid., 180.

58. David Ross, *Aristotle* (London: Methuen, 1974), 237.

59. Cage, *Silence*, 110, 128, 125, 132.

60. Cage, *A Year from Monday*, ix.

61. Ibid., 4.

62. Cage, *Silence*, 173.

63. "The adoption of . . . principles of musical composition by the other arts is probably the single most dominant characteristic of all modernism" (Walter Sokel, quoted in Nahma Sandrow, *Surrealism: Theater, Arts, Ideas* [New York: Harper & Row, 1972], 52).

64. Cage, *Silence*, 40.

65. Cage, *Empty Words*, 51, 65.

66. Cage, *A Year from Monday*, 7.

67. Cage, *M*, 102, 114.

68. Cage, in Richard Kostelanetz, "Conversation with John Cage," in Kostelanetz, *John Cage*, 11.

69. Foreman, *Plays and Manifestos*, 70.

70. Cage, *M*, 3.

71. Heiner Müller, quoted in Elinor Fuchs and James Leverett, "Back to the Wall: Heiner Müller in Berlin," *Village Voice*, 18 December 1984, 64.

72. Ernst Mayr, quoted in Robert Francoeur, *Evolving World, Converging Man* (New York: Holt, Rinehart & Winston, 1970), x.

73. Percy Bridgman, *The Logic of Modern Physics* (New York: Macmillan, 1932), 3.

74. Cage, *Silence*, 65.

75. Kirby and Schechner, "Interview with John Cage," 53.

76. Cage, *Silence*, 128, 64.

77. Cage, in Richard Kostelanetz, "Conversation with John Cage," in Kostelanetz, *John Cage*, 24.

78. Cage, *M*, 69.

79. Cage, *Silence*, 134, 135 (dash present in the original for rhythmic purposes has been omitted). Later, Cage became greatly concerned about the possibility of mass annihilation through nuclear war, an eventuality he considers unacceptable.

80. Cage, *Silence*, 93.

81. Bridgman, *The Way Things Are*, 45.

82. Ibid., 198.

83. Eric Salzman, "Review of Variations IV," in Kostelanetz, *John Cage*, 151 (ellipsis in original).

84. Cage, in Richard Kostelanetz, "Conversation with John Cage," in Kostelanetz, *John Cage*, 18.

85. Jeff Goldberg, "Robert Wilson and 'Einstein on the Beach,' " *New York Arts Journal* 1, no. 1 (1977): 21.

86. While psychiatrists traditionally viewed the patient as a self-contained case and focused their attention on the patient's history, some psychiatrists have come to regard personality as a process and consequently focus their attention on family interactions and patient behavior as a present-time interaction with the therapist who is no longer thought of as invisible or as irrelevant to the behavior. In short, the account of behavior has become more spatial and is expressed in terms of interactions. Such changes, which are consistent with changes in our perceptions of reality generally, of course, affect the examination and understanding of character in drama.

87. Percy Bridgman, *The Nature of Physical Theory* (Princeton: Princeton University Press, 1936), 29.

88. H. Minkowski, "Space and Time" (1908), in *Problems of Space and Time*, edited by John Jamieson Carswell Smart (New York: Macmillan, 1964), 297.

89. Cage, quoting the German mystic Meister Eckhart (ca. 1260–1327), in "More Satie," in Kostelanetz, *John Cage*, 93.

90. Foreman, *Plays and Manifestos*, 186–87; and Foreman, "How to Write a Play," *Performing Arts Journal* 1, no. 2 (1976): 92.

91. Gertrude Stein, "Plays," in *Writings and Lectures, 1909–1945*, edited by Patricia Meyerowitz (Baltimore: Penguin Books, 1971), 81.

92. Cage, *Silence*, 40, 157.

93. According to Wylie Sypher, *The Loss of the Self in Modern Literature and Art* (New York: Vintage Books, 1962), 79–80.

94. Cage, *Silence*, 71; Cage, *A Year from Monday*, 28.

95. Cage, *Empty Words*, 180.

96. Cage, *Silence*, 83.

97. Cage, *A Year from Monday*, 26.

98. Floyd Matson, *The Broken Image* (New York: George Braziller, 1964), 309. This book relates developments in the natural sciences to those in the social sciences.

99. Bridgman, *Reflections of a Physicist*, 93.

100. Cage, in Richard Kostelanetz, "Conversation with John Cage," in Kostelanetz, *John Cage*, 13.

101. Capra, *The Tao of Physics*, 221.

102. Cage, quoted in Richard Barnes, "Our Distinguished Dropout," in Kostelanetz, *John Cage*, 50.

103. Cage, *A Year from Monday*, 98.

104. Werner Heisenberg, *Physics and Philosophy* (New York: Harper & Row, 1958), 96.

105. Cage, *Silence*, 46–47.

106. Cage, *A Year from Monday*, 17.

107. David Bohm, *Causality and Chance in Modern Physics* (London: Routledge & Kegan Paul, 1957), 3.

108. Cage, *A Year from Monday*, 7–8.

109. Ibid., 28, 4.

110. Cage, quoted in Michael Zwerin, "A Lethal Measurement," in Kostelanetz, *John Cage*, 164.

111. Cage, *Silence*, 134 (dash present in the original for rhythmic purposes has been omitted).

112. At the same time that the arts became more spatial, a spatial mode of analysis came into vogue: "Structuralism as it investigates the elements of a structure, the relations among them, and the process of transformation which occurs within the structure, is not primarily concerned with diachronic formation, the order of precedence among the elements. Instead, its concern is with the synchronic, with, as [Michael] Lane puts it, 'relations across a moment in time, rather than through time.' It is not that time is ignored; it is just that it is not emphasized in the 'structuralist vision' in the way that it is in non-structural methodologies. Now, a corollary of the synchronic way of seeing is an absence of interest in causality. Structuralism, because its view is synchronic, does not seek a cause as an explanation of why and how two structures can be said to be of the same class, yet different from one another. Rather, it is interested in ' "laws of transformation" ': 'the law-like regularities that can be observed, or derived from observation, by which one particular structural configuration changes into another.' The question of causality does not arise here" (Isaiah Smithson, "Structuralism as a Method of Literary Criticism," *College English* 37, no. 2 [1975]: 147; quoting Michael Lane, "Introduction" to *Introduction to Structuralism*, edited by Michael Lane [New York: Basic Books, 1970], 16–17).

113. John Cage, symposium proceedings, *Biology and the History of the Future*, edited by C. H. Waddington (Edinburgh: Edinburgh University Press, 1972), 58.

114. Cage, *M*, 153.

115. Cage, quoted in Richard Kostelanetz, "Environmental Abundance," in Kostelanetz, *John Cage*, 175.

116. Cage, *M*, 70.

117. Werner Heisenberg, quoted in David Park, *The How and the Why* (Princeton: Princeton University Press, 1988), 326.

118. Bridgman, *The Way Things Are*, 172, 64.

119. Cage, *Silence*, 39.

120. Ibid., 15.

121. Lincoln Barnett, *The Universe and Dr. Einstein* (New York: W. Sloane Associates, 1957), 34–35.

122. Bridgman, *The Nature of Physical Theory*, 29–30.

123. Cage, *M*, 199. Later Cage would, I think, distinguish the destruction resulting from human action from other natural events; his present ecological concerns make his philosophy less neat.

124. Alvin Toffler, *Future Shock* (New York: Random House, 1970).

125. Cage, *Silence*, 155.

126. Kirby and Schechner, "Interview with John Cage," 60.

127. Christian Wolff, quoted in Cage, *Silence*, 54.

128. Stein, "Plays," 66.

129. Cage, *Silence*, 118.

130. Cage, "Memoir" in Kostelanetz, *John Cage*, 77.

131. Cage, in Richard Kostelanetz, "Conversation with John Cage," in Kostelanetz, *John Cage*, 23, 25.

132. Cage, *Silence*, 130.

133. Cage, *M*, xv.

134. Cage, *A Year from Monday*, 42.

135. Kirby and Schechner, "Interview with John Cage," 55. In this same interview, Cage says that theater is a special occasion involving any number of people, but never just one. Most often, however, it seems that Cage thinks of the theater experience as one that need not entail a special occasion and that need not be shared.

136. Cage, *Silence*, 10, 97.

137. Cage, symposium proceedings in Waddington, *Biology and History of the Future*, 46.

138. Cage, *A Year from Monday*, 54, 157.

139. Ibid., 46.

140. Cage, *Silence*, 97.

141. Ibid., 70.

142. Cage, *A Year from Monday*, 31.

143. Cage, *Silence*, 36.

144. Richard Schechner, ed., *Dionysus in 69* (New York: Farrar, Straus & Giroux, 1970).

145. Bridgman, *Reflections of a Physicist*, 83.

146. Cage, *Silence*, 11.

147. Kirby and Schechner, "Interview with John Cage," 55.

148. Cage, *A Year from Monday*, 6.

149. Cage, *M*, 213.

150. Cage, "Letter to Paul Henry Lang," in Kostelanetz, *John Cage*, 118.

151. Cage, in Richard Kostelanetz, "Conversation with John Cage," in Kostelanetz, *John Cage*, 28.

152. Cage, *A Year from Monday*, 130.

153. Bridgman, *The Way Things Are*, 9.

154. Cage, *M*, 110.

155. David Bohm, quoted in Capra, *The Tao of Physics*, 138. In a comparable vein, Margaret Donaldson ("Language: Learning Word Meanings," in *The Oxford Companion to the Mind*, edited by Richard Gregory [Oxford: Oxford University Press, 1988], 421–23) argues that children learn sentences rather than words first, and in the context of occurrence. Similarly, W. V. Quine asserts that "meaning accrues primarily to whole sentences and only derivatively to separate words" ("Symbols," in ibid., 764).

156. Cage, *Silence*, 9.

157. Jacob Bronowski, *Nature and Knowledge* (Eugene: Oregon State System of Higher Education, 1969), 37.

158. Cage, *Silence*, 194.

159. Aristotle, *Poetics*, chap. 1, 1447a, line 12.

160. Gerald F. Else, *Aristotle's Poetics: The Argument* (Cambridge, Mass.: Harvard University Press, 1967), vii.

161. Cage, *Silence*, ix.

162. Ibid., 98.

163. While Cage's theory allows us to examine both the external world and ourselves as part of the world, it does seem that Cage is interested in anything but himself as subject matter. Certainly the "Diary" is not the sort from which one might gain any intimate knowledge of the author.

164. Cage, *Silence*, 260.

165. Cage, *A Year from Monday*, 12.

166. Johnston, "There Is No Silence Now," in Kostelanetz, *John Cage*, 149.

167. Cage, *Silence*, 35–40.

168. Ibid., 194.

169. Cage, *M*, i.

170. Ibid., i, 107.

171. Cage, *Silence*, i, 109.

Chapter 2

1. Peter Sellars, in David Savran, *The Wooster Group, 1975–85* (Ann Arbor: University of Michigan Research Press, 1986), xvi, 2. The text of *Rumstick Road* is published in *Performing Arts Journal* (Elizabeth LeCompte and Spalding Gray, "Rumstick Road," *Performing Arts Journal* 3, no. 2 [1978]: 92–115); the New York Public Library of the Performing Arts has a videotape of the production and of a discussion between the audience and Spalding Gray held after a performance (nos. NCOV 128 and NCOW 42); and James Bierman has provided a running description of the piece in *The Drama Review* ("Three Places in Rhode Island," *The Drama Review* [T81], 23, no. 1 [1979]: 13–30 [T81 refers to the journal's own numbering system]). Savran, *The Wooster Group*, contains portions of interviews he conducted with Wooster Group members about the development of both *Rumstick Road* and *Point Judith*. According to Erika Munk of the *Village Voice* ("Cross-Left," *Village Voice*, 23 February 1982, 84), "the only reason that the work did not receive an Obie [awarded by the *Village Voice*] is that it used tapes of living people made without their knowledge—which struck some judges as unethical as well as illegal." The denial of the Obie on this account provoked heated correspondence in the *Village Voice* and elsewhere. Subsequently the award was given to *Point Judith*, following the original impetus to award it to *Rumstick Road*.

2. Richard Foreman, *Plays and Manifestos*, edited by Kate Davy (New York: New York University Press, 1976), 192.

3. Spalding Gray, "About Three Places in Rhode Island," *The Drama Review* (T81), 23, no. 2 (1979): 34.

4. Arthur Eddington, quoted in Werner Heisenberg, *The Physicist's Conception of Nature*, translated by Arnold Pomerans (New York: Harcourt, Brace and Company, 1958), 153.

5. Erwin Schrödinger, *Mind and Matter* (Cambridge: Cambridge University Press, 1958), 89.

6. Heisenberg, *Physicist's Conception of Nature*, 24.

7. Spalding Gray, *SoHo Weekly News*, 25 December 1979, 47.

8. "For me, the energy behind the performance of *Rumstick Road* was confessional. . . . It was a confessional act. It was also an act of distancing" (Gray, "About Three Places," 38).

9. In realistic drama the house contains the central characters and forces them to confront one another in its confined space. For Ibsen, the house is a trap, particularly for the woman; freedom lies without.

10. Richard Foreman, "How to Write a Play," *Performing Arts Journal* 1, no. 2 (1976): 86. Allan Kaprow observes that whereas the impressionist painters recorded a world of change in quite enduring materials, the makers of assemblages, environments, and happenings work deliberately in perishable materials, embodying the concept of impermanence in their means; see Kaprow, *Assemblage, Environments, and Happenings* (New York: Harry N. Abrams, 1966), 167–69.

11. His marriage does not show him in a very flattering light either.

12. C. D. Innes, *Erwin Piscator's Political Theatre* (Cambridge: Cambridge University Press, 1972), 1. See also Roger Shattuck, *The Banquet Years* (New York: Random House, 1968), esp. chap. 1, for earlier and closer correlatives (though not primarily theatrical). For the relationship between surrealism and the aesthetic presented here, see Nahma Sandrow, *Surrealism: Theater, Arts, Ideas* (New York: Harper & Row, 1972). For the relationship between futurism and contemporary aesthetics, see Marjorie Perloff, "Why Futurism Now?" *Formations* 4, no. 3 (1988): 1–19.

13. It strikes me that part of the reason this place is so often a room in a house is not just because of the emphasis on family psychology but also because an interior space with artificial lighting is the easiest thing to represent realistically with standard theatrical materials: wood, canvas, and lights.

14. On the diminishment of magnitude in realistic drama, see Joseph Wood Krutch, "The Tragic Fallacy," in *The Modern Temper* (New York: Harcourt, Brace, 1929), 115–43.

15. Percy Bridgman, *Reflections of a Physicist* (New York: Philosophical Library, 1950), 373.

16. Percy Bridgman, *The Way Things Are* (Cambridge, Mass.: Harvard University Press, 1959), 4.

17. Spalding Gray, "Children of Paradise: Working with Kids," *Performing Arts Journal* (13) 5, no. 1 (1980): 65 (the number 13 refers to *PAJ*'s own numbering system adopted in 1979).

18. Spalding Gray, "Playwright's Notes," *Performing Arts Journal* 3, no. 2 (1978): 91.

19. *Sakonnet Point* itself was developed in a space designed for another play and was developed around objects that attracted Gray's attention and that he brought to rehearsal.

20. Alain Robbe-Grillet, *For a New Novel* (Evanston, Ill.: Northwestern University Press, 1989), 21.

21. All the pieces in *Three Places in Rhode Island* rely heavily on the use of tapes, phonograph records, slides, film, and the technology necessary to project them. Phonograph records are very important in *Nayatt School*, at the end of which the cast smashes and burns them and engages in simulated masturbation over them, their hands holding the arms of the record players as well as their genitals. As they stroke ever more rapidly, the amplified sounds of the needles mix in a cacophony of harsh scratchings. This desecration and destruction is disturbing, I think, because these records are not specially made theater props but things from the real world—manifestations of high technology and culture at that—which are being ruined. At the outset, Gray even tells us that one of the records is checked out from the public library!

22. Elizabeth LeCompte, "An Introduction," *Performing Arts Journal* 3, no. 2 (1978): 83.

23. Harold Pinter, quoted in Martin Esslin, *The Peopled Wound* (Garden City, N.J.: Doubleday, 1970), 34.

24. Ibid.

25. Jean Dubuffet, quoted in Wylie Sypher, *Loss of the Self in Modern Literature and Art* (New York: Random House, 1962), 113.

26. At least one can remember much of what happens. Foreman seeks to and succeeds in writing plays that cannot be remembered.

27. Fred Strodtbeck so uses the play in his class at the University of Chicago.

28. *Village Voice*, 23 February 1982, 84; see note 1 above.

29. In performance the name of the psychiatrist is changed, surely in the interest not of protecting the doctor but of avoiding a lawsuit.

30. Walter Kerr, *New York Herald Tribune*, quoted on the back of the paperback edition of Eugene O'Neill's *Long Day's Journey into Night* (New Haven, Conn.: Yale University Press, 1974). Objecting to performances like the one in which Chris Burden had someone shoot him in the arm, Richard Schechner tried to define them as non-art by saying that art, unlike life, can be taken back (Modern Language Association meeting, New York City, 1978). Of course, "primitive" people think of their rituals as efficacious, whereas we tend to think of them merely as art. Presumably, all art psychologically changes those who make, perform, and see it, just as all life changes us, and in that respect nothing can be stricken from the record. Aristotle, however, seems to argue that the greatest drama is that which affects us in particular ways.

31. Joseph Chaikin, *The Presence of the Actor* (New York: Atheneum, 1972), 2.

32. Meredith Monk, quoted in Carole Koenig, "Meredith Monk: Performer-Creator," *The Drama Review* (T71), 20, no. 3 (1976): 53.

33. *New York Times*, 30 March 1980, 48.

34. Jacob Bronowski, *The Origins of Knowledge and Imagination* (New Haven, Conn.: Yale University Press, 1979), 6.

35. Gray, "Playwright's Notes," 89; and Gray, "About Three Places," 38.

36. "A central character tends to move towards his own centrality, toward that part of himself which we will recognize as his dominant passion or his major virtue or error. The bias of centrality holds literary works together; it also holds together the self. A 'person' is someone

whose behavior, however complex, can be referred to a central consistency (a consistency powerful enough to tolerate some genuine inconsistency and even a little irrelevance)" (Leo Bersani, *A Future for Astyanax* [Boston: Little, Brown, 1976], 284).

37. Gray, "Playwright's Notes," 89.

38. Oscar Brockett, *Perspectives on Contemporary Theatre* (Baton Rouge: Louisiana State University Press, 1971), 74.

39. Bronowski, *Origins of Knowledge and Imagination*, 70.

40. Gray, "About Three Places," 39.

41. Gray, "Playwright's Notes," 88.

42. Ibid., 90.

43. Harold Pinter, quoted in Esslin, *The Peopled Wound*, 34.

44. Elizabeth LeCompte, quoted in Lenora Champagne, "Always Starting New: Elizabeth LeCompte," *The Drama Review* (T91), 25, no. 3 (1981): 23. "If I write about a lamp I apply myself to the demands of that lamp. If I write about a flower, I apply myself to the demands of that flower. In most cases, the flower has singular properties as opposed to the lamp. . . . Flower, lamp, tin-opener, tree . . . tend to take alteration from different climate and circumstance and I must necessarily attend to that singular change with the same devotion and allowance. I do not intend to impose or distort for the sake of an ostensible 'harmony' of approach" (Harold Pinter, quoted in Esslin, *The Peopled Wound*, 245–46).

45. C. H. Waddington, *Behind Appearance* (Cambridge, Mass.: MIT Press, 1970), 116.

46. To a limited extent the human figure is decentralized as well: Vawter's arm playing the arm of Gray's brother becomes a central focus; at one point, when he is reading the letter from the neighbor, Gray's head is not lit.

47. Chaikin, *Presence of the Actor*, 11–20.

48. Gray, "About Three Places," 37.

49. "I was with my mother during much of her nervous breakdown and began to empathize with her condition to the point of imitating it. In fact, just prior to making *Rumstick Road*, I began to experience nervous symptoms similar to those my mother had experienced nine years earlier. . . . I was deeply identified with the memory of her madness, and to save myself from becoming that madness, I was able—with the help of Liz LeCompte, Ron Vawter, Libby Howes, and Bruce Porter—to make a theatre piece that was a study of that madness" (ibid., 39).

50. Chaikin, *Presence of the Actor*, 15.

51. Gray, "Playwright's Notes," 88, 91.

52. Ibid., 87–91. George Coates, who improvises with materials in the same way, says that his works are "discovered" by means of group improvisations with objects; see Judith Coburn, "Sho of Shows: George Coates and Co. Meet Poland's avant-garde-niks," *Village Voice*, 12 July 1988, 29.

53. Harold Pinter, quoted in Esslin, *The Peopled Wound*, 246–47.

54. Meredith Monk, quoted in Koenig, "Meredith Monk," 60.

55. Kaprow, *Assemblage, Environments, and Happenings*, 169.

56. Foreman, *Plays and Manifestos*, 145; see also Bronowski, *Origins of Knowledge and Imagination*, 93.

57. Traditionally, dramatic criticism has aimed to be objective, with a goal of describing, interpreting, and evaluating a work as if the commentator were not an important part of that description, interpretation, and evaluation. Recognizing the subjectivity inherent in such traditional criticism, Michael Kirby, as editor of *The Drama Review* from 1976 to 1986, restricted contributors to mere description of performance. Kirby's position was highly problematic, particularly as it related to the contemporary theater so championed by the journal. Although the authors strove to be objective, the selection of the material to be described, the language of the description, and the observations provided were all inevitably subjective. Furthermore, the descriptions did not include the responses of the critics as audience members, nor did they provoke such responses in a reader—where audience response was an essential part of the works.

Another possibility for dealing with the subjectivity of criticism is to take the opposite tack. In the sixties, for example, Jill Johnston turned from providing some of the finest conventional dance criticism (of some very unconventional dance) to openly subjective writing inspired by performances she had just seen or, at an extreme, was on her way to see (Johnston, *Marmalade Me* [New York: Dutton, 1971].

Preferable is something between the two: description in the first person which openly acknowledges that one's associations are personal and limited. No event can be grasped conceptually in its totality. The human mind can see some, perhaps many things in an event, but it can never see everything. Yet just because one's view is limited is not reason to discount it or to abandon the event.

In ways other than its attempt to acknowledge the subjective-objective dilemma, the *The Drama Review* reflected the aesthetics of the theater of which it became the chief exponent. For one thing, the journal did not bury the academic machinery—footnotes—at the end of an article or the bottom of a page, any more than the new theater hides its technology; instead everything was incorporated directly into the text. Furthermore, the presentation was as unrelated to the rhetorical tradition as is an argument or linear action to the plays: indeed, the presentation may have had no argument, and there were usually disjunctive sections. The typescript was often as various as the mixed media of the plays, serving to call attention to the vehicle of discussion—the text. And many photographs eased the reader away from reliance on the text to tell the event.

58. Foreman, *Plays and Manifestos*, 146.

59. Bronowski, *Origins of Knowledge and Imagination*, 69. "Every event, for Whitehead, contains some reference to every other event in the universe. In fact, he argued that its character is determined entirely and completely by the way in which it relates to everything else. Every time-extended occurrence to which we give a name, every stone, or table, or person, is, as it were, a knot in an indefinitely complex four-dimensional network of relations, like one of the junction points in a spider's web that stretches off in all directions" (Waddington, *Behind Appearance*, 114; compare this statement to that of Richard Foreman on page 43, and that of Harold Pinter, note 44).

60. Bronowski, *Origins of Knowledge and Imagination*, 96.

61. Elizabeth LeCompte, quoted in Champagne, "Always Starting New," 20.

62. Bierman, "Three Places in Rhode Island," 22.

63. William Butler Yeats, "Emotion of Multitude," in *Essays and Introductions* (New York: Collier, 1968), 215–16.

64. LeCompte, "An Introduction," 86.

65. C. F. von Weizsäcker, *The World View of Physics* (Chicago: University of Chicago Press, 1952), 178.

66. Ted Kalem, New York *Playbill*, January 1980.

Chapter 3

1. "Landmark 'Chorus' Workshop 'Only Way to Do This Show' for Pressed-for-Time Bennett," *Variety*, 5 October 1983, 109.

2. Discussion between Michael Bennett and co-choreographer Bob Avian, 24 October 1977, New York Public Library of the Performing Arts (NYPLPA) tape, no. NCOW 29.

3. As it was for the silent film comedians who similarly worked without the time constraints and scripts the producers later imposed and whose work is increasingly appreciated.

4. Don Shewey, "The Musical According to Bennett," *New York Times*, 25 September 1983, 1; and Richard Hummler, "150G Nut Means No End in Sight," *Variety*, 5 October 1983, 109.

5. "Landmark 'Chorus' Workshop," 109.

6. Shewey, "The Musical According to Bennett," 32.

7. NYPLPA tape, no. NCOW 29.

8. Ibid.

9. Julius Novick, "This, *This* Is What Show-Biz Is?" *Village Voice*, 3 November 1975, 115.

10. Shewey, "The Musical According to Bennett," 1.

11. Ibid., 32.

12. "Landmark 'Chorus' Workshop," 109. In the discussion between Michael Bennett and Bob Avian (NYPLPA tape, no. NCOW 29), Bennett made the same point about milieu, but there he referred to what he later called the hot musical as "a concept musical." On the development of the concept musical, see Martin Gottfried, *Broadway Musicals* (New York: Abradale Press/ Harry N. Abrams, 1984), 29–37.

13. Narrative forms have been attractive vehicles for contemporary performance because they entail direct communication with the audience and require considerable actor and director invention. The onstage actor/audience was first brought to widespread attention in Peter Brook's *A Midsummer Night's Dream* (1970), where it was perfectly suited to Shakespeare's collective dream-within-a-play and play-within-a-play.

14. NYPLPA tape, no. NCOW 29.

15. Ibid.

16. Novick, "This, *This* Is What Show-Biz Is?" 115. Bennett and Avian said that they choreographed the final number in four hours and never made a change in it. It was their easiest work on the show, they agreed, because they chose to make something deliberately banal and stereotypical (NYPLPA tape, no. NCOW 29).

17. This idea was used earlier in the Open Theater's *Mutation Show*. Close examination of the program for *A Chorus Line* reveals that the dancer who is cast as the dance captain functions as the dance captain for the production.

18. NYPLPA tape, no. NCOW 29.

19. As the play is further removed in time from its origin it tends to become a period piece, and role and character become less interpenetrating. I think that remoteness from Broadway, or at least from a theater town, also makes the play less interactive with its performers. Further, Michael Bennett's death from AIDS in 1987 at the age of forty-four gives the gay character's confession of homosexuality an innocence that also dates the piece.

20. The information in this paragraph is from the NYPLPA tape, no. NCOW 29.

21. Deborah Jowitt, "Dance Makes Musicals Go 'Round," *New York Times*, 23 November 1975, D12.

22. Shewey, "The Musical According to Bennett," 32.

23. Lionel Abel, *Metatheatre* (New York: Hill & Wang, 1963).

24. The fact that the stories the original dancers told, as well as the event of their dancing and telling, are recreated is a layering effect as well, but one the audience may not know about. Similarly, footnotes constitute a kind of suppressed layering.

25. The entanglement is in fact far greater than is apparent from the play, but would be part of the experience of the play for those who know the backstage history: McKechnie, the original Cassie, had previously been a principal dancer in Bennett's *Company*; she won a Tony for her portrayal of Cassie; she was later married to and divorced from Bennett. Cassie, having been a principal dancer, returned to audition for *A Chorus Line* after a period spent out of work and down on her luck. In 1986, ten years after her original portrayal of Cassie, McKechnie returned to the role on Broadway, having spent some of the intervening period in far less successful roles and some of it with an incapacitating arthritis. Although reporters commented on her evident failure to fulfill the promise of her initial success, a new generation of would-be dancers was at the same time inspired to emulate her.

26. The term is from Douglas Hofstadter, *Gödel, Escher, Bach* (New York: Vintage Books, 1980).

27. Hence *A Chorus Line* has spawned numerous imitations, among them *Working*, *Runaways*, *Dancin'*, *Pacific Overtures*, and *Dreamgirls*.

Chapter 4

1. It is also a send-up of Carp's ethnocentrism: Carp asked the class to recall the sensations of a bobsled ride; Morales was chided for her inability to do so. Raised in Puerto Rico, she had never been on a bobsled. Stanislavski did assume the universality of "important" human experiences, but presumably not bobsled rides.

2. Burnet Hobgood, "Central Conceptions in Stanislavski's System," *Educational Theatre Journal* 25, no. 2 (1973): 147.

3. Robert Lewis, *Method—Or Madness?* (New York: Samuel French, 1958), 7.

4. Sonia Moore, *The Stanislavski System* (New York: Viking Press, 1965), 23, 11.

5. Constantin Stanislavski, *Building a Character*, translated by Elizabeth Reynolds Hapgood (New York: Theatre Arts Books, 1949), 289.

6. Sonia Moore, letter, *The Drama Review* (T58), 17, no. 2 (1973): 138.

7. "In the writings of Stanislavski one looks in vain for any mention of philosophers or psychologists, with the single exception of a reference to Ribot, the French psychologist" (John J. Sullivan, "Stanislavski and Freud," in *Stanislavski in America*, edited by Erika Munk [Greenwich, Conn.: Fawcett, 1967], 91).

8. I do not directly examine Stanislavski's influential idea that the work of the actor is creative, nor do I explore his psychology of creativity, which combines the Romantic idea that creativity arises from the unconscious with the modern idea that it can, nonetheless, be fostered. There now exists, however, a vast and rapidly growing body of literature on the psychology of creativity, in light of which Stanislavski's theorizing ought to be considered. See, for instance, D. N. Perkins, *The Mind's Best Work* (Cambridge, Mass.: Harvard University Press, 1981). For ideas on creativity contemporary with Stanislavski's own, see my "Stanislavski, Creativity, and the Unconscious," *New Theatre Quarterly* 2, no. 8 (1986): 345–51.

9. "Do not look for any scholarly or scientific derivations. . . . We do use, to be sure, certain scientific terms . . . as for example, 'the subconscious,' 'intuition,' but we take them in their everyday, simplest connotation and not in any philosophical sense" (Introduction to the first Russian edition of *An Actor Prepares* [1938], in Constantin Stanislavski, *Stanislavski's Legacy*, edited and translated by Elizabeth Reynolds Hapgood [New York: Theatre Arts Books, 1958], 30). Hapgood translates Stanislavski's one word *podsoznanie* variously as both "subconscious" and "unconscious," although the contexts suggest no distinction in meaning; the terms *unconscious*, *intuitive*, *seat of inspiration*, and *superconscious* all seem to refer to the same concept.

10. Jean Benedetti, *Stanislavski: An Introduction* (New York: Theatre Arts Books, 1982), 78. I am wholly dependent on the translations of Stanislavski's work provided by Elizabeth Reynolds Hapgood, David Magarshack, and Christine Edwards and on the accounts of his work provided by Christine Edwards, Jean Benedetti, Vasily Toporkov, and Nicolas Gorchakov. There seems no considerable inconsistency among the translations nor between the translations and the various commentaries provided by other readers of the Russian originals.

11. Constantin Stanislavski, *An Actor Prepares*, translated by Elizabeth Reynolds Hapgood (New York: Theatre Arts Books, 1963), 15.

12. Aristotle, *Physics*, translated by W. Carleton (Oxford: Clarendon Press, 1970), Book 2, chap. 8, 199b, line 15.

13. Konstantin Stanislavsky, *Stanislavsky on the Art of the Stage*, translated by David Magarshack (London: Faber & Faber, 1967), 200.

14. John Herman Randall, *Aristotle* (New York: Columbia University Press, 1963), 63.

15. Constantin Stanislavski, *Creating a Role*, translated by Elizabeth Reynolds Hapgood (New York: Theatre Arts Books, 1961), 79.

16. Stanislavski, *An Actor Prepares*, 241.

17. Stanislavski, *Creating a Role*, 16.

18. Ibid., 55.

19. For Stanislavski's thoughts on the evolution of art and nature, see his *My Life in Art*, translated by J. J. Robbins (New York: Meridian Books, 1956), 566–67: "What is this path of the

progress of art? It is the path of natural evolution. One must travel over it without hurrying. But the Revolution and its generation are impatient. New life does not want to wait, it demands quick results, another and a quickened tempo of life. Without waiting for natural creative evolution, it violates art.... Nature cannot be outwitted. Its true organic creativeness cannot be supplanted either by poverty-stricken or luxurious theatricality. A time will come when the evolution of art shall have completed its pre-destined circle and nature itself will teach us methods and techniques for the interpretation of the sharpness of the new life." According to Darwin, individuals are selected to maximize the contribution of their own genes to future generations—and that is all. Darwinism is not a theory of progress, increasing complexity, or evolved harmony for the good of species, ecosystems, or human culture. Stephan Jay Gould (*Hen's Teeth and Horses Toes* [New York: W. W. Norton, 1983], 259) argues "for a jerky, or episodic, rather than a smoothly gradual, pace of change.... Two outstanding facts of the fossil record [are the] geologically 'sudden' origin of new species and failure to change thereafter (stasis)." His theory (developed together with Niles Eldredge), then, can be characterized as one of punctuated equilibrium.

20. Stanislavski, *Creating a Role*, 80.

21. Stanislavsky, *Stanislavsky on the Art of the Stage*, 129, 200, 106.

22. Stanislavski, *Creating a Role*, 79.

23. When a Stanislavskian actor asks, "What's my motivation?" the answer is to be expressed not as a cause but as an objective: not "my father abandoned me," but "I want to kill him."

24. By 1882 von Hartmann's 1,100-page book was in its ninth edition in Germany; it was translated into French in 1877 and into English in 1884. Around 1870 the "unconscious" was not merely topical for psychologists, it was already fashionable talk among educated people. See Lancelot Law Whyte, *The Unconscious Before Freud* (New York: Basic Books, 1960), 163–64.

25. See Dennis N. Kenedy Darnoi, *The Unconscious and Eduard von Hartmann* (The Hague: Martinus Nijhoff, 1967).

26. Stanislavski, *Building a Character*, 289.

27. Stanislavski, *My Life in Art*, 566.

28. Stanislavski, *An Actor Prepares*, 87.

29. Stanislavsky, *Stanislavsky on the Art of the Stage*, 130.

30. Stanislavski, *Creating a Role*, 55.

31. Stanislavski, *An Actor Prepares*, 171.

32. Stanislavsky, *Stanislavsky on the Art of the Stage*, 92.

33. Stanislavski, *An Actor Prepares*, 151.

34. Stanislavski, *Building a Character*, 61.

35. Stanislavski, *An Actor Prepares*, 150–51.

36. Stanislavsky, *Stanislavsky on the Art of the Stage*, 105–6.

37. "Realism in art is the method which helps to select only the typical from life. If at times we are naturalistic in our stage work, it only shows that we don't yet know enough to be

able to penetrate into the historical and social essence of events and characters. We do not know how to separate the main from the secondary, and thus we bury the idea with details of the mode of life. That is my understanding of naturalism" (Stanislavski, quoted in Nikolai M. Gorchakov, *Stanislavsky Directs* [New York: Grosset & Dunlap, 1962], 143).

38. Stanislavski, *Building a Character*, 280; Stanislavski, *An Actor Prepares*, 242.

39. This was the motto of Stanislavski's theater, the Moscow Art Theatre.

40. Stanislavski, *Creating a Role*, 79.

41. Stanislavsky, *An Actor Prepares*, 151.

42. Stanislavsky, *Stanislavsky on the Art of the Stage*, 199, 58.

43. Stanislavsky, *An Actor Prepares*, 122.

44. Stanislavski, *Creating a Role*, 63.

45. Stanislavsky, *Stanislavsky on the Art of the Stage*, 194. "A sawed-off, choppy gesture is not appropriate for the stage" (Stanislavski, *Building a Character*, 39).

46. Stanislavsky, *Stanislavsky on the Art of the Stage*, 194–95.

47. David Magarshack, *Stanislavsky: A Life* (New York: Chanticleer Press, 1951), 349.

48. Stanislavsky, *Stanislavsky on the Art of the Stage*, 193, 93.

49. Stanislavski, *Stanislavski's Legacy*, 193.

50. Stanislavsky, *Stanislavsky on the Art of the Stage*, 194.

51. Ibid. Stanislavski did not deal with the Aristotelian ideas of recognition and reversal.

52. Stanislavsky, *Stanislavsky on the Art of the Stage*, 58; and Stanislavski, *Building a Character*, 77.

53. Stanislavsky, *Stanislavsky on the Art of the Stage*, 16.

54. Stanislavski, *Building a Character*, 115.

55. Ibid., 266.

56. Moore, *The Stanislavski System*, 35.

57. Of course, this actor's art has in turn come to affect the art of playwriting: the plays of Pinter have almost all their interest in the possible subtexts—so there are few words and many silences. In these the actor's job is to *not* delimit the possible subtexts. In Beckett's plays specifications regarding the actor's placement and gesture are essential parts of the text and not to be altered by actors or directors.

58. Timothy J. Wiles, *The Theater Event* (Chicago: University of Chicago Press, 1980), 20; quoting from Constantin Stanislavski, *My Life in Art*, 361. According to Stanislavski, Chekhov said this frequently.

59. Stanislavski, *An Actor Prepares*, 284.

60. Aristotle, *Physics*, Book 2, chap. 8, 199a, lines 11–15.

61. Stanislavski, *Building a Character*, 19.

62. Stanislavski, *An Actor Prepares*, 294.

63. Stanislavski, *Stanislavski's Legacy*, 172.

64. Stanislavski, *Creating a Role*, 241. "We shall never be able to replace that creative nature by our stage technique, no matter how perfect it is" (Stanislavski, *Building a Character*, 289).

65. Stanislavski, *Building a Character*, 292; Stanislavski, *Creating a Role*, 82.

66. Théodule Armand Ribot, *Essay on the Creative Imagination* (1906; reprint New York: Arno Press, 1973), 57–58.

67. Stanislavski, *Building a Character*, 289.

68. William Wundt, quoted in Whyte, *The Unconscious Before Freud*, 160.

69. Stanislavski, *Creating a Role*, 52.

70. Stanislavski, *Building a Character*, 290–91.

71. Stanislavski, *My Life in Art*, 571, 461.

72. Stanislavski, *Stanislavski's Legacy*, 184. Stanislavski was certainly not the first to assume that even though creativity took place in the subconscious it could nonetheless be approached systematically; Goethe had had the same idea as early as 1832: "The earlier man becomes aware that there exists a craft, an art that can help him toward a controlled heightening of his natural abilities, the happier he is. . . . Here begin the manifold relations between the conscious and the unconscious. Take for instance a talented musician, composing an important score: consciousness and unconsciousness will be like warp and weft" (Johann Wolfgang von Goethe, quoted in Whyte, *The Unconscious Before Freud*, 128–29).

73. Stanislavski, *Creating a Role*, 106.

74. Stanislavski, *An Actor Prepares*, 278.

75. Stanislavski, *Building a Character*, 280–81.

76. Stanislavsky, *Stanislavsky on the Art of the Stage*, 191, 150.

77. See P. V. Simonov, "The Method of K. S. Stanislavski and the Physiology of Emotions" (1962?), in *Stanislavski Today*, compiled, edited, and translated by Sonia Moore (New York: American Center for Stanislavski Theatre Art, 1973), 34–43.

78. Stanislavski, *Creating a Role*, 82. "Symbolism, impressionism, and other isms in the art," Stanislavski wrote, "belong to the sphere of the subconscious and begin where the ultranatural ends" (Constantin Stanislavski, *An Actor's Handbook*, edited by Elizabeth Reynolds Hapgood [New York: Theatre Arts Books, 1963], 138).

79. Stanislavski, *An Actor's Handbook*, 57.

80. Stanislavski, *Building a Character*, 118.

81. Stanislavsky, *Stanislavsky on the Art of the Stage*, 194.

82. Stanislavski, *An Actor Prepares*, 16.

83. Gorchakov, *Stanislavsky Directs*, 333.

84. Stanislavsky, *Stanislavsky on the Art of the Stage*, 195.

85. Ibid., 111, 194.

86. Edward Bullough, " 'Psychical Distance' as a Factor in Art and an Aesthetic Principle," reprinted in *Aesthetics*, edited by E. M. Wilkinson (Stanford: Stanford University Press, 1957), 91–130.

87. "Naturalism cheats the audience of its main pleasure and its most important satisfaction, that of creating with the actor and completing in its own imagination what the actor, the director, and the designer suggest with their theatre techniques" (Stanislavski, quoted in Gorchakov, *Stanislavsky Directs*, 333). That is, the audience's most important satisfaction comes from being shown what it already knows.

88. David Magarshack argues that the Revolution did change Stanislavski's views concerning the role of the actor: "Stanislavski's conception of the actor as a man who is wholly devoted to his art has now been amplified by the conception of the actor-citizen who takes a personal part in the building of a new and better life, the actor, too, who is 'a son of his people,' and whose work on the stage is closely bound up with the best aspirations of his people" (Magarshack, *Stanislavsky: A Life*, 349). I find nothing in the evidence Magarshack provides to show that such change occurred, however. In fact, various statements by Stanislavski indicate that he deplored and discounted revolution: "The former quiet and balanced life of Russia was over"; "revolutions and wars created cruel but interesting moments in the life of man" (Stanislavski, *My Life in Art*, 533, 565). And of revolution in art he wrote: "It is impossible to accept a sermon or a propaganda piece as true art" (from *My Life in Art*; quoted by Magarshack in Stanislavsky, *Stanislavsky on the Art of the Stage*, 72). "The Revolution and its generation are impatient . . . [but] nature cannot be outwitted. . . . A time will come when the evolution of art shall have completed its predestined circle. . . . Much that we have experienced is being repeated at present, and only differs in name from what we knew. . . . The forms and the names are new, but the nature of evolution and its chief laws are the same" (Stanislavski, *My Life in Art*, 566–67).

89. Moore, *The Stanislavski System*, 4; and Stanislavski, *Building a Character*, 246.

90. Stanislavski, *Building a Character*, 260, 18.

91. Stanislavski, *An Actor Prepares*, 194.

92. Nonetheless, I am always surprised at how authoritarian contemporary acting classes based on Stanislavski are.

93. Lewis, *Method—Or Madness?*, opposite p. 34; and Benedetti, *Stanislavski: An Introduction*, 61.

94. Stanislavski, *An Actor Prepares*, 90.

Chapter 5

1. I do not here explain how the concepts I describe in this chapter relate specifically to Beckett and Pinter plays. Game, now-moment, and transformation are, however, key concepts in the acting of their plays; and some of Pinter's characters, like Kate and Anna in *Old Times*, may be understood as interpenetrating. Pinter is not interested in the presence of the actor, though, and the games his characters play are competitive. Beckett requires that the performers serve his text; the American National Theatre, for example, is forbidden from producing Beckett's plays because Joanne Akalaitis radically departed from his stage directions in her direction of *Endgame* there.

2. Theodore Hoffman, "Stanislavski Triumphant," *Tulane Drama Review* 9, no. 1 (1964): 17; Richard Schechner, "Stanislavski at School," *Tulane Drama Review* 9, no. 2 (1964): 211.

3. From Eva Mekler's interviews with a number of well-established acting teachers she concludes that, as disciples of Method teachers themselves, they still use Stanislavskian techniques, but almost never exclusively (Mekler, *The New Generation of Acting Teachers* [New York: Viking Press, 1987], ix).

4. By 1980 Schechner was proposing that each acting student "should follow his own guru" (panel discussion on acting, American Theatre Association convention). In 1967 *TDR* moved to New York University where its name was changed to the *The Drama Review*. Once again under the editorship of Richard Schechner (after a ten year hiatus), *TDR* focuses almost exclusively on performances, not dramatic texts, and accordingly emphasizes its acronym rather than its anachronistic full name.

5. Viola Spolin, *Improvisation for the Theater* (Evanston, Ill.: Northwestern University Press, 1963). After eleven printings the book was minimally revised for a first paperback printing (Northwestern University Press, 1983); except where specified, I refer to the original edition.

6. Eileen Blumenthal, *Joseph Chaikin* (Cambridge: Cambridge University Press, 1984), 209.

7. Richard Schechner, "Aspects of Training at the Performance Group," in *Actor Training 1*, edited by Richard P. Brown (New York: Drama Book Specialists, 1972), 5, 6.

8. Jerzy Grotowski, *Towards a Poor Theatre* (New York: Simon & Schuster, 1968), 125.

9. David Cole, *The Theatrical Event* (Middletown, Conn.: Wesleyan University Press, 1975); and Ernest Theodore Kirby, *Ur-Drama* (New York: New York University Press, 1975).

10. Alain Robbe-Grillet, *For a New Novel*, translated by Richard Howard (Evanston, Ill.: Northwestern University Press, 1989), 23. In a similar vein, Susan Sontag comments on the equation of the self with the suffering self, which is "the latest and most powerful legacy of the Christian tradition of introspection, opened up by Paul and Augustine. . . . For the modern consciousness, the artist (replacing the saint) is the exemplary sufferer. . . . As a man, [the writer] suffers; as a writer, he transforms his suffering into art. The writer is the man who discovers the use of suffering in the economy of art—as the saints discovered the utility and necessity of suffering in the economy of salvation" (Sontag, *Against Interpretation* [New York: Farrar, Straus & Giroux, 1966], 42).

11. Christopher Innes, *Holy Theatre* (Cambridge: Cambridge University Press, 1981).

12. Roger Copeland and Annette Michelson, writing about dance, have tried in different ways to distinguish two contemporary performance modes. Roger Copeland explains that "by making the perceiver preeminent (or at least co-equal with the object of perception), postmodern dance breaks decisively with the primitivist tendency to exalt the experience of the participant. [It places] a high premium on detachment and objectivity, on seeing rather than feeling" (Copeland, "Postmodern Dance and the Repudiation of Primitivism," *Partisan Review* 50, no. 1 [1983]: 114–15); Annette Michelson distinguishes between expressionistic and analytic performance modes (Michelson, "Yvonne Rainer, Part One: The Dancer and the Dance," *Artforum* 12 [January 1974]: 57).

13. Joseph Chaikin, *The Presence of the Actor* (New York: Atheneum, 1972), 6.

14. Ibid., 1, 8.

15. Spolin, *Improvisation for the Theater*, 15, 16, 14. Robert Benedetti echoes the same idea: "Acting is not self-expression; it is self-extension" (Benedetti, *Seeming, Being, and Becoming* [New York: Drama Book Specialists, 1976], 87). Richard Foreman, while not much inter-

ested in acting (and less sunny), is an articulate spokesman for the impulse behind much contemporary theater. Acting, he says, is "to give courage to ourself and others to be alive from moment to moment, which means to accept both flux (presentation and representation to consciousness as reality) and. . .the perpetual constituting and reconstituting of the self" (Foreman, *Plays and Manifestos*, edited by Kate Davy [New York: New York University Press, 1976], 74.

16. Spolin, *Improvisation for the Theater*, 25, 3.

17. For a brief time in the late sixties in Chicago, Sills also ran a theater called the Forty-second Ward Games Theatre in which he engaged the audience in the theater games his mother had devised.

18. Spolin, *Improvisation for the Theater*, 382.

19. Robert Pasolli, *A Book on the Open Theatre* (New York: Avon Books, 1970), 18.

20. Tom F. Driver, *Romantic Quest and Modern Query* (New York: Dell, 1971), 387.

21. Spolin, *Improvisation for the Theater*, 4. As Richard Schechner observes with regard to the importance of the physical response, "*Your body is not your 'instrument,' your body is you*" (Schechner, "Aspects of Training," 29).

22. Chaikin, *Presence of the Actor*, 25.

23. Spolin, *Improvisation for the Theater* (1st paperback edition, 1983), 249.

24. David Selbourne, *The Making of "A Midsummer Night's Dream"* (London: Methuen, 1982), 45.

25. Charles Henry, Goodman Theatre, Chicago, personal communication, 1988.

26. Elinor Fuchs and James Leverett, "Back to the Wall: Heiner Müller in Berlin," *Village Voice*, 18 December 1984, 64.

27. C. H. Waddington, *Behind Appearance* (Cambridge, Mass.: MIT Press, 1970), 116.

28. Charles McGaw, *Acting Is Believing* (New York: Holt, Rinehart & Winston, 1955).

29. Spolin demonstration, American Theatre Association convention, 1972.

30. Charles Marowitz, *The Act of Being* (New York: Taplinger, 1978).

31. Spolin, *Improvisation for the Theater*, 45.

32. Leon Rubin, *The Nicholas Nickleby Story* (Harmondsworth, Eng.: Penguin Books, 1981), 66.

33. Judith Cook, *Director's Theatre* (London: Harrap, 1974), 18.

34. David Selbourne, *The Making of "A Midsummer Night's Dream"*, 115.

35. Foreman, *Plays and Manifestos*, 76.

36. Robert Benedetti, "Notes to an Actor," in *Actor Training 1*, edited by Richard P. Brown (New York: Drama Book Specialists, 1972), 67, 65.

37. J. L. Styan, *Restoration Comedy* (Cambridge: Cambridge University Press, 1986).

38. Similarly, in Pinter's plays the past is not something that can be established; instead it is malleable material for use in the characters' moment-to-moment improvisations.

39. Chaikin, *Presence of the Actor*, 65.

40. Jack Poggi, "Second Thoughts on the Theory of Action," in *Actor Training 2*, edited by Richard P. Brown (New York: Drama Book Specialists, 1976), 27.

41. A theater game that clearly entails competition—tug-of-war—should be followed, Spolin suggests, by a discussion of its outcome in which it is observed that "when one pulled the other fell over, or both fell over, or a stalemate was reached." There is no mention of winners: one infers that what results from conflict is not good (Spolin, *Improvisation for the Theater* [1st paperback edition, 1983], 250).

42. Doon Arbus, ed., *Alice in Wonderland* (New York: Merlin House, 1973), 32.

43. Chaikin, *The Presence of the Actor*, 19.

44. Ibid., 87, 20.

45. Spolin demonstration, American Theatre Association convention, 1972.

46. Meredith Monk, quoted in Carole Koenig, "Meredith Monk: Performer-Creator," *The Drama Review* (T71), 20, no. 3 (1976): 60.

47. Spolin, *Improvisation for the Theater*, 7–8.

48. Chaikin, *Presence of the Actor*, 93.

49. Eileen Blumenthal, "Joseph Chaikin: An Open Theory of Acting," *Yale/Theater* 9, nos. 2–3 (1977): 123.

50. Spolin, *Improvisation for the Theater*, 5.

51. Benedetti, "Notes to an Actor," 73.

52. Chaikin, *Presence of the Actor*, 96, 55.

53. Ibid., 159–60.

54. This description is provided in Pasolli, *A Book on the Open Theatre*, 20.

55. Marowitz, *Act of Being*, 130.

56. Chaikin, *Presence of the Actor*, 6.

57. Spolin, *Improvisation for the Theater*, 25, 37.

58. Ibid., 3.

59. Rubin, *The Nicholas Nickleby Story*, 123.

60. This idea, and not a housing shortage alone, may have helped create the movement of artists and then of middle-class people into loft spaces—spaces that they themselves create.

61. Spolin, *Improvisation for the Theater* (1st paperback edition, 1983), xvii.

62. Chaikin, *Presence of the Actor*, 114.

63. Selbourne, *The Making of "A Midsummer Night's Dream"*, 51.

64. Spolin, *Improvisation for the Theater*, 8–9.

65. Chaikin, *Presence of the Actor*, 102.

66. Rubin, *The Nicholas Nickleby Story*, 59. In Spolin's work, "*every* actor on stage is responsible for everything that happens" (Spolin, *Improvisation for the Theater*, 158).

67. Rubin, *The Nicholas Nickleby Story*, 151.

68. In Brechtian theater the actors are to think of themselves as present along with the roles but not as interpenetrating them.

69. Chaikin, *Presence of the Actor*, 14, 11, 19.

70. Cook, *Director's Theatre*, 18.

71. Spolin, *Improvisation for the Theater*, 13–14.

72. Foreman, *Plays and Manifestos*, 142 (ellipses in original).

73. Robbe-Grillet, *For a New Novel*, 156.

74. Selbourne, *The Making of "A Midsummer Night's Dream"*, 169.

75. Cage, *Silence*, 120.

76. Rubin, *The Nicholas Nickleby Story*, 185.

77. Richard P. Brown, "Foreword," in *Actor Training 1*, edited by Richard P. Brown (New York: Drama Book Specialists, 1972), vii.

78. Richard Schechner, ed., *Dionysus in 69* (New York: Farrar, Straus & Giroux, 1970). For an analysis of the nature of the photodocumentation in the books on *Alice in Wonderland*, *Dionysus in 69*, and other contemporary theater, see my "Recording the Theatre in Photographs," *Educational Theatre Journal* 28, no. 3 (1976): 376–88.

Conclusion

1. Christopher Lasch, "The Minimalist Aesthetic," in *The Minimal Self* (New York: W. W. Norton, 1984), chap. 4. This view is echoed in Arthur Kroker and David Cook's *The Postmodern Scene: Excremental Culture and Hyper-Aesthetics* (New York: St. Martin's Press, 1986), 9: "Western culture itself runs under the signs of passive and suicidal nihilism. . . . Ours is a *fin-de-millennium* consciousness which, existing at the end of history in the twilight time of ultramodernism (of technology) and hyperprimitivism (of public moods), uncovers a great arc of disintegration and decay against the background radiation of parody, kitsch, and burnout."

2. Alain Robbe-Grillet, quoted in Lasch, *The Minimal Self*, 154.

Index

Abel, Lionel, 87

Acting: Chaikin and, 55, 115, 128; Monk on, 55, 68, 119; nature of, 13, 102–3; origins of, 113

Acting Is Believing (McGaw), 117

Acting techniques: in improvisational theater, 112, 115–16, 122, 124–25; LeCompte on, 71–72; in new theater, 4, 31–32, 48–49, 111, 125–26; Schechner and, 72

Act of Being, The (Marowitz), 117

Actor: and the audience, 108, 126–27; Chaikin and the, 123–25; and dramatic character, 102–4, 106–7, 108, 125–26; Grotowski on the, 113; and interaction, 123–26; Robbe-Grillet on the, 113–14; Spolin and the, 119, 123, 124; Stanislavski on the, 102–7, 127

Actor Prepares, An (Stanislavski), 93, 95

Actor's Equity Association: and theatrical workshop agreements, 78–79

Actor Training, 128

Alice in Wonderland, 119, 128; process in, 122

Amadeus, 83

American Center for Stanislavski Art, 94

Anti-theater. *See* New theater

Aristotle: Cage compared to, 5–8, 15–16, 18, 34; and drama, 7–8, 26, 35, 101, 103, 105; influence on new theater, 1–3, 33; and language, 16–17; and observation, 8, 14; *Poetics*, 1–3, 35; and process, 19; Randall on, 6; and realism, 45, 99; theater aesthetic and Cage, 2–3; theory of art, 5, 7–8, 35, 101, 104; theory of nature, 6–7, 15, 17, 29, 30, 35, 94, 95–97, 98, 104, 109

Art: Aristotle's theory of, 5, 7–8, 35, 101, 104; Cage on objectivity in, 40; Cage's theory of, 5, 13–15, 19–20, 26, 29–31, 33–35, 37, 43, 109, 119; Foreman's theory of, 40, 126–27; Johnston on, 14; and nature, 5, 23, 29, 95; and science, 5–6, 18–19; Stanislavski on, 99; Stein on, 29; Waddington on, 117

As You Like It, 115

Audience: actor and the, 108, 126–27; Cage and the, 10–13, 127; and *A Chorus Line*, 83–84, 87, 88, 91; and interaction, 126–27; and *Long Day's Journey into Night*, 44–45; new theater and the, 14, 27, 60, 83–84; and observation, 12–13, 14; Pinter and the, 127; the play and the, 108; Robbe-Grillet on the, 127; and *Rumstick Road*, 52–53, 57, 60, 69; Selbourne on the, 127; Spolin on the, 126; Stanislavski on the, 106, 108, 126; Wilson and the, 127

Bacchae, The: process in, 122

Backstage musical. *See* "Hot" musical theater

Ballroom: Bennett and, 79

Barnett, Lincoln: on causality, 27–28

Beckett, Samuel, 3, 111, 129; Driver on, 115; *Waiting for Godot,* 115

Benedetti, Jean, 110; "Notes to an Actor," 128; on presence, 118; *Seeming, Being, and Becoming,* 128

Bennett, Michael: and *A Chorus Line,* 78, 81, 84–85, 86, 87; and *Ballroom,* 79; and *Dreamgirls,* 82; on "hot" musical theater, 82–83

Bierman, James: on *Rumstick Road,* 72

157

Johnston, Jill: on art, 14; on Cage, 36
Jordan, Pascual, 14
Jowitt, Deborah: on *A Chorus Line,* 87
Judson Dancers, 15

Kalem, Ted: on drama, 73–74
Kazan, Elia, 111
Kerr, Walter: on *Long Day's Journey into
    Night,* 54
King Lear: Breuer's production of, 120
Kirby, E. T., 113
Kirby, Michael: and performance theater,
    43
Kostelanetz, Richard: on Cage, 3

Language: Aristotle and, 16–17; Cage and,
    17, 35; nature of, 16; and reality, 16–17,
    20; in *Rumstick Road,* 61; and theater,
    16–17
Lasch, Christopher, 129
LeCompte, Elizabeth: on acting
    techniques, 71–72; as director and
    co-author of *Rumstick Road,* 42, 47, 63,
    64–65, 68; on *Three Places in Rhode
    Island,* 71
Lewis, Robert, 110; on Stanislavski method
    of acting, 93
Linklater, Kristin, 13
Living Theater: and *Mysteries and Smaller
    Pieces,* 21, 112
Long Day's Journey into Night, 3, 70, 72;
    audience and, 44–45; autobiographical
    content of, 39–42, 44, 45, 57–58;
    characterization in, 41–42, 44, 46, 55,
    57–59; Gray on, 41; imagery in, 72;
    influence on *Rumstick Road,* 41–42;
    Kerr on, 54; O'Neill on, 44; *Point Judith*
    as parody of, 39, 41, 74–76; realism in,
    45–46; *Rumstick Road* compared to, 39,
    42, 47, 55, 59, 63, 72; staging of, 41–42,
    45–46, 55; structure of, 44–45

McGaw, Charles: *Acting Is Believing,* 117
McKechnie, Donna, 87, 146n.25
McLuhan, Marshall, 30
M, 17, 35–36, 37
Maeterlinck, Maurice, 72
Manhattan Project (theater ensemble):
    Gregory and, 119
Marowitz, Charles: *The Act of Being,* 117;
    and improvisational theater, 112, 122

Mayr, Ernst: on process, 19
Method acting. *See* Stanislavski method of
    acting
Midsummer Night's Dream, A: Brook's
    production of, 116, 118, 124, 127;
    process in, 122; staging of, 127
Minkowski, H.: on field, 21–22
Monk, Meredith: on acting, 55, 68, 119
Moore, Sonia: on Stanislavski method, 94
Motherwell, Robert, 65–66
Much Ado About Nothing, 122
Müller, Heiner: on the play, 116–17; on
    Wilson, 18–19
Music: Cage and, 10–13, 15, 17, 22–23,
    25, 26–27, 28–29, 31, 34; as
    performance theater, 17
Musicals, "hot." *See* "Hot" musical theater
Mutation Show, 120
Mysteries and Smaller Pieces: Living
    Theater and, 21, 112

Nature: Aristotle's theory of, 6–7, 15, 17,
    29, 30, 35, 94, 95–97, 98, 104, 109; art
    and, 5, 23, 29, 95; Bronowski on, 62,
    71; Cage and, 16, 17, 32–33, 111;
    concept of, 32–33; improvisational
    theater and, 112–13; Stanislavski
    method and, 94, 95–98, 109, 111, 113;
    Stanislavski on, 95–96, 97–98. *See also*
    Process; Reality
Nayatt School, 39, 71, 75
New theater: acting techniques in, 4,
    31–32, 48–49, 59–60, 111, 125–26;
    Aristotle's influence on, 1–3, 33; and
    the audience, 14, 27, 60, 83–84; Bohr
    and, 1, 4; Brustein on, 2; chance in,
    26–27, 122; *A Chorus Line* as, 77–78,
    80–81, 83, 86, 90–91; and field, 24–25,
    31–32; Hayman on, 2; and human
    behavior, 120–21; and improvisational
    theater, 112; nature of, 1–2, 60, 129;
    Nicholas Nickleby as, 83; and
    observation, 9–10; *Point Judith* as,
    75–76; and process, 20–21, 90–91;
    Stanislavski method and, 93, 111–12,
    113; *Tulane Drama Review* and, 111–12;
    Wilson and, 20–21, 29, 70; Wooster
    Group and, 20–21. *See also* Performance
    theater

Rumstick Road, 3; audience and, 52–53, 57, 60, 69; autobiographical content of, 39, 40–42, 43, 47–48, 51–54, 59, 63, 68, 69; Bierman on, 72; characterization in, 41–42, 47–48, 51, 53, 60–61, 63–65; A Chorus Line compared to, 81, 82, 86; compared to Long Day's Journey into Night, 39, 42, 47, 55, 59, 63, 72; creation of, 42–43, 47–48, 61, 63–64, 65, 66, 74, 78; Gray as co-author of, 40, 42, 47, 53, 54, 59, 61–63, 66; Gray on, 40–41, 52, 63, 64, 66; Gussow on, 59, 72; imagery in, 49–51; lack of structure in, 68–69, 73; language in, 61; LeCompte as director and co-author of, 42, 47, 63, 64–65, 68; Long Day's Journey into Night's influence on, 41–42; as multimedia production, 49; parodied in Point Judith, 75; performance of, 43, 47–48, 49–50, 52–53, 55–57, 63, 66; as performance theater, 42–43, 47–51, 55–57, 64, 65–66, 67–69; realism and, 53–54, 55–57; source documents of, 40–41, 42–43, 47–49, 51–52, 54, 57, 60–61, 65, 68, 70, 74; staging of, 41–42, 48–49, 50, 53, 55–56, 59, 67–68, 70; technology in, 50; and violation of privacy, 47–48, 53–54, 61

Sakonnet Point, 39, 43, 50, 71
Schechner, Richard, 20, 112; and acting techniques, 72; Dionysus in 69, 31–32; Environmental Theatre, 6; on Stanislavski method, 111
Schrödinger, Erwin: and causality, 22–23; on objectivity, 40; and the self, 130
Science: art and, 5–6, 18–19; Bridgman on, 6; Cage's theater aesthetic and, 5–6; process and, 19; Stanislavski and, 110
Second City (improvisation company): Sills and, 115
Seeming, Being, and Becoming (Benedetti), 128
Selbourne, David: on the audience, 127; on interaction, 124
Self: Cage and the, 130; Chaikin and the, 130; Robbe-Grillet on the, 129–30; Schrödinger and the, 130; Spolin and the, 130

Sellars, Peter, 39; production of The Count of Monte Cristo, 116, 124
Serban, Andrei, 20
Silence, 35, 37
Sills, Paul, 112; and Second City, 115
South Pacific: Bogard's production of, 120
Space-time. See Field
Spolin, Viola, 15; and the actor, 119, 123, 124; on the audience, 126; and Chaikin, 112–13, 114, 119, 121–22; on improvisational theater, 114–16; Improvisation for the Theater, 112, 124; and interaction, 124–25; on presence, 117, 119–20; and the self, 130
Stage design: Brook and, 124; Chaikin and, 124; and interaction, 123–24; Rubin on, 123. See also "staging" as subheading
Stanislavski, Constantin, 4, 13; on the actor, 102–7, 127; An Actor Prepares, 93, 95, 109; on art, 99; on the audience, 106, 108, 126; background of, 93, 94–95; Building a Character, 93, 95, 109; Creating a Role, 95, 109, 110; and creativity, 106–7; on dramatic character, 100–103; on his method of acting, 93–94, 95–96; and human behavior, 96–98, 99; on nature, 95–96, 97–98; on the play, 99; and science, 110; and theater, 93–94, 95, 98–99, 101; on the unconscious, 97–98, 104–6; Wiles on, 103; writing style, 94–95, 109–10
Stanislavski method of acting: Chaikin and, 112; Hoffman on, 111; and improvisational theater, 113, 116, 117; influence of, 93–94; Lewis on, 93; Moore on, 94; and nature, 94, 95–98, 109, 111, 113; nature of, 93–94, 96, 102–7, 109; and new theater, 93, 111–12, 113; presence and, 118; and realism, 99; Schechner on, 111; Stanislavski on, 93–94, 95–96; and text of the play, 103
Stapp, Henry: on observation, 8
Stein, Gertrude, 22; on art, 29
Stella, Frank: on observation, 12, 114

Technology: Cage on, 17–18, 34–35; in Rumstick Road, 50
Tempest, The: Falls's production of, 116; process in, 122